JOYCE'S WEB

T0374946

Literary Modernism Series

THOMAS F. STALEY, EDITOR

Joyce's Web

THE SOCIAL UNRAVELING OF MODERNISM

Margot Norris

University of Texas Press
Austin

Requests for permission to reproduce material from this work
should be sent to Permissions, University of Texas Press, Box 7819,
Austin, TX 78713-7819.

⊚ The paper used in this publication meets the minimum requirements of American National Standard for Information Sci-
ences—Permanence of Paper for Printed Library Materials, ANSI
Z39.48-1984.

Library of Congress Cataloging-in-Publication Data

Norris, Margot.
    Joyce's web : the social unraveling of modernism / by Margot
Norris. — 1st ed.
        p. cm. — (Literary modernism series)
    Includes bibliographical references and index.
    ISBN 0-292-72255-9
    1. Joyce, James, 1882–1941—Political and social views.
2. Literature and society—History—20th century. 3. Social
problems in literature. 4. Modernism (Literature) I. Title.
II. Series.
PR6019.O97764 1992
823'.912—dc20   92-15209

To John Hannay (1949–1988)
In loving and grateful memory

Contents

Acknowledgments

Joyce's Web: The Social Unraveling of Modernism is about the social production of modern art, specifically Joyce's art. In this spirit,
I was obliged to reflect on my own book's production, on the way
that scholarship, too, is socially produced, by webs of institutional
support, professional interactions, and social relationships. The first
of these were crucial for the timely completion of this work: a fellowship from the John Simon Guggenheim Memorial Foundation in
1988–1989, which gave me a year's leave for research and writing,
and which was supplemented by a University of California President's Research Fellowship in the Humanities. I finished the writing
with additional support from Terence Parsons, Dean of Humanities
at the University of California, Irvine, and from an Irvine Research
Fellowship that allowed me to spend two months in Ireland—my
first extended visit to that marvelous country after twenty years of
studying Joyce. While writing my second chapter on Pound's efforts
to secure grant support and patronage for Joyce, I was mindful of my
own generous referees taking time to write letters on my behalf. I
thank them warmly. While the institutional support provided the
money to release research and writing time, I enjoyed direct research
assistance from my resourceful graduate student, Catherine Whitley,
who especially deserves credit for much of the historical information found in Chapter 5. And my colleague James McMichael first
read and commented helpfully on the completed manuscript.

But it is the indirect intellectual influences that are more difficult
to attribute and that oblige me to attempt to give a particularized
face to a unique scholarly community, that by now has a history of
several decades, and that extends across nations and continents. It
is sometimes derided with the misleading commercial epithet "the
Joyce industry" and sometimes chided, as in a recent *James Joyce
Broadsheet*, for narcissism and self-indulgence. But I honestly believe it functions as a uniquely open, democratic, and highly social-

ized and humanized community of scholars. Its earliest benefits came to me while I was still a graduate student at SUNY Buffalo, when Bernard Benstock agreed to serve as an outside reader for my manuscript, David Hayman got me permission to see the *Finnegans Wake* notebooks, and Fritz Senn responded warmly to the reading of the *Wake* made possible by the Parisian fads then invading American academies. Later Thomas Staley gave me my first teaching job at the University of Tulsa, the home of the *James Joyce Quarterly*, and Suzette Henke invited me to serve on my first panel at an International Joyce symposium in Dublin in 1976. I was launched, not only into a scholarly career, but into a community that tirelessly stimulates and encourages new participants with fresh ideas and novel approaches, thereby keeping the scholarship sharp and challenging. Morris Beja deserves credit for steering the International James Joyce Foundation's policies and practices in directions that foster heterogeneity and cosmopolitanism at Symposia and in publication. Karen Lawrence's leadership will clearly continue them. I see modernism's social history at its very best—fostering experimentation and nurturing new talent—in these Joycean institutions, which include the journals and publication projects of Thomas Staley, Robert Spoo, Richard Pearce, and Ellen Carol Jones. Several of the chapters in *Joyce's Web* have had the advantage of readings and criticisms from some of their, and other, journals, and I owe special thanks for permission to reprint pieces to *PMLA*, which published a version of Chapter 6 called "Narration under a Blindfold: Reading Joyce's 'Clay,'" in the March 1987 issue; the *James Joyce Quarterly*, which published a draft of Chapter 8, "Modernism, Myth, and Desire in 'Nausicaa,'" in Fall 1988; *Modern Fiction Studies*, which printed the first version of Chapter 5, "Stifled Back Answers: The Gender Politics of Art in Joyce's 'The Dead,'" in the Autumn 1989 issue; and *Joyce Studies Annual 1990* in which "The Politics of Childhood in 'The Mime of Mick, Nick, and the Maggies'" first appeared.

After two decades as a Joyce scholar, the benefits of the Joyce community have begun to emerge from a different direction, from students and younger scholars who obliged me to recognize new directions and concerns in the discipline. My classes, graduate and undergraduate, at the University of Michigan and the University of California at Irvine, have shaped and sharpened many of the arguments in this book through their pedagogic challenge. Derek Attridge's interrogation of my heliotropic valentine to Joyce in Copenhagen in 1986 had more impact than he knows on my turning away from romance and sexuality in exploring the problem of women in Joyce, and turning toward class, labor, and history. This shift, in turn, required the prior work on Joyce and feminism pioneered by Bonnie Scott, Shari Benstock, Mary Power, and many others. At the same time, the work of Patrick McGee, Cheryl Herr, and Vicki Mahaffey was prodding me to look at problems of culture and style as politicized and historicized elements of the Joycean text. The resulting shifts and torsions are inscribed in *Joyce's Web.*

Meanwhile, in my everyday writing and teaching of Joyce, I have worked so closely with Kimberly Devlin for so many years that I suspect much of my Joyce has come from her Joyce. At the same time, her support and friendship have extended far beyond the professional, and she has conspired, along with her husband, William Dahling, and our friend Vincent Cheng, to make the study and celebration of Joyce a movable feast for me. These circles of overlapping work and play within the field of Joyce studies make the institutional boundaries fluid enough to accommodate non-academics whose enthusiasm and acumen have much enriched our collective enterprise. I am especially grateful to have been so warmly received and nurtured by both southern and northern California *Finnegans Wake* circles, whose influence insures that my defections from Joyce study in future will be quite temporary. Finally, there is an honorary Joycean to whom I owe an especially tender thanks: my mom, Helga Barisits, who has replaced my son Josef on my Joyce travels, but who brings to my professional life the same familial warmth.

Abbreviations

CW	*The Critical Writings of James Joyce*, ed. E. Mason and R. Ellmann (1989)
CWOW	*The Complete Works of Oscar Wilde* (Harper & Row, 1989)
D	*Dubliners* (Modern Library, 1969)
E	*Exiles* (Viking Press, 1966)
EP	*Epiphanies* (University of Buffalo, 1956)
FW	*Finnegans Wake* (Viking Press, 1967)
JA	*The James Joyce Archive*, ed. M. Groden et al. (1978)
JJ	R. Ellmann, *James Joyce* (Oxford University Press, 1982)
Letters I	*Letters of James Joyce*, vol. 1, ed. S. Gilbert (1966)
Letters II	*Letters of James Joyce*, vol. 2, ed. R. Ellmann (1966)
Letters III	*Letters of James Joyce*, vol. 3, ed. R. Ellmann (1966)
OW	R. Ellmann, *Oscar Wilde* (1988)
P	*A Portrait of the Artist as a Young Man*, ed. C. Anderson (1968)
P/J	*Pound/Joyce: The Letters of Ezra Pound to James Joyce, with Pound's Essays on Joyce*, ed. F. Read (1967)
SH	*Stephen Hero*, ed. J. Slocum and H. Cahoon (1963)
SL	*Selected Letters of James Joyce*, ed. R. Ellmann (1975)
U	*Ulysses*, ed. H. Gabler (1986)

PART I
The Artist

CHAPTER ONE

Textual Raveling: A Critical and Theoretical Introduction

1. Joycean Canonization and Modernism

Consider the difference: Joyce's *Finnegans Wake* begins its critical history denounced as an unreadable book, and ends its critical history celebrated as an unreadable book. Inscribed in the difference of this false identity is the history of postmodern thought, whose momentum *Finnegans Wake* has ridden like a dark horse to a victory I will perversely question.[1] The question I will raise—perversely, because the postmodern intervention greatly abetted my own Wakean project—is whether the price of *Finnegans Wake*'s premature and oblique canonization as a postmodern work has not been Joyce's own more enduring historical power. This question reflects not only my own shift away from the ahistoricism of my earlier approach to Joyce (*The Decentered Universe of 'Finnegans Wake'*) but also the increasingly historical perspective of the contemporary critical and theoretical debates on the nature of the avant-garde and modernity, of modernism and postmodernism, that center largely on the relationship of modern art to social practice. Within this debate, the figure that still emerges as politically most suspect and contested is that of highly experimental art—a historical focus that makes *Finnegans Wake*'s ideological status central to the contemporary controversies over the politics of modernism and postmodernism.

To scholars familiar with Joyce's critical history, these controversies must seem old, having been fought from the thirties through the fifties on the left on both sides of the Atlantic,[2] with Edmund Wilson and Lionel Trilling defending Joyce's progressive liberalism in the United States, while the Soviet bloc marxists, notably Karl Radek at the 1934 Soviet Writers Congress, and later Georg Lukacs, denounced his ahistoricism, his existential solipsism, and his retrogressive formalism. But the marxist privileging of realism in its pursuit of a genetic or mimetic relationship of art and history, has begun to wane. The question of the social and historical significance of Joyce's art is currently revisited in the light of several significant ideological realignments made possible by, among others, the Frankfurt school's broadened understanding of the possibilities of art's social engagement, and by the increasing embrace of the "historical avant-garde" by the left. As a result, the question at the heart of current debates is whether linguistic and philosophical disruptions— of the kind that produce powerful paradigmatic shifts in intellectual history without addressing themselves to society's ideological practices—can or should be thought of as harboring revolutionary potential of a kind that can properly be called "political."

This question depends on a theorized understanding of the relation of what has come to be called the symbolic order (an ontopsychological conception of social power) to history conceived in the more structural materialist sense of traditional marxist philosophy. This focus is difficult to maintain in the face of post-structuralism's counterarguments that history must be construed as a discursive phenomenon or linguistic event,[3] or the rhetoricizing of history by theorists like Jean-François Lyotard and Jean Baudrillard who locate its power in names and signs. But Peter Buerger in his *Theory of the Avant-Garde* sets the terms for this debate in a way that challenges post-structuralism's attempts to steer the metaphysical radicalism of Wakean language into a politically progressive direction. Unlike Theodor Adorno, who finds in the non-instrumentality of art, its uselessness and absence of function, the tacit power to critique an instrumentalistic society, Buerger construes modernism's noninstrumental aestheticism as signifying the artistic autonomy that makes modern art the institutional collaborator of modern bourgeois ideology. "Lukács and Adorno argue within the institution that is art, and are unable to criticize it as an institution for that very reason" (lii). Specifically, an art that pretends to autonomy disavows its origin in the social realm and its reproduction of its foundational society's own oppressive practices. As the historical alternative to this aesthetic modernism flouting its independence from social and political responsibility—the construction of a modernist Joyce in opposition to a propagandistic Irish revival, for example— Buerger's thesis promotes the "historical avant-garde" of the early twentieth century (dadaists, surrealists, expressionists, etc.) as using the insights into the ideological function of artistic autonomy made visible by aestheticism to launch a system-immanent critique— that is, a self-criticism against the very institution of art that spawned it. Given Joyce's historical situation at the precise moment when the avant-garde's self-critique was made possible by its confrontation with aestheticism's disavowal of art's social origin, Buerger's political plotting of the art of modernity suggests a means of rehistoricizing *Finnegans Wake* to restore its significance as a text of the politically volatile thirties.[4]

By rehistoricizing the practice of periodization, Buerger's theory discloses the ahistoricism of the traditional critical constructions of the modern period, that by focusing on the shift from realism to aestheticism within the work of art, occlude the social function of the institution of art. This reformulation of the project of literary history should give particular priority to the practices resulting from artistic reception—canonization, for example—as a way of linking even apparently autonomous art to the ideological uses to which it may be put. In Anglo-American modernism, the revaluation of the poetic tradition was intertextualized both in poetic and critical practice by T. S. Eliot and Ezra Pound, who followed a Nietzschean mandate with respect to the use and abuse of history that ensured that art would serve autotelic ends. The privileged moments of their refigured literary history were positioned to empower the present life of modern art, and their implication of Joyce in this program is made explicit in the teleology betrayed by Eliot's syntax, when he praised Joyce's use of Homeric myth in *Ulysses* as "a step toward making the modern world possible for art" (178). But Eliot's gesture in his essay, of coding myth as a dehistoricizing method for the dehistoricizing of art, practices the disavowals upon which the ideology of artistic autonomy is founded. For Eliot's formalistic polemic mutes the historical anxiety over the cultural crisis, intellectual controversy, and censorship that nearly caused the production of *Ulysses* to founder and which gave his endorsement and support of Joyce such urgency. The success of that early modernist strategy extends into our own *fin de siecle*, where, amid sweeping and general discussions of aesthetics, Alvin Kernan invokes Stephen Dedalus as *the* aesthetic theorist:

> *Aesthetics,* a term coined expressly to designate romantic art values, has stressed the formal properties of art, above all, style. Style achieved in every aspect of the work, sound patterns, syntax, imagery and tropes, characters, and plots culminating in the wholeness, harmony and radiance, in Joyce's terms in *Portrait of the Artist,* of the perfected work of art. (22)

I would stress here that if Kernan distorts Joyce's strategy, by conflating his aesthetics with those of Stephen Dedalus, his move
merely emphasizes a chief ground for Joyce's canonization. The
canonical privileging of a discursive moment within Joyce's novel,
making the highly ironized and historicizable aesthetic theory of
Stephen Dedalus the synecdoche for modern aesthetics, betrays
an ideological choice to reinforce the very artistic autonomy that
a study like Kernan's, with its focus on censorship, copyright,
and other aspects of literary and artistic production, precisely
undermines.

In this study of Joyce, I will take as my target one of the "effects"
of his canonization—which I will both relate to and distinguish
from his texts and their interpretive constructions. The specific
"canonization effect" that troubles me in the case of Joyce is that of
the *doubling* cited above: Joyce canonized for an ahistoricism and
apoliticism that appears to repeat Stephen's heroic *Non-Serviam*
from *Portrait.* But although this effect represents neither the diver-
sity nor the consensus of Joyce's critical history, it nonetheless functions as a defining feature of Joyce's place within modernism, or, at
any rate, the mythology of a modernism whose great cultural contour has been the triumph of an arguably deconstructive poetics obsessed with the metaphysics of style and form (Riddel). In its crudest
version then, this "effect" is the equation of Joyce with the aestheticism of modernism, but an equation redolent with modernism's
suppressed romantic plot of the heroic artist saving art's power to
transcend its degradations in the modern world. Kernan makes the
romanticism of modern art explicit when he equates Wordsworth's
"spots of time" with Joyce's "epiphanies," and finds the romanticist
poet surviving all along the historical and political spectrum: "Sometimes they took up their stance on the left, like Blake and Shelley,
sometimes on the right like Yeats and Pound, but always, like
Joyce's Stephen Dedalus, they refused to bow—non serviam—to the
bourgeois family, religion, nation, and language that they felt cast
nets over their souls" (17). The postmodernization of *Finnegans
Wake,* celebrating the unreadability and freeplay of the text, participates ideologically in the same tradition of positioning Joyce's art
as the *other* of social life and material reality, as a metaphysical
epiphany, as it were.

Because it repeats the premise of artistic autonomy, art's freedom
from history and social determination, I will assimilate the postmodernization of Joyce to the trope of the aestheticism that deter-

mines Joyce's most significant ideological use as a canonized writer. But I hope to attack this mythology (too weighty, I would argue, to be a straw man) using Joyce himself as the critical probe. Specifically, I will argue that Joyce historicizes his own modernist aestheticism by grounding it in the nineteenth century liberal tradition's separation of art from social life. I will follow Seamus Deane in finding the source of the trope of the "poetic Celt" that is the historical mythology behind Stephen Dedalus in Matthew Arnold's ideological maneuver, and the beginnings of its immanent critique in Joyce's complex and incisive use of Oscar Wilde as the intertexted figure of the violence that the myth of aestheticism inflicts, materially and historically, on the Irish artist. Following Buerger's implicit internalization of Herbert Marcuse's formulation of "affirmative culture," I will argue that it is Wilde's aestheticism that makes visible and clear to Joyce the way the myth of artistic autonomy allows bourgeois society (and its historically dominant British culture in his own time) to use art as the idealistic supplement to heal the spiritual lacks and deprivations its materialism and commercialism produces; "art thus stabilizes the very social conditions against which it protests" (Buerger 11). Joyce's texts challenge, I will argue, the bourgeois legitimation of modern art's autonomy by exposing how art's aesthetic discourse tells political lies about itself. Joyce's texts, too, tell such lies—but Joyce provides multiple mechanisms whereby they are repeatedly caught. In the end, Joyce's texts can be made (through a paradoxical process of "unreading readings") to yield their own negation of artistic autonomy by betraying their genesis in Irish colonialism and lower class poverty, in reputable and disreputable fundraising and patronage, in censorship and amateur publishing. Joyce's texts betray that the forgery or deception practiced by an art putatively forged in the smithy of the soul, takes the form of amnesia regarding the complex economic, social, cultural, and political forces that forged it in history.

The Joycean text, then, I will argue, is capable of an ideological self-correction aimed specifically at the socially empowering features of its own aesthetic modernism. The strategy of this self-critique is to implicate the very qualities in which Joyce's emplacement as a modernist resides—the hard, clean, luminous epiphanic effects for which he is honored—in domestication of the oppressive history, colonial and continental, he is believed to have transcended with his art. In other words, I find a self-critique audible in a dispersed field of silent counterdiscourses, that gesture through the artistic self-congratulation and aesthetic pyrotechnics that shape the most characteristically modernist of Joyce's formal and stylistic self-displays. But instead of treating these textual self-corrections as the effect of historical contradictions that inscribe themselves into all textual discourses—as, for example, Franco Moretti treats the discursive tensions of *Ulysses*—I will adopt the more dramatic, but theoretically retrograde, practice of personifying these effects as Joyce's intention. This practice entails a price in theoretical self-contradiction: by reconsolidating Joyce as the controlling and designing author, I will be recuperating a leftist or socialist version of the very figure I wish to banish—that of the heroicized artist. But I would justify my strategy on polemical grounds—that a powerful countermyth is needed to oppose the powerful mythology of Joyce as modernist artist created by the collusion of Richard Ellmann's monumental biography with the Icarean trope of *Portrait*.

The adversary position I take toward Ellmann is not toward his text—which remains indispensable to Joycean scholarship and exemplary as a work of scholarly biography—but toward the specific features of its canonizing effects. Unlike the amusing parataxis in *The New Yorker* cartoon of Joyce's refrigerator—which attempts to redomesticate and rebourgeoisify the selfsublimation of Joyce's art—the Ellmann biography's blatant patronization of the way Joyce negotiated his material circumstances—poverty, money, class, social relations, politics—serves to firmly demarcate and valorize the separation of his art from his material and domestic life. Perhaps more than other literary biographies, the Ellmann biography reinforces the ideology of artistic autonomy by trivializing and denigrating what falls outside Joyce's art, including, as Robert Scholes has argued, Joyce's socialist and other political tendencies. The effect has been precisely that of a Marcusean affirmation: of implying that Joyce's artistic achievement transcends and redeems the problematic personal and political history out of which it is born, and which it negates. A new structural trope is needed to suggest a countermyth that neither merely juxtaposes the artistic and the social, the mundane and the sublime (as the cartoon does), nor represses and devalorizes the one in the interest of the other, as the Ellmann biography does. My own preferred trope will take the form of the gender contradiction implicit in our contemporaneous, Americanized, sense of Joyce's name, and mythically evoked, in my title *Joyce's Web*, to suggest that, like a modern Penelope, Joyce imbricates and interweaves the life of the art in ways that ravel modernism's myth of aesthetic and artistic autonomy.

2. Joyce, Feminism, and the Ideologically Self-Critical Text

To unravel the cruder of heroic high modernism's canonization effects, I plan to translate Joyce's ideological role in its history into
the countertrope of raveling Penelope: the artist as silent and cunning, to be sure, but also as securing with self-effacing and devious
textual practices and labor the ground against which the male heroic
epic may be narrativized. While Odysseus battles and adventures
abroad, "Penelope stay-at-home" (9:620) preserves his abandoned
native social fabric against colonization and consumption by the exploitive and parasitic suitors. Her strategy is to create a recuperable
time—a delay or reprieve prior to making a personal and political
commitment to a new marriage and a new king—by resorting to the
distaff ruse of weaving a shroud for her living father-in-law whose
completion she defers by unraveling it every night. This Odyssean
episode of a politically active text(ile) production serves me as
countermyth to the forcible separation of art and labor that Theodor
Adorno and Max Horkheimer, in *Dialectic of Enlightenment*, inscribe into the Odyssean Sirens episode to launch their critique of
the Enlightenment and its effects on modern thought. In this book I
plan to explore the Joycean *oeuvre* as a Penelopean text(ile): a writing whose opposition to heroic modernism I will type in a complex
figure of woman's material labor as political performance. In Joyce's
own text, I find this opposition inscribed in the parataxis of Stephen's bombastic final preparations to fly by his nets ("And the air
is thick with their company as they call to me, their kinsman, making ready to go, shaking the wings of their exultant and terrible
youth") and the prosaic female processing of recycled textiles.
"Mother is putting my new secondhand clothes in order" (252). I
will cast Joyce as a modern Penelope, unraveling in silent and submerged textual strategies the modernistic formalism that consolidates his power as an artist of (and, as Irishman, prostituted to) the
dominant culture.

By invoking a female trope recently wedded especially closely to
the modernist woman writer (in Susan Stanford Friedman's *Penelope's Web: Gender, Modernity, H.D.'s Fiction*), I oblige myself to
enter the contemporary feminist debate on Joyce's political status—
a debate extraordinarily useful for exploring larger relations of
theory, history, and gender. The sharp polarization of feminist response to Joyce—Anglo-American feminism's indictment of Joyce
for misogyny, on the one hand, and French feminism's political recuperation of his experimentalism as sharing the disruptions of
écriture féminine, on the other—focuses, in these dominant con-

temporary feminisms, a set of methodological and metaphysical differences in whose intellectual genealogies modernism (and Joyce
himself) share. The utilitarian Victorian grounding of the work of
Sandra Gilbert and Susan Gubar, for example, with its investment
in a liberal political tradition intent on reforming oppressive conditions and restoring the disenfranchised to the coveted authority and
power of the dominant order, sets itself psychologically and philosophically against much that is textually disruptive and avant-garde
in modern writing. Victorian (and patriarchal) values remain implicit in Gilbert and Gubar's approach: a privileging of representation over performativity, of realism over *écriture*, a faith in the presence and unity of the subject rather than delight in its disruptions,
and a commitment to the authority of the authorial voice rather
than to an unmasterable play of styles. Joyce, in their reading, may
therefore be indicted, ideologically, by inferences drawn from his
character's private and decontextualized musings on female speech
and female intelligence. "Clearly, in endowing Bloom with such
speculations, Joyce is taking upon himself the Holy Office of pronouncing that woman, both linguistically and biologically, is wholly
orifice" (232). We are reminded of the weakest critical moments of
Kate Millett's otherwise groundbreaking *Sexual Politics*, when she,
too, allows herself to assume that what male characters or narrators
say is what male authors invariably mean ("Paul Morel is of course
Lawrence himself" [246] or "Tommy Dukes, one of the author's
humbler mouthpieces" [242]).

French feminists in some cases (like Hélène Cixous [*The Exile of
James Joyce*]) arrive at feminism from, if not through, modernism,
and therefore reflect a theoretical disposition drawn from a Continental philosophical tradition that foregrounds the metaphysical
possibilities of the performative nature of language. Informed by the
traditions of Freud and Nietzsche and their problematization of discourse, they are least interested in crudely referential functions of
language—for example, the sort of "pronouncements" men make
about women. Instead, they recognize writing as an ontological gesture, a mode or *mise en scène* of being, whose significance resides
not in what is said, but in the relation between the performance of
saying and the significatory power structures of the symbolic order.
For Gilbert and Gubar, Joyce speaks in the same monological voice
of male authority and mastery ("'Oxen of the Sun' presents us with
a parabolic wresting of patriarchal power from the mother tongue"
[260]) however traditional or experimental his styles. For French
feminism, Joyce's anarchic disruptions constitute a philosophically
revolutionary gesture:

As capitalist society is being economically and politically choked to death, discourse is wearing thin and heading for collapse at a more rapid rate than ever before. Philosophical finds, various modes of "teaching" scientific or aesthetic formalisms follow one upon another, compete, and disappear without leaving either a convinced audience or noteworthy disciples. . . . Only one language grows more and more contemporary: the equivalent, beyond a span of thirty years, of the language of *Finnegans Wake*. (Kristeva 92)

But however political these formulations, they are not grounded in history, either Joyce's or modern literature's. Because their disruptive locus is the emplacement of the subject in a transhistorical symbolic order—for example, that of the family or that of the libidinal organization of the body—the revolutionary potential of the problematized discourses they privilege is ontopsychological rather than material or historical. The danger, for feminism, in politically valorizing a writing like that of *Finnegans Wake*, is precisely that of producing feminism without women—a feminism of no benefit to historical or material women.

However much *Finnegans Wake*'s experimentalism may be coded in feminist typologies as "preoedipal," "semiotic," *jouissance*, and the like,[5] the reference of its disruptive powers to family, language, or pleasure nonetheless fails to address its historical moment or demonstrate its social relevance. The historical and political recuperation of *Finnegans Wake* remains more a matter of polemical assertion than of critical demonstration, even in the hands of poststructuralist critics with a marxist bent. Colin MacCabe finds little contradiction between deconstruction's ahistoricism and marxism's historical progressivism. "What is subverted in the writing is the full Cartesian subject and this subversion is a political event of central importance," he writes of *Finnegans Wake*. "When Lenin called for a 'new kind of party,' he was challenging the assumption that those who wished to transform social relations could organise in a discrete area called 'politics.' . . . And it is in terms of the desire for 'a new kind of party' that one can understand Joyce's texts as revolutionary in their commitment to the overthrow of the possibility of contemporary (both his and still ours) political discourse" (152–153). But Gayatri Spivak, in contrast, remains unpersuaded by this general type of argument. "I have already expressed my dissatisfaction with the presuppositions of the *necessarily* revolutionary potential of the avant-garde, literary and philosophical. There is something even faintly comical about Joyce rising above sexual identities

and bequeathing the proper mind-set to the women's movement"
(169). Spivak's dismissal of Joyce's feminism as a joke ("faintly comical") serves, in its glibness, less as critique than as brash resistance
to male canonical appropriation and assimilation of feminism. But
the danger of Spivak's refusal to concede that the male writer could
rise above sexual identity sufficiently to achieve feminist insight is
that it puts more general possibilities of historical progress—including woman's ability to rise above sexual identity—into question. At stake, to my mind, in both Anglo-American and French
feminism's critique of Joyce, is the question of the use and abuse of
history, in a Nietzschean sense. Both feminist traditions practice a
polemically mandated ahistoricism that, in each case, erases, elides,
or "forgets" its male intellectual antecedence. French feminism
"forgets" Nietzsche in joyful and properly submerged obedience to
his own example of a proper erasure and amnesia of historical debts
and precedents in the interest of a present and living exercise of
power. The birthright of a Nietzschean daughter is the originary
myth of her intellectual orphanage—as though she sprang full-grown
from her own body and intellect. In contrast, Anglo-American feminism's reformist model maintains a therapeutic utilitarian historical practice of chronicling gender narratives around the moral axis
of oppression, suffering, and disenfranchisement. Its literary history
becomes the genealogy of a crippled female tradition produced by
male literary misogyny. The implicit historical focus of Gilbert and
Gubar's *No Man's Land* is less the analysis of the remarkable intellectual and political forces in mid- to late nineteenth century England that brought about the suffrage movement and woman's powerful cultural emergence, than the polemical re-creation of woman
as a literary spectacle of insult, injury, and suffering.

The relation of the contemporary feminisms (using Gilbert and
Gubar synecdochically for a major tendency in the Anglo-American
tradition) to Joyce's work and status serves to illustrate the problems
created by dehistoricizing "the political" in literary study. In the
case of Joyce's history this problem is especially complicated because a variety of disparate but converging forces have tended to
conspire to canonize him (or critique his canonization) on essentially ahistorical grounds. Seamus Deane describes this practice in
his essay on "Joyce and Nationalism" when he writes, "Repudiating
British and Roman imperialisms and rejecting Irish nationalism and
Irish literature which seemed to be in service to that cause, he
turned away from his early commitment to socialism and devoted
himself instead to a highly apolitical and wonderfully arcane practice of writing. Such, in brief, is the received wisdom about Joyce

and his relationship to the major political issues of his time" (168). Ellmann's biography hewed this thesis into the Joyce history (as Robert Scholes has criticized), and the myth he thereby established was scarcely undone when, enlightened by the Trieste library, Ellmann conceded in his revisions of the 1977 *The Consciousness of Joyce*, "Literature is a revolutionary instrument, however round-about it may move" (79). This is not to say that there have not been powerful refigurations of Joyce as a political writer in recent years—a scholarly trend inaugurated by Ellmann's student, Dominic Manganiello, whose *Joyce's Politics*, Cheryl Herr writes, "testifies to the profoundly political nature of Joyce's writings" (7). But the full range of possibilities for historical progress that might have been produced in male consciousness by a variety of oppressive conditions and their intellectual effects in the late nineteenth and early twentieth centuries have still to be explored. Joyce's gender thinking, in particular, needs to be resituated in the socialistic dramatic tradition of Ibsen, Hauptmann, and Shaw, and their translation of socially determined critiques (colonial, working class, gender) into dramaturgical experiments addressed to the progressive power of a living art and culture.

Bonnie Scott in her early study of *Joyce and Feminism* researched and historically situated much of Joyce's intellectual background—a background itself highly implicated in his modernism—with respect to theories and attitudes toward gender and feminism.[6] Feminist critics outside the Joyce community have paid scant attention to this aspect of the Joycean history, and have failed or refused to test Joyce's alleged misogyny against the rather remarkable historical phenomenon of an Irish adolescent male at the turn of the century coming to intellectual consciousness and maturity through a complex and subversive modernity that makes gender—both in progressive and misogynistic versions—one of its key issues. It is not difficult to muster evidence that Joyce received his insights from male rather than female thinkers, and that he followed the path of Ibsen and Hauptmann, rather than Strindberg and Schopenhauer, with respect to gender politics; I would contend that Carolyn Heilbrun is simply wrong when she writes "Joyce admired Ibsen and ignored his most profound contribution" (*Women in Joyce* 215). One could argue that it was precisely the "feminine" curriculum of modern languages (Scott) he studied in his Jesuit schools rather than the classical Greek he would have been taught in the more conventional English public schools from which his Irish Catholicism and poverty barred him, that gave Joyce early models of radical modernity—the Nietzschean revision of classical philology, for example, that ultimately forms his use of Homer in *Ulysses*. His uniquely progressive Continental education dominated Joyce's intellectual development, and spawned a remarkable cultural activism, during his late teens.

If we consider his earliest publications and intellectual projects, his review of Ibsen's *When We Dead Awaken* in 1900, his translations of Gerhart Hauptmann's *Vor Sonnenaufgang* and *Michael Kramer* in the following year, and the 1901 publication of "The Day of the Rabblement," we see Joyce as an eighteen- and nineteen-year-old boy profoundly agitated by a modern, experimental literature whose political relevance to modern-day Ireland he extols urgently in every conceivable venue available to him. Joyce's first published work is a review of Ibsen that particularly praises the Norwegian's sympathetic portrayal of oppressed woman, "Ibsen's knowledge of humanity is nowhere more obvious than in his portrayal of women," and virtually credits him with an early version of something proleptic of *écriture féminine*: "He amazes one by his painful introspection; he seems to know them better than they know themselves. Indeed, if one may say so of an eminently virile man, there is a curious admixture of the woman in his nature" (CW 64).

The young Joyce's outrage at the Irish Literary Theatre's decision to back away, in the face of threatened censorship, from the production of modern Continental drama in Dublin, evinces his keen sense of the revolutionary potential of this modern art for his own contemporary society. The young Joyce cites a compendious list of modern writing in "The Day of the Rabblement" that includes, among others, Tolstoy, Turgenev, Flaubert, Maeterlinck, Strindberg, and D'Annunzio. But he singles out Ibsen for special emphasis—"the old master who is dying in Christiania" (CW 72)—and Gerhart Hauptmann, the writer Joyce nominates as Ibsen's most worthy successor. Joyce wrote to Stanislaus on 15 March 1905, "I believe that Ibsen and Hauptmann separate from the herd of writers because of their political aptitude—eh?" (SL 59).

If we keep this biographical gesture in mind when we read *Stephen Hero*—the young Joyce frustrated, as Stephen is, by Dublin's refusal and failure to use the modern art of the Continent as a progressive lens for exploring its own oppressive colonial and bourgeois situation—a very different artistic agenda may be discerned in the young artist of both life and art than the aesthetic modernism privileged by Ellmann. Ellmann's sense that Joyce admired an individualistic, aesthetic, and heroic Ibsen rather than the progressive socialist celebrated by Shaw, and initially adopted as a nationalistic model by Yeats, Moore, Martyn, and other figures of the Irish revival, is reflected in other, unsubstantiated arguments that Joyce consistently separated himself from the feminist agendas of his compatriots. "The Day of the Rabblement" was published privately, together with "A Forgotten Aspect of the University Question," by Joyce and Francis Skeffington. Ellmann argues that the two young men separated their essays in the preface ("each writer is responsible only for what appears under his own name") because "neither agreed with the other's position" (JJ 88) without offering any further evidence for this rationale. Ellmann thus creates the long-lived assumption that Joyce feared contamination of his work by Skeffington's feminist text, which advocated equal status for women at the university, and that modernism's and feminism's agendas, beyond their common censorship by institutional authority, were incompatible and irreconcilable. But if we contest this assumption, we leave open a different possibility—namely, that Joyce saw the suppression of modern art's living critical use in society related to Skeffington's promotion of higher education for women. This possibility casts a rather different light on Stephen's Ibsen crusade in *Stephen Hero*, one that sharply foregrounds the unusual role Joyce lets the overworked mother play in that novel, as the key addressee and consumer of the new modern art whose suppression her artist son so vigorously protests.

At this point I wish less to produce a feminist reading of *Stephen Hero* than to demonstrate that this early text (which ought perhaps to be construed as the novel Joyce wanted to write first, and perhaps most, rather than the discarded residue of *Portrait*'s refinement) explicitly thematizes and dramatizes Joyce's early obsession with the critical uses and functions of modern art. This obsession is textually and historically repeated and re-versed during this period: inscribed in Joyce's essay ("Drama and Life") and Stephen's essay ("Art and Life"), dramatized in Ibsen's censorship and Joyce's protest against that censorship, repeated in Joyce's own censorship in Dublin, it was a living drama of modern art urgently striving and failing to present itself to a populace whose institutions repel it against the people's best interests. In *Stephen Hero*, Stephen argues for a Nietzschean historical use of art ("The poet is the intense centre of the life of his age to which he stands in a relation than which none can be more vital" [SH 80]), and Joyce stresses throughout Ibsen's status as a *living* author ("I never heard of his name before. Is he alive at present?—Yes, he is" [SH 84]). Yet in this Irish cultural climate that refuses to read Ibsen or allow him to be read ("The young men of the college had not the least idea who Ibsen was but from what they could gather here and there they surmised that he must be one of

the atheistic writers whom the papal secretary puts on the *Index*"
[SH41]), the most unlikely figure in the world—the harassed mother
ironing clothes while interrogating the apostasies of her son—becomes one of the first readers of Ibsen. "What does Ibsen write,
Stephen?" (SH84) she asks, and Stephen offers her the plays to read.
Joyce is writing here, I would contend, the passionate living rationale behind "The Day of the Rabblement," namely that people like
his mother *need* Ibsen. As a dramatized plea for female literacy, this
scenario of Mrs. Daedalus, reading—while her children die around
her—Ibsen's ideological critique of nineteenth-century idealizations
of *Kindermord*, serves as the populist version and counterpart of
Skeffington's essay in favor of admitting women to university.

Mrs. Daedalus *needs* Ibsen because she does not know why her
children die. "Do you know anything about the body?" she asks her
son. "There's some matter coming away from the hole in Isabel's . . .
stomach. . . . The hole . . . the hole we all have . . . here" (SH 163).
Her aphasia (uttered in life by Mrs. Joyce about Georgie [EP 171]) is,
in a sense, ideological and political, for she cannot name the perito-
nitis that kills Isabel, as it killed Joyce's brother George as well as
countless poverty-stricken children suffering from typhoid and other
contamination-produced diseases at the turn of the century, because
she does not recognize it as belonging to what Mary Lowe-Evans
calls "the discourses of population control" in the Ireland of Joyce's
time. "Joyce was a poor Irish-Catholic Dubliner," Mary Lowe-Evans
writes, "the son of a woman who experienced seventeen pregnancies
and died at the age of forty-five" (26). Infantile, juvenile, and mater-
nal mortality inscribed themselves historically on the bodies of Irish
women and children. "How many children had she," Cranly asks
Stephen of his mother in *Portrait:* " 'Nine or ten,' Stephen answered.
Some died" (P 241). In *Stephen Hero,* under the intertexted tutelage
of Ibsen and Hauptmann, agency is restored to Stephen's cold "Some
died":

> Isabel was lying upstairs in the backroom, day by day growing
> more wasted and querulous. The doctor came twice a week now
> and ordered her delicacies. Mrs. Daedalus had to set her wits to
> work to provide even one substantial meal every day and she cer-
> tainly had no time to spare between accomplishing this feat, ap-
> peasing the clamour at the halldoor, parrying her husband's ill-
> humour and attending on her dying daughter. (SH 151)

Isabel dies because she is the least effective of her family's creditors.
And while modern literature cannot save her, it can at least spare

her the violence of ideological sentimentalization in her mother's heart. "I hope you're not going to mention Little Nell in the *Old Curiosity Shop*" (SH 86), Stephen tells her, fearing Dickens has corrupted the meaning of Ibsen's *Wild Duck* for his mother. At the very least, Ibsen may help to prevent the hole of Irish woman's self-understanding from being glued with Victorian treacle.

In having the agency of modern art mediate, however ineffectually, Mrs. Daedalus's self-figurations as *pietà* in his first attempt at a novel, the young Joyce complicated his inaugural *Kuenstlerroman* with a powerful immanent critique of undeniable historical specificity. Set in the twilight of Ibsen's career in order to problematize the passing of his cultural legacy and ideological power upon the furthest and most provincial reaches of Europe, Joyce emplaces his own novel of artistic development within a late nineteenth-century tradition of art as social praxis. Joyce's inscription of this living literary history into his text constitutes a project resonant to a modern conception of marxist critical practice, like that of Tony Bennett:

> I want to suggest that the proper object for Marxist literary theory consists not in the study of texts but in the study of reading formations. By a reading formation, I mean a set of discursive and inter-textual determinations which organise and animate the practice of reading, connecting texts and readers in specific relations to one another. (70)

By privileging gender as a specific feature of such a "reading formation" in *Stephen Hero*, I hoped also to demonstrate a way of historicizing Joyce's gender practice in a tradition of progressive and avant-garde writing.

3. Intertexted Weavings

My aim, in this discussion of Joyce and feminism, has been to argue that the young Joyce—poised on the verge of the modernism that marked *Portrait*, and that emblematized him as the most aestheticist, apolitical, and ahistorical of the high modernists—began with a highly developed and clearly demonstrable sense of, and commitment to, the social function of art. But, derived from a dramaturgical tradition whose initial realism was quickly experimentalized, Joyce's socialist project is rarely polemicized—except in the notoriously bombastic first ending of the 7 January 1904 sketch of *Portrait* that has the poet see "messages of citizens . . . flashed along the wires of the world" to the unborn multitudes:

Man and woman, out of you comes the nation that is to come,
the lightning of your masses in travail; the competitive order is
employed against itself, the aristocracies are supplanted; and
amid the general paralysis of an insane society, the confederate
will issues in action. (P 265)

In its broader scope, the problem of artistic social praxis is inscribed
in the Joycean *oeuvre* in forms of Penelopean weavings, intertexted
figures of palimpsests and imbricated writings that perform rather
than announce their social functions—all the while, like Penelope's
raveled and rewoven shroud, they efface their labor and its critical
and social significance.

Joyce's most famous figuration of the aesthetic gesture, Stephen's
theorizing of beauty as a set of formal relations in *Portrait,* explicitly
performs aestheticism's excision of material and social labor from
the aesthete's idealistic concerns:

Stephen pointed to a basket which a butcher's boy had slung inverted on his head.
—Look at that basket, he said.
—I see it, said Lynch.
—In order to see that basket, said Stephen, your mind first
of all separates the basket from the rest of the visible universe
which is not the basket. The first phase of apprehension is a
bounding line drawn about the object to be apprehended. An esthetic image is presented to us either in space or in time. . . . But,
temporal or spatial, the esthetic image is first luminously apprehended as selfbounded and selfcontained upon the immeasurable
background of space or time which is not it. (P 212)

This passage illustrates how aesthetic theorizing is founded on the
disavowal of the material and social relations of life, and how the
apprehension of the beauty of the basket depends on eliding its
status as a commodity, a produced object representing the transformation of human labor, as well as its social function as an implement of labor. Stephen, ignoring the young Joyce's own lesson from
Ibsen that art should represent "men and women as we meet them
in the real world" (CW 45), cuts the butcher boy out of the picture
altogether, but not without leaving us the problematic residue of
that decapitated head still presumably within the inverted basket.
Phantom figures of labor remain behind all sorts of luminously apprehended selfbounded and selfcontained images and effects in the
Joycean text—which both extirpates them and makes their extirpa-

tion by aestheticism visible to the reader. The social unraveling of modernism in my subtitle is effected by Joyce's strategy of problematizing the aesthetic theory that has come to emblematize aesthetics in general (Kernan), and modernist aesthetics in particular, by recovering its implied violence.

The trope of the raveled textile of Penelope—that allows me to figure the Joycean textual practice as one of imbricating art, labor, and gender—has other palimpsestic versions in figures of the Joycean text, including a repeated figure for Stephen's poetic production that takes forms of double-sidedness like that theorized in Derrida's *Post Card*. At least three of Stephen's poems are written (or not written) on paper that is already inscribed with what he himself would eventually refer to as the language of the market-place: the aborted poem about Parnell attempted "on the back of one of his father's second moiety notices" (P 70), the villanelle scribbled on the cardboard of a cigarette packet ("Smoke went up from the whole earth, from the vapoury oceans, smoke of her praise" [P 218]), and, of course, the vampire poem in "Proteus" ("mouth to her mouth's kiss" [U 3:398]) penned on a strip torn from the bottom of Deasy's letter to the newspaper about hoof and mouth disease. Beyond the wit of the associations, a more serious point is made; Stephen's art, however much it strives to epiphanize itself and thereby transcend its material and social context, is literally inscribed in the textualization of Ireland's political and economic life. Stephen can only write on the back or in the margins of texts of British commercial power: the impotence of the Irish writer figured as the inability to pen a poem to Parnell on the back of a landlord's eviction threat. Nor is this figure of the socially imbricated text of art a mere conceit, as the physical manuscript evidence of Stanislaus's diary indicates. George Healey in his preface to *The Complete Dublin Diary of Stanislaus Joyce* describes that artifact as speaking in its materiality of the poverty of the household in which it was produced: "It consists of 230 pages of writing on sheets cut to about eight by six and a half inches. These sheets, most of them previously used on one side, were culled from old business letters, school exercises, ledger paper, notebook leaves, and similar odds and ends. At least one sheet is a palimpsest; the diarist erased a whole page of something else to gain a usable page for himself" (viii). Furthermore, it turns out that four of Joyce's early essays—"Force," "The Study of Languages," "Ecce Homo," and "Drama and Life," according to Jill Perkins (3)—survived originally as scrap paper recycled by Stanislaus for the diary, "preserved because Stanislaus subsequently used the versos of their pages for his own writing." For Joyce this scarcity

of the most literal material basis of art, the implication of paper in
the poverty of the familial social economy, exists as a historical fact
before it is appropriated as a trope for the artistic mode of production. Its ideological impact, however, resides in Stephen's, the narrative's, and the reader's occlusion of this textual thickening as the
economic and social condition of art.

These examples of the palimpsestic thickening of the Joycean text
with materiality are intended to introduce the textile strategy that
I metaphorize as weaving and raveling by offering textual displacements—parataxes, dialogisms, heteroglossias, elisions and patches,
scars and sutures (to reinsert the various forms of violence that produce the trouble surfaces of Joycean writing)—as a political effect. I
intend, then, to strategically supplement and complicate what recent politicalizations of Joyce have begun to stress. "Much of his
writing can easily be read as one sustained allegory of Irish society
and politics during the nineteenth and early twentieth centuries"
(215), Vincent Pecora has written. But the techniques I will explore
for their social and political effects retain much of the textualism of
my post-structuralist and postmodernistic training. Only I hope to
give the postmodernistic features I will uncover in the texts, their
fragmentariness and patchiness, for example, an etiology that is
more political and less hypertextual and logopoetic than that of deconstructive approaches. In its self-referentiality and self-reflexivity,
I hope to show in the Joycean language an avant-garde intention (in
Buerger's sense) of criticizing, rather than reinforcing, the autonomy,
separatism, and ultimate transcendentality of modern art. To do so
I need to trace the aporia in the historical success of Joyce's canonization, namely, that the cultural success of the avant-garde (its
status as "high art" in the contemporary museum) is its failure
and its death. Compared with the truest and most self-destructive
historical manifestations of avant-garde art—for example, the self-
consuming forms of ephemeral Dada performance whose Zurich
conjunction with Joyce Tom Stoppard celebrated in *Travesties*—a
Joycean avant-gardism appears as bourgeois self-parody. Indeed, it
would have been better had *Finnegans Wake* really been the hoax
that many believed it to be in its earliest history: as hoax, Joyce's
last text would have been the ultimate avant-garde act, the most
obscene violation of art's responsibility to itself, to its own institution. Consider the flamboyance of that gesture: an unintelligible 627
page text, written in an alien "other" language—something like
"choctaw," as Pound called it (P/J 237)—that would have represented a reckless waste of seventeen years of unceasing labor, an
indisputable talent, a growing international reputation, a generous

and life-sustaining patronage, all in order to produce a malicious counterfeit of art whose only purpose and profit could have been to assault the literary establishment by violating its faith in genius and devotion to art. It would have been magnificent—but *de trop:* its social cost hugely disproportionate to its social usefulness. Instead, *Finnegans Wake's* texticidal strategies are less radical, nihilistic, and suicidal: art survives, but in a self-critical form that places its own truth and beauty under ethical and political skepticism. Its textual effects—not only the *Wake's*, but also those of the earlier fictions it disfigures and revises—form a dialectical and heteroglossic manifestation. In them, Joyce is no longer making the modern world possible for art, but rather making art answer to the conditions of a modern world that uses art to lie about itself.

My approach, then, is not properly an ideological analysis of the Joycean text, since I do not scrutinize the values and assumptions that work through Joyce in the form of his cultural materials and that inscribe their role in his social construction as an artist upon his art. By mythologizing Joyce's own textual strategies as implementations of a chosen and self-conscious social labor, I realize that I am privileging him, among the high modernists, as the "socialist artist" he proclaimed himself to his brother in 1905 (L II, 89). Such a reading contributes to an emergent critical ideology that has begun to make Joyce the "good boy" of modernism. But while not being able to avoid the political heroicizing of Joyce altogether, I wish my emphasis to be shifted more to the exploration of the progressive possibilities of experimental texts. Specifically I would like to delineate how Joyce uses texts as a *mise en scène* of ideological formation, as a stage on which we can watch discourse executing ideological projects of which it is unaware. Joyce interplays textual discourses and the silences which give them birth as politically implicated structures. Because of this negative element in his strategy, the dependence of his discourse upon absences and silences and gaps, his dramatization of ideological formations has become more visible since marxist criticism has developed philosophical tools for interrogating texts against the pressures of their formal unity and the seeming plenum of their discursive "presence." Fredric Jameson discusses the impact of Louis Althusser's refiguration of "the work of art":

> It follows, then, that the interpretive mission of a properly structural causality will on the contrary find its privileged content in rifts and discontinuities within the work, and ultimately in a conception of the former 'work of art' as a heterogeneous and (to

use the most dramatic recent slogan) a schizophrenic text. In the case of Althusserian literary criticism proper, then, the appropriate object of study emerges only when the appearance of formal unification is unmasked as a failure or an ideological mirage. (56)

In similar language, Terry Eagleton formulates Macherey's negative model of ideology as a discursive paradigm whose literal structures I intend to seek in the Joycean text: "An ideology exists because there are certain things which must not be spoken of. In so putting ideology to work, the text begins to illuminate the absences which are the foundation of its articulate discourse" (90).

My approach transgresses the proper task of ideological criticism— "Its task is to show the text as it cannot know itself, to manifest those conditions of its making . . . about which it is necessarily silent" (Eagleton 43)—because it largely displaces focus from Joyce and his production of the text in history to Joyce's narrative discourse and its ideological formation within the Joycean text. I treat the Joycean text then not as a cultural phenomenon but as a *representation* of a cultural phenomenon, or, to shift to my preferred model—which I believe is also Joyce's, given his crucial early interest in experimental drama—the *staging* of a cultural phenomenon. This approach is consistent with my previous efforts to approach the Joycean text psychoanalytically, not as a psychic production but as Joyce's representation or staging of a psychic production—that is, *Finnegans Wake* not as dream (Attridge, Begnal, Bishop) but as textual staging of dream-work, as the production of psychoanalytic paradigms in textual form. I would like to contend, then, that my theoretical shift from the structuralist and post-structuralist influences I acquired (sometimes in garbled form) from the scant and fresh translations available while I was formulating my initial approach to *Finnegans Wake* nearly twenty years ago, is less a defection than a reflection of the changed critical possibilities that the mutual awareness and consequent self-reflexion of deconstructive and historical theories have produced during the last two decades.

My critical procedure is, then, a raveling of Joyce's raveled text, a teasing apart and reknitting of writing intertexted with itself as gaps in early works become visible only when they are sutured by extended narratives in later works, as later works rewrite and revise earlier texts that themselves give the later ones a different significance. I will ravel "Clay," for example, by stitching into its elided narrative of washerwomen's labor, its suppressed story of what women do and say when they work, the extended poetic work song of the launderwoman voices of "Anna Livia Plurabelle." At the same time, I will draw the significance of this interpolation from a nineteenth-century project that attempted to turn classical philology on its head (Samuel Butler's *The Authoress of the "Odyssey"*) by restoring female domestic materialism to the origin of the Western classical epic. This meaningful intertextuality is not merely logopoetic—an art that obsessively draws self-referential attention to the ineluctability of its own verbal status—but also ideological. I will draw attention to the social and historical determinations that make the complex narrative and allusive relations that I find troubling and riving the Joycean text—the imbrications, contradictions, supplementarities, and dissonances—ideologically functional. My procedure thus flouts post-structuralism's warnings against the "reading" of *Finnegans Wake* ("the aim is not to produce a *reading* of this intractable text, to make it more familiar and exorcise its strangeness, but on the contrary to confront its unreadability," [*Post-structuralist Joyce* 10]) but does so in the interest of retrieving—from the more general linguistic productivity that deconstructive theory explores for its metaphysical ruptures—the specificities of class inflection, rhetorical purpose and cross-purpose, and historical reference that restore the *Wake* to literary history as a social text. I side, then, with Patrick McGee when he argues, "The reading that excludes all readings withdraws from the political and social space in which textual productivity is realized in practice. It retreats into the idealism or fetishism of the text." (6)

Joyce's writing is produced within the institution of art at a historical moment that exerts enormous pressure upon art to live in untruth. In its commitment to aesthetic formalism, to verbal craft and classical discipline, modernism proclaims its autotelic constitution, its redemption of modernity by transcending its social and economic degradations, at the very moment that capitalism and censorship, colonialism and world war, class struggle and revolution, inscribe themselves on its production, reception, and form. Joyce, I will argue, negotiates this cultural paradox of modern art's self-representation in a way that runs him afoul of Georg Lukács' privileging of realism as the premier form of socially responsible representation, but that aligns itself with the oblique and playful anti-mimeticisms of the historical avant-garde. Like Penelope's weaving, Joyce's art is devious and self-destructive. He reproduces in the surface narratives of *Portrait* and "The Dead," for example, the dominant ideology's narratives of artistic legitimation in Arnoldian alternatives to Saxon Philistinism. But in addition to the self-critical ironizations that Wayne Booth and Hugh Kenner uncovered early in the critical history of the Joycean text, I will try to uncover larger narrative maneuvers of self-repeal and sub-textual counterreadings that allow the Joycean text to incriminate and indict itself—both for its aesthetic effects and its bourgeois values. I hope to show the Joycean text continually disrupted by its own silences, by voices that it represses, by stories it suppresses and displaces, by eruptions of countertextual challenges ("stifled back answers" I call them in "The Dead") that cause it to confront its blindness toward its own oppressiveness. Weaving it to its historical roots in late nineteenth- and early twentieth-century dramaturgical experiment, I locate Joycean avant-gardism in a dramatic and dynamic textual performativity whose end is not autotelic, as deconstruction would argue, but political: modern art's confrontation with its own extrusions of the ideologically unprofitable.

The demonstration of this thesis will be carried out in subsequent chapters, through a patchwork strategy of raveling and re-weaving that produces readings and unreadings of a series of related texts. I will organize these raveled readings around three mythologized tropes in the Joycean *oeuvre*—artist, woman, and child—that track both their representations, especially their aestheticized and epiphanic figurations, and their mutism, what they can't say, in order to articulate their dialogical occupation of the Joycean text. Because this kind of critical activity is plotted into the Joycean text through negative structures and relations—gaps, dissonances, fragmentations, lies—my readings will never be quite *there* in any conventional sense. They will depend on listening for the inaudible, and rely on speculation, though—I hope—speculation driven by pressures of disturbance within the texts. At the same time one can point to increasingly compelling archival evidence of Joyce's own raveled composition practice in the work of Joyce's manuscript scholarship—especially David Hayman's recently published *The "Wake" in Transit*. I will appeal to this evidence only sporadically, in spite of my conviction that it confirms the sort of intertexted procedures I believe I consistently uncover. At the same time, I would go beyond archival scholarship in finding in Joyce's composition practice at least the rudiments of an ideological agenda.

By alluding to the workshop materials in the *Archive*, I wish to stress that Joyce's lifelong awareness of labor as a suppressed issue of art may be grounded in a writing practice whose mark as labor, however mental, thus remains indisputably clear to us. Terry Eagleton writes of Joyce's art, "art instead was a productive *labour*, a massive life-consuming substitute for the social identity denied by a stagnant, clericist, culturally parochial Ireland" (154). In his own writing practice of weaving the strands of old ideas together (Hayman calls Joyce's composition "an endlessly unfolding and self-enfolding process text, a Penelope's web that includes the reader in its perpetual elaboration and unmaking" [7]), I believe Joyce, who clearly had Hauptmann in mind as a model during his "Work in Progress" (*Our Exagmination* 91), may have intended to demythologize his textual weaving as Gerhart Hauptmann did when he restored it to the history of labor. Joyce considered Hauptmann's *The Weavers*, his drama of the 1844 riots of the Silesian textile workers, a "masterpiece," calling it (with a gloss on Yeats) "'a little immortal thing';" (SL 117). My point, of course, is not that Joyce's labor was hard, oppressive, or even strictly material—although he once boasted to Myron Nutting that the old notes from *Ulysses* he sorted to begin the *Wake* weighed twelve kilos (JJ 545). But the analogy of the *Wake*'s composition with the material raveling of weaving is useful because it draws attention to Joyce's material salvage of textual detritus—the scraps and discards of earlier writing—that doubled, arguably, as ideological detritus. In the notebook Thomas Connolly first introduced as *James Joyce's Scribbledehobble: The Ur-Workbook for Finnegans Wake*, and that is now designated as Buffalo Notebook VI.A in *The James Joyce Archive*, the beginning of the *Wake* as an interweaving from the early texts is made abundantly clear: "Joyce divided this notebook into forty-seven sections, and gave each section a title drawn from one of his previous literary works, beginning with *Chamber Music* and ending with the various parts of *Ulysses*" (viii). The features of this composition procedure first caught my attention because of their similarity to the psychoanalytic textuality of dream formation: the dream's raveling and reweaving of discarded and trivial psychic material into new and significant (if seemingly unintelligible and surreal) dream texts. In my early psychoanalytic approach to *Finnegans Wake* (*The Decentered Universe*) I lacked a waking referent, a source for the manifest content, as it were, for interpreting the *Wake* as a dream. That referent has emerged, and can now be found, in the early Joyce works themselves, as Kimberly J. Devlin has demonstrated textually in *Wandering and Return in "Finnegans Wake,"* and Hayman's study of the notebooks has reinforced archivally. But while it would now be possible to read *Finnegans Wake* as the textual unconscious of the early Joycean *oeuvre*, its study as their political unconscious seems more compelling at the present time.

   Although the content of the *Scribbledehobble* entries is so cryptic that they have been used as little more than word lists, I find that they make sense when related to certain chapters which are "patched" in my sense, and when one looks for the neglected or marginalized element. For example, the entries under "Nausikaa" in *Scribbledehobble* confirm my sense that that chapter is precurser to the children's games of Book II, Chapter 1, of *Finnegans Wake*, "The Mime of Mick, Nick, and the Maggies." The entries referring to children especially ("little sufferers," "baby went asleep" [113]) foregrounds the children in "Nausicaa," the Caffrey twins and Baby Boardman, whose presence is a largely uninterrogated excrescence, a gratuitous addition to the *Odyssey* episode in which no children appear at all. The question of why Joyce should add gratuitous children to chapters becomes particularly interesting in light of the ways children are ideologically profitable (for example, the martyrdom and miniature Parnellization of little Stephen as contributing to the mythologizing of the heroic artist in *Portrait*) or unprofitable in the Joycean text, like the slum children who appear in the margins of the *Dubliners* stories as so much vermin:

> A horde of grimy children populated the street. They stood or ran in the roadway or crawled up the steps before the gaping doors or squatted like mice upon the thresholds. Little Chandler gave them no thought. He picked his way deftly through all that minute vermin-like life. (71)

But in the strange twist Joyce gives the angel references in his "Nausikaa" entries in *Scribbledehobble* (angel references seemingly proleptic of the game "Angels and Devils or colours" in the *Wake*'s "Mime") a Hauptmannesque version of childhood like that in the play alluded to by Jolas in *Our Exagmination* (91) as one of Joyce's technical dream analogues seems to be evoked. Joyce's note, "colour crept back into her face: girl's dream of death she still lives: angel of slums," (113) seems, I would speculate, an allusion to Hauptmann's *Hannele's Himmelfahrt* in which the playwright invented a technique that combines naturalism and surrealism to dramatize the delirium of a young, abused girl dying in a poorhouse. I see in the "Nausikaa" notes of *Scribbledehobble* Joyce's preparatory moves to interweave a fantasy of happy childhood ("Lucia's girl's tea-party" [114]) with a historical reality of poverty, disease, hunger, and mortality among the Irish young of the turn of the century. This argument, which I will elaborate at length in my last chapter, had its genesis in a troubling elision in Jacques Derrida's brilliant and influential essay on *Finnegans Wake* ("Two Words for Joyce") which draws its metaphysically charged two words, HE WAR, from the children's chapter, the *Wake*'s "Mime of Mick, Nick, and the Maggies," and dilates them into a deconstruction of ontotheology, without referring to the children at all. Derrida's occlusion of the children in his meditation reinforces my sense that except in psychoanalytic theory, children tend to be metaphysically as well as ideologically unprofitable. For the purpose of restoring them to history, the "Mime" is better explored through the cultural lens of Walter Benjamin's lifelong interest in the culture, pedagogy, and reading that shape children's social life and experience.

In the ensuing chapters I plan to retrieve other marginalized and suppressed figures, or certain features of their aspects, that weave themselves through the Joycean texts: the artist's body of poverty in the next three chapters, concluding with a look at "Shem the Penman's" parody of modernist resistance to its ideological betrayal in the *Wake*; the abjection of old maids in "The Dead," "Clay," and "Nausicaa;" the vulgar speech and labor of washerwomen in "Anna Livia Plurabelle;" and the fractured, gestural discourse of Irish children in "The Mime of Mick, Nick, and the Maggies." My aim, however, is neither to restore these submerged figures to representation, nor to show Joyce giving them muted voice. Rather, I hope to explore their subversive function in pressing against the aesthetic style and bourgeois ideology of the narrative effects, the silences of their ideological penury implicitly interfering with Stephen's eloquent theorizing or Molly Bloom's sexualized, focalized discursive abundance. The anomaly of my writing a feminist study without addressing Molly Bloom is produced by my countertextual and materialist focus on anti-aestheticist formations in the Joycean text. My focus throughout this book, then, is not on artist or woman, per se, but rather on Joyce's critique of their implication in modern art's self-aestheticization.

This project is enabled by the benefit, and spurred by the cost, of the more widespread postmodernization of modernism, in which Joyce's late work, especially, has been given a privileged role. John Carlos Rowe describes "modern" movements as "generally characterized by their postmodern desires: quite simply, the guiding motivation for the artist is to exceed the boundaries and limitations of modern society and its discursive conventions" (156). In the resulting recanonizing effects of postmodernizing modernists like Marjorie Perloff and Joseph Riddel, the shift of interest from "lost generation" novelists and "homemade" poets to avant-gardists like Gertrude Stein and Djuna Barnes mirrors the shift of interest from Joyce's early texts to the logopoeia of the more experimentalized forms of the late *Ulysses* chapters and *Finnegans Wake*. It is the cost of this maneuver, in the form of the writing's removal from history, that I hope partly to redress in this study. My narrative for

restoring the Joycean text to history as a rehistoricizing agent follows the contours of Peter Buerger's argument for the emergence of
the historical avant-garde: Joyce, affrighted by Oscar Wilde's betrayal by aestheticism's denial of history, turns to the progressivism
of Continental drama for artistically self-critical forms. He finds in
Ibsen the invention of an institutional and generic *mise en abyme*,
a staging of staging, for example, in *A Doll's House*, the indictment
of bourgeois drama become internalized as the ideological model of
bourgeois behavior. Joyce translates this model of an ideologically
critical metatextuality by producing a writing of writing that likewise indicts art's production of itself, in Wilde's terms, as a beautiful
unreal thing. If Gabriel Conroy "wanted to say that literature was
above politics" (188), Joyce's texts nonetheless show that it is not.
This book, I hope, will show Joyce showing that it is not.

CHAPTER TWO

Patronage and Censorship: The Production of Art in the Social Real

PETER BUERGER'S HISTORICAL NARRATIVE of the late nineteenth century crisis in the institution of art might well double as a description of Joyce's *Portrait*:

> The apartness from the praxis of life that had always constituted the institutional status of art in bourgeois society now becomes the content of works. Institutional frame and content coincide. The realist novel of the nineteenth century still serves the self-understanding of the bourgeois. Fiction is the medium of a reflection about the relationship between individual and society. In Aestheticism, this thematics is overshadowed by the ever-increasing concentration the makers of art bring to the medium itself. (27)

Buerger's argument drives an extremely useful historical wedge into the self-problematization that becomes the institutional discourse of modernism. But at the same time, the simplicity of this equation of modernism with aestheticism ruptures when translated from Buerger's resolutely European moorings into the history of Anglo-American and English modernism. There the relationship between the institutional discourses of the art—exemplified, for example, in the writings of the poet-critics—and the commerce of publication, becomes highly heterogeneous and complex. Pound thematized and theorized the commercialization of the modern work of art in his poetry; Stein's "autobiography" gave modern art a genderized and collectivized production history; and Eliot, Woolf, and Marianne Moore—poets whose work exemplifies Buerger's logopoetic aestheticism—produced art contiguous to their editorial work and involvement with the publishing industry. But Joyce's seeming escape from contamination by the commerce of art (since he supported himself chiefly by language instruction prior to patronage) made him more readily assimilable to the institutional ideology of aestheticism.

The story of the production of Joyce's art actually consists of many imbricated plots that overlap intellectual production (what Joyce read, saw, heard, and thought; his library, cultural materials, and records; literary discussions and influences), textual production (workshop materials, composition strategy, drafts, revisions, and publication schedules), and the social production recorded with exemplary precision in the Ellmann biography (friendships, patronages, and their role in finding pensions, grants, support, and alternative publishing). But if Ellmann supplies the commercial and social history of Joyce's artistic production, he also denigrates it in the interest of superimposing Stephen's heroic narrative of artistic idealistic ambition upon Joyce's own.[1] The result has been that treasured idealistic, egotistic, or aggressive clichés of Joyce's aspirations (to serve as priest of the eternal imagination, to forge in the smithy of his soul the uncreated conscience of his race, to wage war on language, to keep generations of professors and their assistants busy trying to understand his works) have etched themselves as legendary shibboleths on the story of Joyce's art. But Ellmann's privileging of intellectual and textual production, while marginalizing the social and economic forces, exemplifies a more general ideology of artistic autonomy that Buerger grounds in the artist's historical escape from the division of labor. "Being arrested at the handicraft stage of production within a society where the division of labor and the separation of the worker from his means of production becomes increasingly the norm would thus be the actual precondition for seeing art as something special" (36). Modernism, with its emphasis on the craft of writing, particularly promotes this ideology, and my own disappointment as a student on first reading the Pound/Joyce correspondence, and finding it simply business letters rather than a discourse of genius, was symptomatic of that engendered perception. The theorized analysis of the complex nexus of legal, commercial, and ideological constraints on modern art—well underway in Continental literature (Berman) and certain areas of Anglo-American modernism (Benstock)—could fruitfully be extended to the study of Joyce. Such a project would, of course, extend far beyond the scope of this book—although I hope to make certain introductory gestures toward sketching a material and social production history of the Joycean text that, I will argue, reenters the writing to rupture its aestheticist content and form. Although Buerger does not locate avant-garde self-criticism as a socially progressive content in the work of art, I will locate it as both a submerged and invisible content, and a disruptive formal process. My answer to a question suggested by Buerger's historical narrative of modernism—why would an art produced by struggling against official censorship and commerical neglect develop amnesia regarding just these conditions of its genesis—is that Joyce's texts both forget (and convulsively remember) their material and social history in order to inscribe a greater fullness of their historical moment within themselves. An art like Joyce's—born out of a million small social and commercial transactions, loans, donations, grants, favors, requests, obligations, contracts, threats, deals, negotiations—pretends to idealistic status as the product of soul in order to expose the contradiction between its institutional discourse and its commercial reality.

In Joyce's texts, I will argue, art lies about itself in order to tell the truth about its lying. Artistic self-representation in the Joycean text, which has traditionally been focalized in the figure of an existentialized Stephen, is better sought in the continuous raveling of idealistic and historical narratives of artistic genesis, development, and function. The familiar story of art as soul and as form in *Portrait* can be found told side by side, in opposition to, or as the reverse of, the story of art as social and material commodity throughout the Joycean *oeuvre*. In the fictional texts it is generally less compartmentalized than in Joyce's early non-fiction, where it splits dramatically into the private and the public: the Aristotelian and Thomistic speculations of 1904, for example, that rehearse Stephen's aesthetics theory, coexist with a body of published criticism, reviews, and essays (now collected as *The Critical Writings*) whose frequent burden is the artist's (especially the Irish artist's) suppression, attack, and neglect by society and its apparatus of constraints. These neglected critical writings,[2] generally dismissed as hack work undertaken for money, are themselves, by virtue of that very fact, double in function—a part of the material mechanism for enabling the production of art, and self-reflection on the social conditions of artistic production. As such, they articulate Joyce's counterargument to the modernist aestheticism of his fiction, by providing a sharp history of art's resistance to, and suppression by, civic and commercial systems responsive to a hegemonic order: Catholic protest against the heresy of Yeats's *The Countess Cathleen* ("Day of the Rabblement" 1901), the Irish artist's persecution in "Oscar Wilde: The Poet of 'Salomé'" (1909), "Bernard Shaw's Battle with the Censor" (1909), Joyce's exclusion from the Irish literary establishment ("The Holy Office" 1904), his abuse by publishers ("Gas from a Burner" 1912), etc. Sometimes the political history of artistic production becomes attached as a dissonant paratext to the fiction. Joyce's letter of appeal for help with his censorship problems with Maunsel and Company was printed by Pound in *The Egoist*, in January 1912, a fortnight before the first serial installment of *Portrait*; it was titled "A Curious History" and contained the Crown's rejection of Joyce's appeal for help ("it is inconsistent with rule for his Majesty to express his opinion in such cases" [Pound/Joyce 22]). A more famous later paratext was, of course, Judge Woolsey's decision—preempting the text of the 1934 Random House edition with its legal and official exoneration of *Ulysses* from obscenity. The new Gabler edition of *Ulysses*, necessarily prefaced with discussions of editorial practice, marks the now solidly canonized status of *Ulysses* in its prefatorial shift from the book's cultural to its scholarly controversy. But in replacing the book's historical relevance with its contemporary relevance, the new editions of *Ulysses* efface the turbulent cultural history that dramatized its socially oppositional function in the twenties and thirties. The theorized retrieval of that function is needed to complicate the ideological grooves into which canonization has tended to settle the text.

The cursory sketch of the production history that I will offer in the next section is intended less to rehearse the by now familiar facts than to reknit them into a different genre and a different plot. In constructing the Joyce biography on the model of a novel plot, the obstacles to means and access for producing art (money and contacts) have become easily coded into moral terms, as problems of character in the bourgeois individual. Furthermore, licensed by Joyce's own precedent of invariably translating his most serious official conflicts and trials into highly farcical terms, his problems of penury, censorship, and publication misadventure have emerged as the comic and vulgar subplot of the noble and heroic spiritual odyssey. What tends to be overlooked in constructing the production history in this way is a rather significant paradox in the ideological constitution of modernism. As an artistic movement committed to being, except for the disciplines of its self-determined formal craft, the freest cultural enterprise on earth, modernism encountered constant and concrete proof—in its multiple and numerous collisions with governments, laws, commerce, and social censure—of its incontrovertible embeddedness, dependence, and potency as a social and political phenomenon. Yet modernism's self-representation of its autonomy generally denies this self-knowledge. By exploring carefully the intertwined impact of censorship and patronage on Joyce, I hope to emplace his production history within the superstructural problems produced by the colonial and class context in which he was obliged to create.

Joyce's censorship problems, and their impact on his work and livelihood, changed over time and varied by country. The early problems with the publication of *Dubliners* were most acute because censorship in that case took the form of a prior restraint which interfered with production, while the American obscenity laws banning *Ulysses* interfered chiefly with distribution. But in each case, censorship usefully revealed both society's deepest ideological investments and its sense of vulnerability to art's power to challenge and damage its self-image. George Bernard Shaw, whose Fabianism gave him much practice in these matters, defended *Ulysses* by troping it as a critical mirror: "If a man holds up a mirror to your nature and shows you that it needs washing—not whitewashing—it is no use breaking the mirror. Go for soap and water" (JJ 576). The ground of the legal objections to Joyce's work shifted from country to country and publisher to publisher: in England it was censored on a variety of grounds by Grant Richards (*Letters* I, 60–64); in Ireland his press inexplicably objected to references to King Edward VII, and feared libel charges by the individuals and commercial establishments named in the texts; in America Joyce's work incited legal prosecution for frank sexual representation and obscene language. Ireland betrayed a particularly poignant colonial abasement by protecting the honor of its British imperial overlord at the expense of its artist. Joyce, outraged by the demand of his Irish publisher, Maunsel, that he delete or alter references to the late Edward VII in "Ivy Day in the Committee Room" explained in "A Curious History": "I declined to do either, pointing out that Mr. Grant Richards, of London, had raised no objection to the passage when Edward VII was alive, and that I could not see why an Irish publisher should raise an objection to it when Edward VII had passed into history" (*Pound/Joyce* 21). Furthermore, the Irish fear of libel from commercial establishments Joyce named in his fiction suggests other Irish internalizations of the commercial spirit Matthew Arnold associated with Saxon Philistinism. In these early censorship problems, Joyce and his society enact a classic liberal scenario that poses art as society's adversary culture.[3] Joyce's own response, later sublated into the martyred and Parnellized figure of the artist in *Portrait*, took farcicalized form in the vulgar, aggressive broadside "Gas from a Burner." Here Joyce viciously satirized the craven cowardice of Maunsel and Roberts ("I'll penance do with farts and groans/ Kneeling upon my marrowbones" [CW 245]), as well as their political hypocrisy in overlooking similar indecencies in the texts of Ascendancy writers ("Written by Moore, a genuine gent/ That lives on his property's ten per cent" [CW 243]). But the sanction of prior restraint that Sally Dennison calls a "quirk of the law" (80)—making printers liable[4] to prosecution for printing politically offensive, libelous, or obscene material—made commercial publishers retreat from questionable texts like Joyce's. At the outset of his career, then, censorship contravened Joyce's artistic production in ways that threatened both his ability to create and to earn even the deferred benefits that might make art self-supporting. At the same time he was writing *Portrait*, Joyce experienced in his quarrels with officialdom and commerce the material exigencies of art's social genesis and historical emplacement. *Ulysses*'s later problems with censorship and piracy sufficiently interfered with distribution and income that *Finnegans Wake* might never have seen the light of day without the private patronage Patrick Parrinder calls an "anachronistic form of literary financing" (200), and Russell Berman specifies as belonging to "precapitalist forms of renumeration" (55).

1. Patronage as Communist "Grace"

One of Joyce's most subtle and complex inscriptions of his own ideological dilemma as an Irish artist can be found in a story that is not about art at all. "Grace"—traditionally construed as a salvation myth structured on the scaffolding of Dante's *Divine Comedy*—stages a narration's ideological collusion in denying and suppressing the violence of Irish economic oppression. The narrator carefully misleads the reader into interpreting as a *moral* fall—an accidental tumble down some steps caused by drunkenness—what was, in all probability, a violently conducted financial transaction: Tom Kernan's discipline by a loan shark's "muscle" for delinquent payment.[5] At the same time, by trumpeting the institutional and dogmatic power of the Church, the narration nearly mutes the small moments of "grace" that flower in the story, and that redefine it not as a divine gratuity (an illogically unrequested and unrequitable benefit) but as a human gratuity. Mr. Fogarty, we learn, will function as the commercial and moral opposite of the moneylenders, bringing a half-pint of a special whiskey to the ailing Kernan even though "there was a small account for groceries unsettled between him and Mr Fogarty" (D 166).

Joyce recognizes, I believe, the useful function served by an ideology that makes debtorship, especially sponging or cadging unrepayable loans, a farcical Irish stereotype in the land in which the "gombeen-man" made usury and extortion (at a customary rate of sixty percent interest on loans) a monumental historical problem.[6] By privatizing and satirizing the symptoms of a depressed and un-

dernourished economy as human foibles and weaknesses, as misfor-
tunes brought on private individuals by the follies of their drinking
and profligacy, the oppressions of a system that gives the individual
virtually no affordable credit, that is, little "grace" to achieve any
measure of economic control, are concealed and exonerated. Joyce,
as Irish artist, was victimized by this ideological maneuver both in
life and in the literary tradition. In imitation of the most famous
Ibsen protagonist, he played, like Nora Helmer, the wastrel and the
spendthrift to gain the needed indulgence and leverage to keep multiple sources of credit liquid and available while he pursued the
elusive artistic success that should, but never would, make his art
self-supporting. His biographers eventually took his own implicit
permission to lampoon his economic "ineptitude" according to a
bourgeois ideology that rewards thrift and sobriety and excoriates
indulgence and profligacy, to reduce Joyce to a sort of socioeconomic
clown.[7] Ellmann makes special display of Joyce's galling importu-
nity and ingratitude, "As proud as he was needy, Joyce conferred his
debts like favors; his friends were permitted to recognize their duties," (JJ 163) and even Brenda Maddox does not spare the Joyces
implicit chiding for their "contradictory" lifestyle: indulging themselves with restaurant meals, operas, and finery while borrowing
money for food and rent. In general, Mr. Deasy's economic and
moral maxim—that an Englishman's proudest boast is that he paid
his way—is applied flat-footedly to Joyce, and he is treated as having
never earned what he lived on. At the same time this countermyth
omits his own broadly ironic sense of Deasy's boast, that the British
Empire, of course, made its colonies, including Ireland, pay its way,
and like Haines ("Pay up and look pleasant, Haines said to him,
smiling" [U 1:449]) takes their "hospitality" for granted. Joyce is
inscribed into the mythology of a dominant ideology that legitimates art by idealizing genius and heroicizing its struggles against
society's Philistine values, but that farcicalizes the artist's material
struggle "to be fed," as Kenner puts it.[8]

Russell Berman argues that writers of the late nineteenth and
early twentieth century were keenly aware of the effects of the book
industry on their lives and art. "The dynamic of the capitalist book
industry, with its basic opposition of publisher and author, entrepre-
neur and producer, not only impoverishes the writer but also robs
him of his autonomy and thrusts him into a new form of servitude"
(61). But Joyce's censorship problems threatened to keep him out of
the market altogether, and bar his entry into capitalist book production; modern poetry—unsuitable for mass distribution—was likewise extruded. As an Irish artist of no independent means, Joyce's

situation differed, economically, in degree rather than in kind from that of the peasant or sharecropper also living under conditions of deferred production that necessitate access to credit. It is no wonder that Ezra Pound, taking upon himself responsibility for locating credit for aspiring artists in such an era of artistic commodification, became obsessed with its frustration to the point of wishing to reinvent the economic system. Eventually Joyce's stars crossed favorably under the intersection of two individuals disturbed in different ways and for different reasons by the evils of usury. By bringing Joyce to the attention of Harriet Shaw Weaver, Pound found for him his "grace," the gratuitous generosity necessary to produce a work so monumentally experimental no commercial establishment would have underwritten it.

Pound's obsession with usury led him, as we know, to appropriate Major Douglas's theories of Social Credit and eventually embrace fascism in the hope that Mussolini would implement Social Credit doctrines. Harriet Shaw Weaver gave her money to Joyce and became, as we acknowledge only furtively, a communist. While Pound's political principles are taken seriously in light of his later treason and incarceration, Harriet Shaw Weaver's tend to be trivialized and misunderstood in order to avoid confronting the rather startling historical truth—that Joyce's last work owes its existence, economically, to the political principle of a British feminist who spent the last quarter century of her life as "Comrade Josephine," a member of the Communist Party active in the Upper Montagu Street cell.[9] The farcical countermyth of a dependent, demanding, ungrateful Joyce is better served by making Weaver a female "saint" to modern art, a spinster sublimating her own creative frustrations in selfless service to genius, rather than a woman with a lifelong history of political activism as a Labour Party member that included an effective stint of East End social work and membership in the Pankhursts' Women's Social and Political Union before she became director of *The New Freewoman* and editor of its later incarnation as *The Egoist*. In 1923, at a time when *Ulysses* was bringing Joyce huge acclaim, but no money—since it was banned in most of the English speaking world—Miss Weaver made over to Joyce the capital from the bequest of her late aunt Emily Wright in the amount of twelve thousand (12,000) pounds:

> The suggestion made, long after the event, that Harriet should have kept her capital and given James Joyce a yearly income, was presumably considered by Harriet at the time. But, aware of the risks, she preferred to make over the capital, with certain safe-

guards. She was not interested in having Mr Joyce as her pen-
sioner; she wished to see him a free man. Her own freedom, too,
was involved. She was still living on "usury"—her own word for
unearned income—and her sense of guilt had not abated. But she
gave herself some relief by passing on the inheritance. (Lidderdale and Nicholson 225)

By privatizing Weaver's gift as an act of personal generosity, this significant point is lost: that the "grace" of which Joyce became the
beneficiary was that of a carefully reasoned and expressly marxist
political analysis, theory, and praxis. Weaver recognized and responded, by her act, to her own and the Irish Joyce's embeddedness
in the political matrix of the modern postcolonial world.

Joyce's response to this gift is generally regarded as greedy, irre-
sponsible, and exploitive: failing to properly husband the fund, and
therefore continuing to dun Sylvia Beach for money,[10] and plaguing
Miss Weaver with many personal importunities for assistance. But
such a moral construction obscures the ideological contradictions
within this anomalous and unprecedented form of artistic relationships and dependencies. The modern "democratized" form of patronage invented both abroad and in the States to fund both experimental and minority art depended on an effacement of actual social
and economic power relationships that was as violable as it was necessary. On the one hand modern patrons were obliged, by the artistic
ideology of the time, to guarantee autonomy and aesthetic freedom;
on the other hand, that freedom was entirely revocable, as the case
of the Harlem Renaissance writers revealed most clearly. Langston
Hughes was dropped by his patron Mrs. R. Osgood Mason, when,
according to Houston Baker, he wrote "an 'engaged' poem, a 'socialist' response to the opening of a luxury hotel in New York when so
many were starving" (110). Joyce was, of course, in no such danger
from Miss Weaver, although an earlier experience, when the American Mrs. McCormick withdrew her patronage—presumably because
he refused her offer to have Jung psychoanalyze him—had given him
a taste of the indignities of patronly caprice (JJ 466). But if he owed
Miss Weaver neither artistic nor political debts, he was nonetheless
"scrupulously aware of his obligations towards his patron" (200), as
Parrinder points out. Joyce's complex and inconsistent behavior toward Beach and Weaver—grateful, demanding, dignified, wheedling,
tactful, insensitive, etc.—might therefore be considered his imperfect, but altogether human, adjustment to an emotionally ambiguous and contradictory set of relations—complicated by differences
of nationality, wealth, gender, and temperament—that had continu-

ally to be invented as they were lived. Without excusing his behavioral lapses, Joyce must be seen as transforming Miss Weaver from a bank into a friend with all the emotional risks that such greater familiarity and intimacy entail. Her overdetermined roles as confidante, editor, secretary, agent, friend, and, at the last, Lucia's nurse, enmeshed her in a far broader set of Joycean dependencies than just the financial. But they suggest, too, the resistance of both patron and protegé to a model of alienated and commodifiable labor in favor of recognizing the complicated integrations of social, psychological, professional, and financial needs that underlie artistic production. Joyce's eye problems and the disruptions of Lucia's illness were no less serious than worry over money, and Miss Weaver's support increasingly took on a holistic character until Lucia's inevitable deterioration doomed her efforts, and with them her friendship with the Joyces, to failure.

An important departure from bourgeois censures of Joyce's social behavior with respect to money was Phillip Herring's major address at the Venice Joyce Symposium in 1988, where he made the anthropological argument that the Irish social system may traditionally have fostered a more generous set of social attitudes toward various forms of economic exchange: earnings, debts, gifts, loans, and other financial dealings. "He demanded much of patrons and friends, but his generosity was also great," Herring notes. "But, you say, Joyce was no Indian. No, but his behavior was typical of three tribes who may claim him, the Irish, who in early days had communal property (grazing land, for instance), the socialists, who claimed his allegiance for the first decade of this century, and the artistic bohemians, with their typical contempt for ownership and property" (92). Herring's point is significant because it opens the door for reconsidering the ways that a dominant ideology of economic individualism would itself oppress the Irish as colonial subjects. The Joyces' willingness to owe, to incur unrepayable obligations, to acknowledge their social and economic dependence, could be construed as a commitment to the truth of their social situation rather than to the mythology of self-sufficiency, self-support, and individualistic independence that was the luxury of Joyce's contemporaries of the Irish Ascendancy—Moore, Martyn, Lady Gregory—who enjoyed the moral and material luxury of living on their estate rents. Miss Weaver's true "grace" then was not the money in itself, nor her generosity in itself, but her recoding of her gift as the correction of a system that inequitably allowed her to live on unearned income while Joyce labored unceasingly without the ability to earn. If the material benefit of her patronage translated, paradoxically, into the autonomy necessary to sustain modernist experimentation and avant-gardism, its socialistic motivation must have possessed for him even greater psychological significance, when set against his own fear, iterated in fiction and non-fiction, of becoming enmeshed in a colonial history of Irish artistic degradation and betrayal.

Joyce's bitterest writing as an Irishman and an Irish artist was his 1909 essay for *Il Piccolo della Sera* on "Oscar Wilde: The Poet of 'Salomé.'" This essay displays Joyce's keen insight into his ideological peril as an Irish artist on the verge of committing himself to a fiction that appears to celebrate aestheticism as the Irish mode of art. Hugh Kenner too detects self-reflection in both the name of Stephen Dedalus ("was that name not almost certainly modelled on the name another Dubliner fabricated on similar principles to cover his anonymity in exile, a martyr Sebastian, a fabulous wanderer Melmoth . . . Sebastian Melmoth, the last persona of the fallen Oscar Wilde?" [*Pound Era* 272]) and in the timing and aim of Joyce's project—"Joyce seems to have begun what was finally the *Portrait* just after Oscar Wilde died; was it to have offered a lower-class Catholic analogue to Wilde's upper-middle-class Protestant career." Joyce's essay was written on the occasion of a performance in Trieste of Richard Strauss's opera *Salomé*, whose words are based on Wilde's poem. But its poignant depiction and analysis of Wilde's persecution and fall has little to do with the poem or the opera. Instead it bitterly laments the fate of the colonial artist who submits to British domestication. Named after "Oscar, nephew of King Fingal and the only son of Ossian in the amorphous Celtic *Odyssey*, who was treacherously killed by the hand of his host as he sat at table," Oscar Wilde's fate seemed prophesied in his name as well as in the vulnerability to which his idealism and aestheticism exposed him, "Like that other Oscar, he was to meet his public death in the flower of his years as he sat at table, crowned with false vine leaves and discussing Plato" (CW 201). Wilde was betrayed by Pater and Ruskin, whose theories of beauty he sought to implement by cloaking himself in the persona of Apostle of Beauty—a trope that hid a very different social reality: "From time to time his medals, trophies of his academic youth, went to the pawnshop, and at times the young wife of the epigrammatist had to borrow from a neighbour the money for a pair of shoes" (CW 202). By ornamenting and beautifying himself in aestheticism, Joyce implies, Wilde made himself the British aristocracy's whore. It is that, not his homosexuality, that appears to have been his sin, for it made him vulnerable to the hypocritical betrayal of a British public that eventually hunted him down for their sport:

His friends abandoned him. His manuscripts were stolen, while
he recounted in prison the pain inflicted on him by two years
of forced labour. His mother died under a shadow. His wife died.
He was declared bankrupt and his goods were sold at auction.
His sons were taken from him. When he got out of prison, thugs
urged on by the noble Marquis of Queensbury were waiting in
ambush for him. He was hunted from house to house as dogs
hunt a rabbit. One after another drove him from the door, refusing him food and shelter, and at nightfall he finally ended up under the windows of his brother, weeping and babbling like a child.
(CW 203)

The irony of Wilde's aestheticism, that it failed to put him "above
politics" by interposing a shield of beauty between himself and the
social realities in which he lived—Irish, homosexual, economically
vulnerable—was not lost on Joyce. Nor was the failure of the lancet
of Wilde's wit to sting the conscience of his public.

Joyce contextualizes Wilde in an Irish comic tradition to which
he himself is destined to be consigned, but whose political fate he
clearly aims to escape: "In the tradition of the Irish writers of
comedy that runs from the days of Sheridan and Goldsmith to Bernard Shaw, Wilde became, like them, court jester to the English"
(CW 202). Joyce sharply notes here the way the colonial configuration of the market—obliging Irish artists to placate British expecta-
tions in the interest of gaining access to a far wider English language
reception—causes them to submit to particularly veiled, and therefore particularly intractable, forms of patronization and abasement.
The barbs of Irish satire and wit, like the licence of the court jester
or the fool, signify not any real freedom or critical power but quite
its opposite, the seemingly free speech that can be readily allowed
because its domination is assured by the subject's absolute subjection. How perilously near Joyce felt this threat to himself this anecdote (that Ellmann treats as collegiate farce) makes clear: "Gogarty wrote to an Oxford friend, G. K. A. Bell (later a bishop), about
Joyce's artful dodges to subsist without formal employment, and
Bell replied that he wept for Joyce," Ellmann reports, and reprints
the comical letter Joyce had Gogarty send Bell in response:

Dear Sir: My friend Mr Gogarty informs me that my conduct is
to you a source of amusement. As I cannot long continue to
amuse you without supporting my corporal estate (station) I take
the liberty to ask you to forward three guineas etc." (JJ 165)

Joyce here preempts the role of court jester, making overt his position of beggar with the fool's impudence rather than the indigent's
pathos. But the "Telemachiad" makes clear that Joyce always saw as
already politicized Gogarty's mediations between himself and his
various Oxford friends (Gordon), and gives Stephen's pained reflec-
tions on these roles a very different tone: "A jester at the court of
his master, indulged and disesteemed, winning a clement master's
praise. Why had they chosen all that part?" (U 2:49). Indeed, the
triangle of Oxford friend, Mulligan, and Stephen becomes the cast
of Stephen's nightmare of history—which Haines considers to
blame for the Irish plight—a cast invested in the tropes of the Raj.
With Haines and Mulligan as "the panthersahib and his pointer" (U
3:277), Stephen becomes, like Wilde, sport and prey of the imperial
nightmare.

Harriet Shaw Weaver's bequest, translating philanthropy into political "debt," saved Joyce from being intellectually pimped to the
British upper class—as Wilde was, and as Stephen is by Mulligan.
Prior to the time of that secure income, Pound improvised fundraising for Joyce with a keen sense of its psychological perils. "The public demand for a work being in inverse ratio to its quality," Pound
wrote to Joyce in 1915, "one exists by chance and [a] series of igno-
minies" (P/J 42). Pound's strategies deployed diverse means to mini-
mize the indignity. By shrewdly using modernism's extrusion from
commerce and the market as a moral lever with potential donors, he
tuned his argument to an Arnoldian key: "Mr Joyce's work has been
absolutely uncorrupted. He has lived for ten years in obscurity and
poverty, that he might perfect his writing and be uninfluenced by
commercial demands and standards" (P/J 39). He appealed as much
as possible for institutional support, thereby giving his fundraising
on Joyce's behalf an increasingly corporate character. "If you are
hard up, there is as you may know a Royal Literary fund, or some
such thing for authors in temporary distress. De la Mare has just
been given a pension. And if you arent worth ten De la Mares I'll eat
my shirt," (P/J 36) Pound wrote Joyce. He further saved pride by eschewing diplomacy, and making his argument aggressive rather than
ingratiating. When he wrote to Llewelyn Roberts, the Secretary of
the Royal Literary Fund, he assaulted the pensioning of De la Mare
("I might say that it seems to me ridiculous that your government
pensions should go for the most part to saving wrecks rather than in
the fostering of letters. Thus you give a pension to De La Mare . . .
he is a man who has written a few charming poems, who has been
worried to death, who is practically at the end of his tether and who

is unlikely to write anything more of any value" (P/J 39) as much as he praised Joyce's talent ("a really great writer like Joyce, capable of producing lasting work"). At the same time Pound dealt with the national and class snobberies that would have torpedoed efforts on Joyce's behalf by interposing powerful intermediaries between his request and the funding establishment. It was only thanks to Yeats' intercession with Edmund Gosse ("You need not thank me," Yeats wrote to Joyce, "for it was really Ezra Pound who thought of your need. I acted at his suggestion, because it was easier for me to approach the Fund for purely personal reasons. We thought Gosse [who has great influence with the Fund people, but is rather prejudiced] would take it better from me" [P/J 40]) that Pound's campaign yielded Joyce a £75 stipend. Gosse's 'prejudice' against Joyce was clearly that of the Oxfordian Haines toward Stephen—"A ponderous Saxon. He thinks you're not a gentleman" (U 1 : 51).[11] Another £100 was secured by Pound for Joyce through Yeats, Moore, and Lady Cunard from the Civil List in an effort that involved getting Prime Minister Asquith's secretary, Edward Marsh, to read Joyce's books. Here too, Pound makes his mendicancy less odious by abusing the prospective patron—wisely, behind his back: "Lady Cunard is your very good friend, she has been trying to stir up * * * * * to publish you. She got the little beast to read the Portrait for himself, and he has professed an admiration for 'Death' [sic] in Dubliners. Lady C. has even gone the length of inviting the pig to see her a couple of times and enduring the sight of his face while she tried to instill sense into his soapy kurranium" (P/J 78). Miss Weaver, in making over the capital of her bequest to Joyce as a redistribution of income, spared him a lifetime of such indignity and worry.

This complex material motor of artistic production in history inscribes itself, seemingly as a subplot—but actually as a counterplot to aestheticism—throughout the Joycean *oeuvre*, but particularly in the "Telemachiad." To be sure, it is displaced and upstaged by the familial melodrama—the mythic search for the father and the guilt over the mother. But underneath these highly interiorized and aestheticized concerns, the first three chapters of *Ulysses* fictionalize what even Lukács would need to acknowledge as a network of social and material relations, the artist's efforts "to be fed" within the colonial matrix of Joyce's own history. Stephen and Haines stage the confrontation of young Irish and British intellectuals at the turn of the century in all the crudity of its political differential: a reciprocal fear of murder, as the indigent Stephen utters his first lines of the novel as a fear of Haines—who in turn is suffering literal nightmares of terror dreaming the reprisal of his subaltern "hosts." At the same time both live in the daylight reality of the Sassenach's raw social and material advantage, as Haines travels Ireland in tennis flannels, armed with Oxford credentials, a bejewelled silver cigarette case (Stephen writes villanelles on the back of cardboard cigarette packs), access to the Irish literary scene, to publication (of borrowed Irish witticisms), and, for good measure, his guncase ("Where is his guncase?" [U 1:57])—with a gun, John Gordon suggests, he may have brought to shoot crows. [589]). Stephen's first lines of the novel, "Tell me, Mulligan . . . How long is Haines going to stay in this tower?" [U 1:47] virtually serve as proleptic political allegory. Stephen even implies the heart of the problem, when he points out to Haines that the rent the Irishmen pay for the tower is paid to the secretary of state for war (U 1:540).[12] The Irish rents, the peculiar real estate of the tower implies, support the British military's ability to repel Irish liberation.

If "Telemachus" reinscribes the problem of Saxon patronage ("I intend to make a collection of your sayings if you will let me. . . . Would I make any money by it? Stephen asked. . . . I don't know, I'm sure" [U 1:480–493]), "Nestor" translates Joyce's actual Triestine "job" of teaching into the colonial situation. Again, he preserves both the psychological effects and the analysis of the institution, as he dramatizes the social dishonor to which teachers, both tutors and classroom teachers, were vulnerable in his day. Brenda Maddox writes of Joyce's work as a private language tutor in Trieste, "Joyce's frustration was as social as it was sexual. Signorina Popper was typical of Joyce's students, wealthy and leisured, and the way that these attractive young girls, as much as their parents, treated him as a servant rankled him" (117). In "Nestor" Stephen feels similarly vulnerable to his students' overbearance, "In a moment they will laugh more loudly, aware of my lack of rule and of the fees their papas pay" (U 2:28). Joyce carefully plots the chapter on Stephen's *job*, the "formal employment" Ellmann expects aspiring young artists to pursue, to fall on payday, in order to stage the complex integration between the school's pedagogical ideology of teaching imperial history and Milton to Ireland's wealthy young scions ("Welloff people, proud that their eldest son was in the navy" [U 2:24]), and Stephen's payment in both money and propaganda by the misogynistic, antisemitic Tory who is his master and headmaster. In both "Telemachus" and "Nestor" Joyce criticizes education as the institution of Enlightenment liberation, the disseminator of art and culture, reproducing intact the colonial and class oppressions (Kershner) that trammel the Irish artist as much as his familial or religious or patriotic nets.

2. Ibsen, Censorship, and Art's Social Function in *Stephen Hero*

Joyce's difficulties in being fed as an artist were, then, complicated
by a censorship law executed through prior restraint that threatened
to abolish his access to the market, and to the initiatory, if deferred,
income that could eventually make his art self-supporting. Furthermore, by making the British printer of offensive matter "as guilty of
breaking the law as the publisher, and equally subject to criminal
prosecution" (JJ 220), censorship was exercised at the most material
level of textual production. Joyce was outraged at this overdetermination of the printer as ideological guardian of culture, asking his
publisher, Grant Richards, disingenuously and sarcastically, to explain the printer's "mysteries . . . for example, how he came by his
conscience and culture, how he is permitted in your country to com-
bine the duties of author with his own honourable calling, how he
came to be the representative of the public mind." Joyce concluded
with a rather brutal assertion of the bourgeois division of labor, "But
I cannot permit a printer to write my book for me. . . . A printer is
simply a workman hired by the day or by the job for a certain sum"
(*Letters* II, 142–43). But although Joyce's anger appears directed at
the printer, he is clearly responding to the absurdities of a system
that displaces the execution of its ideological coercions onto "a
workman hired by the day or by the job for a certain sum." As Sally
Dennison points out, for printers fear necessarily replaced conviction: "Printers had everything to lose and nothing to gain by setting
in type stories that were even the slightest bit questionable" (80).
The immediate and devastating effect of this law on Joyce was to
turn his publication history into one of the most compelling nightmares of publishing misadventure in modern letters.[13] Its nadir
came when the publishing firm of Messrs. Maunsel, three years after
signing a contract to bring out *Dubliners*, demanded from Joyce a
thousand pound security to indemnify them against prosecution, and
threatened to sue him for expenses on grounds that by submitting
to them a book with libelous content, Joyce had broken his contract
(JJ 331). Joyce's reaction was nearly homicidal, as he wrote to Nora
12 August 1912: "For a long time today I thought of spending the
last money I have on a revolver and using it on the scoundrels who
have tortured my mind with false hopes for so many years" (*Letters*
II, 311). After these melodramatic temptations, Joyce made Maunsel
a sensible offer to buy the edition, which had already been typeset,
only to be told by the printer that "the copies would never leave his
printing-house" and "that the type had been broken up, and that the
entire edition of one thousand copies would be burnt the next day"

(P/J 23). These crushing obstacles were, of course, ultimately transformed into a series of modern publication triumphs by the extraordinary private publishing enterprises of London and Paris that made
Joyce their beneficiary.[14] In his own version of Joyce's publication
history, Pound wrote, "Eighty percent of such literature of my generation (from 1910 to 1930) as has any solid value, has been published only via specially founded 'amateur' publishing houses" (P/J
247). Established in the interest of procuring artistic freedom at all
costs, alternative publishing transformed legal and social censorship
into its enhanced opposite. Dennison argues that Joyce gained an
unprecedented freedom for experimental play from Shakespeare and
Company's willingness to indulge such costly revisions in the last
stages of producing *Ulysses* as no commercial publisher could have
or would have sustained.

But if the happy ending of modernism's bruising publishing history is artistic autonomy and free experimentation, then the paradox of its aesthetic triumph as an effacement of its violent material
genesis, is all the more ideologically problematic. Joyce's own account to John Quinn in 1917 of the genesis of *Dubliners* creates a
strange sense of that text as a miraculously resurrected body with
its social and political scars and mutilations magically repaired:

> Ten years of my life have been consumed in correspondence and
> litigation about my book *Dubliners*. It was rejected by 40 pub-
> lishers; three times set up, and once burnt. It cost me about three
> thousand francs in postage, fees, train and boat fare, for I was in
> correspondence with 110 newspapers, seven solicitors, three so-
> cieties, forty publishers and several men of letters about it. All
> refused to aid me, except Mr Ezra Pound. In the end it was pub-
> lished, in 1914, word for word as I wrote it in 1905. (*Letters* I, 105)

Where in Joyce's texts is this kind of material, social, and political
production and distribution history—of a martyred genesis, a nearly
aborted literary beginning, an ongoing illegitimacy—inscribed, except possibly in the opening of the 1934 Random House edition in
which Judge Woolsey dismissed *Ulysses* with an insulting exoneration—in effect, like a whore with insufficient allure to inflict any
serious social damage?

Joyce curiously confronted this dilemma of historical self-inscrip-
tion virtually before the fact. That is, he wrote about the problem of
the censorship of modern art during the composition of *Stephen
Hero*, in the years from 1904 to 1906, before his own publication
problems reached their critical pitch in 1912. *Stephen Hero* turns

three related instances of historical censorship and self-censorship—
Joyce's minor skirmish with the University College censor over his
Ibsen paper, the Irish Literary Theatre's retreat from Continental
drama after the *Countess Cathleen* protests, and the censorship of
"The Day of the Rabblement," Joyce's protest over the incident—
into a perceptive critique of Ireland's institutional confrontation
with modern art. Homer Obed Brown's caveat against dismissing
Stephen Hero as mere *juvenilis* (by reminding us that *Stephen Hero*
was being written at the same time as the technically polished *Dubliners* stories [61]) is needed to grant to this early, unpublished text
such a measure of sophistication. But *Stephen Hero* problematizes
in an ideologically complicated way the oedipal role Harold Bloom,
for example, might assign to literary influence. In "Day of the Rabblement" Joyce pointedly elides Shakespeare as a viable literary fore-
bear for the Irish, and proclaims their dramatic-poetic orphanage:
"A nation which never advanced so far as a miracle-play affords no
literary model to the artist, and he must look abroad" (CW 70). By
embracing the Norwegian Ibsen, Joyce eludes the imperial control
of either a classical (Aeschylus) or a British (Shakespeare) master
poet, while, at the same time, declaring an Irish literary allegiance
without the parentage of Yeats or the Irish revival. Ibsen represents
to the Irish writer at the turn of the century an alternative to British
poetic or dramatic models, a censored and censured oppositional figure, an abandoned and betrayed inspiration of Irish literary nationalism, and a flouting of ideological assumptions about the primacy
of dead poets in canonicity. Ellmann reports that as late as 1915,
Joyce still shocked friends by arguing Ibsen's superiority to Shakespeare: "But they began to talk of Ibsen, and Joyce proved Ibsen's
superiority to Shakespeare so eloquently that he won Feilbogen
over" (JJ 398). Joyce's championship of a censored, silenced, and unread Ibsen replaces genetic descendence with voluntary adoption,
national filiation with political allegiance, poetic debtorship with
ideological defense. Embracing a great poet with no influence, Joyce
becomes father to his own paternity, as it were, or—in an algebra
that rivals Stephen's *Hamlet* theory—his own literary grandfather.
He thus finds in his adoption of Ibsen a self-actualizing alternative
to either literary parricide or Bloomian misprision.

Translated into a grammar of identification, Joyce first champi-
oned Ibsen, then tried to imitate him, and finally *became* Ibsen,
when he was able to embed his first two phases as implications in a
larger critique of bourgeois resistance to Ibsen's own critical art. The
first stage included his paper on "Drama and Life" before the University College Literary and Historical Society on 20 January 1900,

followed by publication of his essay on "When We Dead Awaken" in the 1 April 1900 issue of the *Fortnightly Review*. By September of the same year, William Archer, Ibsen's English translator, rejected a play called "A Brilliant Career," now lost, that Joyce had written in the Ibsen manner, perhaps inspired by George Moore and Edward Martyn's *The Bending of the Bough*, which he saw at the Irish Literary Theatre in February of that year. Ellmann's judgment of this lost play ("It is hard not to exclaim, with *Finnegans Wake*, 'Ibscenest nansense' " [JJ 79]), is based on a plot sketch by Stanislaus Joyce and should be set aside. But clearly Joyce began his creative career by trying to write like Ibsen. However, his later, bolder experiment in *Stephen Hero*, written between 1904 and 1906, gives Ibsen a role in Ireland's use and abuse of literary history, and thereby translates his influence from one of personal artistic filiation—Ibsen as the foreign role model that can save the Irish artist from bastardy as illegitimate heir to Shakespeare and the English tradition—into a progressive cultural force whose potent criticism might have saved the Irish from destroying Parnell. Ibsen's (absent) presence as stifled progressive cultural force in *Stephen Hero* also inaugurates a construction of artistic development that foregrounds the ideological, by making the locus of artistic experience not what the artist produces, what he suffers, or even what he feels and thinks—as *Portrait* does—but *what he stands for*. Unlike the Stephen of *Portrait* who stands, narcissistically and autotelically, for himself, the Stephen of *Stephen Hero* stands, however ironically and hypocritically, for progressive art.

In *Stephen Hero* Joyce takes silent and cunning revenge on the Irish revival for keeping Ibsen off the Irish stage. In a maneuver whose effects can still be felt in contemporary critical commonplaces, he erases the Irish literary establishment's key role in importing Ibsen to Ireland, and thereby emasculates their movement as a major player in modern continental art. Joyce, after all, did not come upon Ibsen by chance or accident, even though he codes Stephen's discovery of Ibsen as a cosmic pulse or wind ("he felt the morning in his blood: he was aware of some movement already proceeding 'out in Europe' " [SH 35]), or as mystical lightning of the sort that struck St. Paul ("the minds of the old Norse poet and of the perturbed young Celt met in a moment of radiant simultaneity" [SH 40]). But Joyce knows perfectly well that he owes his knowledge of Ibsen to the nationalist Irish literati, who recognized an affinity between Norway's colonial struggles against Sweden and their own country's aspirations. As early as 1889 the leaders of the Irish revival, W. B. Yeats, George Moore, and Edward Martyn had issued a "famous manifesto" proclaiming Ibsen's significance in *Beltaine*, the Irish theater journal: "Everywhere critics and writers, who wish for something better than the ordinary play of commerce, turn to Norway for an example and an inspiration" (Setterquist 19). George Bernard Shaw's "The Quintessence of Ibsenism" had appeared in 1891. When Joyce in 1918 wrote the programme notes for the English Players' production of Edward Martyn's *The Heather Field* (which he had seen performed in Dublin at the turn of the century), he made special mention that Martyn "follows the school of Ibsen and therefore occupies a unique position in Ireland" (JJ 454). Irish writing of the time actually expressed considerable progressive continental influence. George Moore wrote a number of works under the influence of continental naturalism: *The Mummer's Wife* (1885), for example, for which Zola wrote an introduction to the French edition; *Strike at Arlingford* (1893), a play about a miners' strike; *Esther Waters* (1894), the story of a servant-girl Joyce praised with qualification as "fine, original work" (CW 71), and *A Drama in Muslin* (1887) of which Ulick O'Connor writes, "That Moore was capable of seeing the true economic situation of the country through the imperial sham, is shown by his observation that the national income derived from the peasantry, apart from a few distilleries and breweries in Dublin" (67). B. J. Tysdahl writes, "Joyce's essays reveal that by advocating Ibsen he thought of himself as taking up an *avant-garde* position, which pleased him immensely. He preferred to overlook the fact that Ibsen had champions in Ireland earlier than himself" (23).

But the logic of Joyce's erasure of his debt to Yeats, Moore, and Martyn, for Ibsen, must not be construed as mere personal egotism. The young Joyce put himself on the record, in the face of censorship, of excoriating in "The Day of the Rabblement" the Irish Literary Theatre for reneging on its commitment to continental art in *Beltaine:* "The official organ of the movement spoke of producing European masterpieces, but the matter went no further. Such a project was absolutely necessary. The censorship is powerless in Dublin, and the directors could have produced *Ghosts* or *The Dominion of Darkness* if they chose" (CW 70). The logic of why "such a project was absolutely necessary" is made perfectly clear in *Stephen Hero*. In its most striking instance it is thematically implicated in censorship, when one of the mourners at Isabel's wake entertains the company with tales of the censor, "the task which a friend of his in the Castle had in examining prohibited books" (SH 166). The point is made paratactically that the occlusion or misreading of wretched social conditions, Isabel's death in poverty and squalor, is displaced by preoccupation with immorality in art and culture ("Such filth, he said. You'd wonder how any man would have the face to print it" [SH 166]). The Irish either cannot read, because texts are censored or self-censored, or, corrupted by Victorian conventions, misread what they can get. Mrs. Daedalus, in dire need of feminist self-understanding, reads Ibsen's *A Doll's House* and "found Nora Helmer a charming character" (SH 86). Mr. Daedalus, who infers from the title "that *Ghosts* would probably be some uninteresting story about a haunted house" (SH 88), has little chance of seeing a version of his own ruinous profligacies as *paterfamilias* in the dissipations of Captain Alving. And even the socialist McCann misreads *Ghosts* as a brief for celibacy (SH 52) rather than as a critique of social hypocrisy and sexual repression. The Irish Literary Theatre, to Joyce's mind, fails to give Ibsen's plays body and voice. Unstaged, without production, they cannot work their critical effects on an Irish population that—could it have examined its own hypocrisies and illogicalities, and measured how ideologically incommensurate Parnell's adultery was to the historical colonial crimes his leadership might have abated—might have saved itself much sooner. Unread, unstaged, and therefore robbed of social impact, Ibsen becomes to young Dublin intellectuals an item of trivial pursuit in their parlor game of "Who's Who?"—"The answer 'Norway' gave Stephen the clue at once and so the game ended" (SH 46). For thus reducing Ibsen to a purely negative ideological signifier, Joyce metes poetic justice to the Irish nationalist literary revival by henceforth draining it of continental philosophy and influence, and thus reducing it to the effete esoterica of "the mystical set" (SH 81).

In the cultural milieu of *Stephen Hero*, Joyce reproduces the intense preoccupations with the function of art in turn-of-the-century Ireland that the competing interests of nationalism, aestheticism, and liberalism fueled. Having marginalized literary nationalism for the reasons cited above, Joyce staged Stephen's testing of Ibsen's critical potency and usefulness against the intellectual liberalism of the Jesuits of the College:

—So this Censor of yours is inspecting my essay?
—Well. He's liberal-minded . . .
—Ay. (SH 89)

The President's sense of art's social function is ostensibly bound up with notions of spiritual and social improvement and elevation as he insists, like Father Butt (who recommends *Othello* to his students for just that reason) that art have "a high moral aim." But in

the course of Stephen's interview with the President it becomes
clear that he has not read Ibsen either ("May I ask you if you have
read even a single line?—Well, no . . . I must admit . . . " [SH 93]),
and that he, too, judges him on purely ideological grounds: "I understood he had some doctrine or other—a social doctrine, free living,
and an artistic doctrine, unbridled licence—so much so that the
public will not tolerate his plays on the stage" (SH 93). The President's liberalism, yoking both artistic and critical functions to the
progressive agenda of instruction and elevation, masks the claims of
unnamed authority behind the force of consensus. "All the world
recognises Eschylus as a supreme classical dramatist," he tells Stephen—who retorts, "O, the world of professors whom he helps to
feed" (SH 97). A more overt political translation behind the privileging of Greek culture is made by the College orator during the debate
on Stephen's paper when he alliteratively proclaims: "Greek art . . .
is not for a time but for all times. It stands aloof, alone. It is 'imperial, imperious and imperative' " (SH 101).

With cant about morality, the priest masks the political agenda
that he betrays almost inadvertently: "Our people have their faith
and they are happy. They are faithful to their Church and the
Church is sufficient for them" (SH 97). This complicity of Church
and imperialism to keep subversive art and criticism in Ireland
shackled—"It represents the sum-total of modern unrest and modern freethinking" (SH 91)—masks as high-minded utopianism the
oppressive authority of hegemonic culture. Ibsen is censored in order to maintain the lie of Irish contentment under colonial and
Catholic rule: "Yes, we are happy. Even the English people have begun to see the folly of these morbid tragedies, these wretched un-
happy, unhealthy tragedies. I read the other day that some playwright had to change the last act of his play because it ended in
catastrophe—some sordid murder or suicide or death" (SH 98). The
President of the College could be describing the fate, and pronouncing judgment, on Ibsen's *Ghosts* with these words. But while Stephen's pressure against the President's liberal obligation to bow to
open-mindedness and tolerance in criticism staves off censorship,
and while he reads his paper, Joyce himself suffered at least one
more major blow from British intellectual liberalism. F. R. Leavis,
reviving Father Butt and the College President's notion that great art
must conjoin virtuosity of form with the moral tradition of high
seriousness, summarily excludes Joyce from *The Great Tradition* of
the English novel. Treating Joyce's technical innovations as "a dead
end, or at least a pointer to disintegration," he groups Joyce and his
literary heirs, Djuna Barnes, Henry Miller, and Lawrence Durrell,

among those with "the wrong kind of reaction against liberal ideal-ism" (26).

If Ibsen fails to serve as a political mirror in which bourgeois so-ciety might learn to decipher the discourses of its own hypocrisies and delusions and learn to analyze the systems of oppressive social and economic relations that produce them, so *Stephen Hero* as a text likewise failed to inspire recognition of its attempts to mirror the failed and stalled operation of modern art as a cultural and po-litical force in contemporary society. Joyce apparently made numer-ous attempts to publish the text before he decided to totally recast it as *Portrait*—on the basis of what Joyce learned by writing "The Dead," Brown argues (61). In May 1927, Joyce offered the manuscript to Sylvia Beach in the context of a set of tense transactions with her. He had been demanding money from her all that spring, and al-though she committed her exasperation and resentment chiefly to an unsent letter written on 12 April 1927 (209), a milder form of her rebukes may have been transmitted to Joyce. Possibly to redress his importunities, Joyce wrote to her sometime in April or May of 1927, "Since you go and pay several hundred francs postage (!) on these scribblers etc of mine it is possible you may wish to have the MS of *Dubliners*. . . . I have also a heap of MS in Trieste that I forgot all about until this instant about 1500 pages of the first draft of the *Portrait of the Artist* (utterly unlike the book)" (*Letters to Sylvia Beach* 117). In 1935, Shakespeare and Company offered this manu-script for sale in a catalogue in which Sylvia Beach had written, "When the manuscript came back to its author, after the twenti-eth publisher had rejected it, he threw it in the fire, from which Mrs. Joyce, at the risk of burning her hands, rescued these pages" (SH 7). Theodore Spencer notes that "No surviving page of the manuscript shows any signs of burning" (SH 8), but even if its mul-titudinous rejections and its martyrdom are apocryphal, *Stephen Hero*—a text that if it argues against anything it is the commodifi-cation of art—ironically meets a fate of pure commodification: un-read, unremembered, but able to fetch money purely on the prestige of its aestheticist twin, *A Portrait of the Artist as a Young Man.*

CHAPTER THREE

Stephen Dedalus, Oscar Wilde, and the Art of Lying

JOYCE'S PORTRAITS OF THE ARTIST, the Stephens in *Stephen Hero*, *Portrait*, and *Ulysses*, and Shem in *Finnegans Wake*, constitute ideological ravelings whose donnée is the historical emplacement of the Irish artist in confrontation with his or her modernity. This emplacement takes the form of an avant-garde gesture of a desublimating self-portraiture that interrogates its own self-aestheticizing impulse (an impulse implicated in, and directed toward, issues of gender) by critiquing not only artistic narcissism (Norris) but its status as a privatized form of art's social institutionalization. If, for example, the artist of *Portrait* is a kind of *Mona Lisa*, a depiction of art aestheticizing itself, then the artist of "Shem the Penman" might be Duchamp and Picabia's *L.H.O.O.Q.*, the *Mona Lisa* with moustaches—"anna loavely long pair of inky Italian moostarshes glistering with boric vaseline and frangipani" (FW 182.27)—the avant-garde graffiti artist's defacement of high art to critique art's privileges, pretensions, and symbolic functions both inside and outside the museum (Feshbach, Loos). Furthermore, like Duchamp's own most provocative play directed (as in his transvestite self-portraits as Rrose Sélavy) toward gender, Joyce's critical ravelings also track art's use and abuse of woman (as artist and as object) to mark the political issues of the late nineteenth and early twentieth centuries. The fulcrum of these institutional interrogations is aestheticism—because, as Buerger argues, aestheticism makes the institutional ideology of art visible and apparent. Joyce's historical moment, his maturation in the 1890's that marked the twilight of an aestheticism led, among others, by one of his own Irish countrymen—therefore makes possible an immanent critique that coincides with the project of the "historical avant-garde."

Duchamp serves as a useful analogue for Joyce because he demonstrates the avant-garde's shift in using artistic intertextualism less for logopoetic than for ideological self-reference. If Dada interrogates the waning power of the Renaissance aura, Joyce, I will argue, carefully works Stephen's portraiture, and self-portraiture, through Romanticism's decadence in Aestheticism (aestheticism as romanticism minus the politics) and in its highly self-disciplined form as Modernism. Throughout these portraitures I will track Joyce's deployment of what one—adapting Buerger's sense of immanent critique—might call Ibsen's avant-gardist naturalism: an exposure of art as an environment that "entwined itself in the deepest layers of the personality" (Williams 141). If, in a theatrical play like *A Doll's House*, Ibsen represents character as deeply theatricalized— Nora Helmer unconsciously enacting ideologically constructed gender roles against her own best psychological and moral self-interests—Joyce goes him one better by aesthetically incriminating the very representations that show artistic character as deeply aestheticized, as fashioning itself from aesthetic figurations.

In Joyce's early texts the problematizing of novelistic form betrays the ideological regime of formal conventions and poetic practice— for example, naturalism's stripping of the emotional and aestheticist enhancements that permit subjectivity to soak into, and retexture, the environment. Nowhere do we find a more dramatic contrast between a naturalistic representation of art's institutionalization, and a romanticizing of artistic function than by comparing the literary censorship episodes in *Stephen Hero* and *Portrait*. In *Stephen Hero* the revealing interview with the President of the college ends inconclusively, and Stephen reads his paper more in the absence of a definite ban than by dint of having won the priest over to his theories of modern art. The discussion that follows his reading of the paper before the Literary and Historical Society consists largely of ideological discourses ("conceived in a spirit so hostile to the spirit of religion" [SH 102]; "the moral welfare of the Irish people was 'menaced by such theories'" [SH 103]; "Mr Daedalus was himself a renegade from the Nationalist ranks: he professed cosmopolitism" [SH 103]) whose liberal gestures of strained fairness and tolerance blunt their political force. The grand episode of Stephen's championship of modernism in the face of censorship and opposition ends in an anticlimactic whimper, "The vote of thanks was passed unanimously but without enthusiasm" [SH 105]. By the time Stephen rejoins his friends on the way home, who seem to have already forgotten his paper, and who only from politeness remind themselves to offer him insincere condolences ("Stephen was touched by this show of friendship but he shook his head as if he wished to change the subject. Besides, he knew that Madden really understood very little of the paper and disapproved of what he understood" [SH 105]), it is clear that Stephen's efforts on Ibsen's behalf have failed and produced only indifference. Narratively, modern art in *Stephen Hero* has taught the artist its social futility as Ibsen is assimilated to Dublin's intellectual complacency and paralysis. The cry of literary bolshevism with which the early sketch of *Portrait* closes is the logical outcome of *Stephen Hero*'s plot. But the self-critical possibilities of *Stephen Hero* are restricted because its naturalistic indictment of society for martyring modern art is not delivered in a self-indicting form.

Portrait, on the other hand, shifts the martyrdom of art onto the martyrdom of the artist. In place of *Stephen Hero*'s naturalistic treatment of artistic reception and effect, *Portrait* internalizes, naturalizes, and aestheticizes censorship. The modern, progressive Ibsen is replaced by the Romantic Byron as the artist's hero and cause. The prosaic setting of the college is replaced by the gothic atmospherics of the Clonliffe Road at night, where in the gloomy dusk Stephen is menacingly attacked by his schoolfellows. The dry narrative prose of *Stephen Hero* is transformed into the rhetoric of romantic algolagnia, "His sensitive nature was still smarting under the lashes of an undivined and squalid way of life" (P 78). The diffuse and inconclusive college debate is replaced by a lurid beating, "Struggling and kicking under the cuts of the cane and the blows of the knotty stump Stephen was borne back against a barbed wire fence" (P 82). The ideological discourse about the nature and function of art is replaced with the tropes of heresy and the inquisitional interrogation and confession, "—Admit that Byron was no good./—No./—Admit./—No./—Admit./—No. No." (P 82). The naturalistic narrative of the fate of modern art in modern society has been replaced by this histrionic drama that is deliberately and explicitly theatricalized. Stephen's attack by Heron and his friends on the Clonliffe Road is presented as a revery stimulated by his mock caning by the same gang of boys, as he waits behind the stage of the Belvedere auditorium ready to do his bit of acting in the play *Vice Versa*. Censorship has become deinstitutionalized and subordinated to heroic fantasies of artistic martyrdom, Stephen suffering senselessly for art in order to legitimate his growing social isolation, idealistic transcendence, and self-dramatization. *Portrait* makes its intertexted forms and conventions complicit with its lie about the nature and function of censorship in modern culture. Expressed differently, *Portrait* attempts to contain art's "outside"—its effects and reception and its encounters with law and economics, on the inside of its forms.

Joyce's curious transition from a naturalistic depiction of art's cultural operations within his contemporary Irish society in 1904 to the romanticized figurations of the artist as *poète maudit* in the tradition of Verlaine's accursed and martyred modern poets doomed to alienation and rejection from bourgeois society is mediated—I will agree with Hugh Kenner (*Pound Era* 272)—by Joyce's embrace and dramatization of the problematic that Oscar Wilde's aestheticism posed for modern Irish art. Wilde's example of aestheticism's untenability in the modern world would have allowed Joyce—even before he "modernized himself" in *Portrait*—to preemptively grasp modernism's "failure," or the failure of the version of modernism Suzi Gablik describes in *Has Modernism Failed?*:

> Those who defend modernism claim that art need not serve any purpose but should create its own reality. . . . For the committed modernist, the self-sufficiency of art is its salvation. Aesthetic experience is an end in itself, worth having on its own account. The only way for art to preserve its truth is by maintaining its distance from the social world—by staying pure. (20–21)

Joyce might have borrowed Stephen's phrase to call this sense of modernism's aestheticism "Tame essence of Wilde" (U 9:532). His own 1909 essay on Wilde suggests that he would have possessed a historical perspective on the Paterian Oxford tradition behind the *l'art pour l'art* of the *fin de siècle* in England, and would also have grasped its decadent social implications. It is no simple caricature of aestheticism that Joyce inherits from Wilde and deploys in his own texts, but an aestheticism capable of theorizing itself, of mocking itself, and of raveling itself—as Wilde's "De Profundis" ravels *The Picture of Dorian Gray*—that Joyce inherits from Wilde.

The beginnings of Joyce's self-critique of aestheticism can be found in *Stephen Hero*, in the curious discrepancy between Joyce's essay on Ibsen and Stephen's essay on Ibsen. If we compare Joyce's essay "Drama and Life" with the essay Stephen presents to the University College Literary and Historical Society in the novel, we realize that they are not the same text. Joyce's essay contains an explicit warning against aestheticism:

> A yet more insidious claim is the claim for beauty. As conceived by the claimants beauty is as often anaemic spirituality as hardy animalism. . . . Beauty is the swerga of the aesthete; but truth has a more ascertainable and more real dominion. Art is true to itself when it deals with truth. Should such an untoward event as a universal reformation take place on earth, truth would be the very threshold of the house beautiful. (CW 43)

In this remarkable reworking of the Keatsian tropes of beauty and truth, Joyce opens art to its own reflection of a "more real dominion" that is clearly outside of itself, and whose coincidence with "beauty" is deferred until a utopian moment of revolution, "such an untoward event as a universal reformation." Stephen's essay, described but not presented in the novel, appears to flout this warning as it adds to the core of Joyce's tenets the core of Stephen's Thomistic aesthetic theory as this will be developed and presented more fully in *Portrait*. Joyce marks this difference by having Stephen change the title of his essay from "Drama and Life" to "Art and Life" (SH 81). The result is a strange concatenation of contradictory discourses that superimpose a commitment to Ibsenite realism upon a Thomistic essentialism that maintains the autotelicity of art—"He proclaimed at the outset that art was the human disposition of intelligible or sensible matter for an esthetic end" (SH 77). The college President may be excused for being confused by this strange amalgam of Thomistic scholasticism, avant-garde dramatic theory, and what he correctly recognizes as a remnant of *l'art pour l'art*. "I suppose you mean Art for Art's sake" (SH 77) he asks Stephen, and Stephen does not disagree: "I have only pushed to its logical conclusion the definition Aquinas has given of the beautiful . . . *Pulcra sunt quae visa placent*. He seems to regard the beautiful as that which satisfies the esthetic appetite and nothing more" (SH 95).

Joyce's object in mixing the Ibsen theory with that of Aquinas is to discredit Stephen's grasp of Ibsen, and to bring to an ironic closure (with historical resonances) Ibsen's failure to produce a progressive critical effect upon the Irish. In his implicit shift from critical to aesthetic values in his paper, Stephen reflects the aesthetically rationalized resistance to Ibsen among the Irish—a criticism of the prosaism of Ibsen's language and the vulgarity of his concerns that especially troubled Synge (Setterquist) as well as Arthur Power. By telling his friend, "Indeed if I remember rightly Synge disliked the plays of Ibsen. He dealt with what Synge calls 'seedy problems' " (Power 34), Power provoked Joyce into a spirited defense of Ibsen's feminism: "You have not understood him, he said, neither his purpose nor his psychological depth, as opposed to Synge's romantic fantasy . . . The purpose of *The Doll's House*, for instance, was the emancipation of women" (Power 35). Yet notwithstanding his championship of Ibsen, no one abuses Ibsen's feminism more scandalously than Stephen in *Stephen Hero*. Stephen grasps the implicit political analogy Ibsen so carefully draws between marriage and prostitution in *A Doll's House* clearly enough to reproduce it in the discourse of material marxism to Cranly:

A woman's body is a corporal asset of the State: if she traffic with
it she must sell it either as a harlot or as a married woman or as
a working celibate or as a mistress. But a woman is (incidentally)
a human being: and a human being's love and freedom is not a
spiritual asset of the State. (SH 202)

Incidentally? Stephen who elsewhere betrays his misogyny by calling
women "marsupials" and treating the plump Emma Clery throughout the text as a warm mammal, goes on to pervert Ibsen's feminism
by transgressing the not so fine line between libertarianism and lib-
ertinism. Abruptly demanding from Emma a single night of sex
without emotional or social encumbrance, he later justifies this assault to Lynch and Cranly (who tell him he must have been mad)
with the lofty political argument that he was saving her from simo-
niacal entrapment in the State's sexual economy. Disciple of Ibsen
that he is, Stephen has consistently ridiculed McCann's feminist polemic along with the chastity McCann advocates to keep his politics
sexually disinterested. With respect to women, Stephen is guilty of
the ultimate Ibsen sin, *hypocrisy*, by using progressive ideology to
further a lust that unlike Ibsen—who supported an illegitimate
child for many years—he will ground in neither economic, social,
nor emotional responsibility. Stephen, disciple of Ibsen, is a pro-
grammatic cad. "Would you like me to seduce her?" he asks Lynch
about Emma. "Very much. It would be very interesting" (SH 191). I
would then reformulate Heilbrun's claim that "Joyce admired Ibsen
and ignored his most profound contribution" (215) by arguing that it
is not Joyce, but Stephen, who admired Ibsen and ignored his most
profound contribution, but whose hypocrisy the text betrays and
exposes.

The theoretical shift from *Stephen Hero* to *Portrait*, which replaces Ibsen, the progressive, controversial, contemporary thinker,
with Aquinas, the canonical scholastic, and which deinstitutional-
izes Stephen's theories, moving them out of the university, where
they were subject to censorship and public debate, into the arena of
the privatized dialogue, the elitist intellectual confidence, seems like
a retrogressive maneuver on Joyce's part: a shift of attention away
from art's social function to the self-display of individual genius. But
Joyce had, I believe, a subtler and more critical end in view. By foregrounding *theory* itself in *Portrait*, Joyce had his text make a deliberate gesture of self-enclosure: an announcement of art as bounded
and determinate (like the aestheticized basket atop the butcher boy)
that appears to swallow up the novel itself. The difference between
the 'inside' and 'outside' of art ("Shall we put life—real life—on the

stage?") that the young Joyce explicates as the problem of realism in
"Drama and Life" (CW 44), is in *Portrait* collapsed as a problem of
metarepresentation. Stephen's aesthetic theory stages the question
of how the hermetic seal of aestheticism can be cracked, once
theory has shut the window of realism Joyce had Lona Hessel open
at the end of "Drama and Life" (CW 46). The solution, I propose, is
intertextuality: the staging of theory as a staging of theory enclosed
in a spiral that winds through Wildean aestheticism into Irish literary history typified by Wilde and Yeats in London telling each other
after Christmas dinner, theories of unreal art. Aesthetic theorizing
in *Portrait* is staged as a plebeian version of the dialogue that structures Oscar Wilde's theory of aestheticism in the essay "The Decay
of Lying: An Observation," which belonged to the volume *Intentions* Joyce had in his Trieste library (Gillespie 102).

By shifting the form of the theory from a third person narration in
Stephen Hero presented largely for its content by an often sarcastic
narrative voice who refers to its rhetoric as "eloquent and arrogant
peroration" (SH 80), to first person speech that foregrounds itself and
that displays its own beauty, Joyce imitates Wilde's strategy by letting *Portrait* dramatize aestheticism's aestheticizing of itself. The
Wilde essay, whose importance Ellmann signifies by calling it "the
locus classicus for the expression of the converging aesthetic ideas
of writers everywhere" (OW 304), functions as a significant, if silent,
intertext in *Portrait* whose function Joyce doubles, again silently, in
Ulysses, when Stephen borrows from it his epigram for Irish art as
"the cracked lookingglass of a servant." The dialogical form of the
essay was doubled in life as well as in fiction. In his biography of
Oscar Wilde, Richard Ellmann describes how Wilde introduced the
essay to Yeats at Christmas dinner at his Tite Street house in London in 1888. "After dinner Wilde brought out the proofs of 'The Decay of Lying,' which James Knowles was to publish the next month
in the *Nineteenth Century*. It could hardly have found a more willing listener" (OW 301). Wilde presenting his essay to Yeats recapitulates the dialogical form of the essay itself, in which Vivian reads his
paper, "The Decay of Lying: A Protest," to his friend Cyril (Vyvyan
and Cyril were the names of Wilde's sons): a dialogue recapitulated
in turn in Joyce's fiction, when Stephen formally narrates his aesthetic theory to Lynch in *Portrait*. Lest the homology between the
dialogues be missed, Joyce formally marked their similarity with the
code of smoking: "Shall I read you what I have written?" Vivian asks
Cyril, who replies "Certainly, if you give me a cigarette" (CWOW
971); "If I am to listen to your esthetic philosophy give me at least
another cigarette," Lynch tells Stephen (P 207).

Wilde, who traced the concept of aestheticism and the aesthetic poet to Plato's *Symposium*—and who invokes him in this essay to justify lying, "Lying and poetry are arts—arts, as Plato saw, not unconnected with each other" (CWOW 972)—structured "The Decay of Lying" into a Socratic dialogue that would simultaneously allow him to show wealthy, idle, young men disporting themselves intellectually in English country houses. Joyce's social displacement of this structure by displaying poor, idle, young men disporting themselves intellectually on Dublin's mean streets in itself already ironizes Wilde's aim to have art occlude the real environment: "Art begins with abstract decoration, with purely imaginative and pleasurable work dealing with what is unreal and non-existent" (CWOW 978). But this tension of environment resisting an artistic theorizing that would negate it becomes the textual drama of Stephen's aesthetic lecture to Lynch in *Portrait*. "A crude grey light, mirrored in the sluggish water, and a smell of wet branches over their heads seemed to war against the course of Stephen's thought" (P 207), the text tells us, and a little later Stephen's voice is drowned out by commercial traffic, "A long dray laden with old iron came round the corner of sir Patrick Dun's hospital covering the end of Stephen's speech with the harsh roar of jangled and rattling metal" (P 209). The competing "discourses" of theory and environment are staged in *Portrait* as the agon of dialectic, of propositions contesting the disputed truth of the nature of representation. This dispute is extended to a dialogism of competing vocational discourses, as Stephen epiphanizes the artist in order to drain his vocation of the materialism that infects his Philistine peers: "We are right, he said, and the others are wrong. To speak of these things and to try to understand their nature and, having understood it, to try slowly and humbly and constantly to express, to press out again, from the gross earth or what it brings forth . . . an image of the beauty we have come to understand—that is art" (P 206). The poetic rhetoric of Stephen's theory plainly universalizes as inchoate matter ("gross earth") that which is "outside" and therefore "unfit" for art—by implication extruding realism's and naturalism's matter on the ground of a representational problematic. While giving his gross earth greater urban, class specificity—"As for that great and daily increasing school of novelists for whom the sun always rises in the East-End"— Wilde's Vivian likewise resorts to similar material tropes of rudiment to indicate deficient representation: "the only thing that can be said about them is that they find life crude, and leave it raw" (CWOW 974).

Stephen's theorizing is punctuated and interrupted by an analo-

gous vocational discourse of the marketplace: "Did you hear the results of the exams? . . . Griffin was plucked. Halpin and O'Flynn
are through the home civil. Moonan got fifth place in the Indian.
O'Shaughnessy got fourteenth" (P 210). By extruding and excising
this commercial language as product of the "gross earth," Stephen
performs an ideological maneuver upon the institution of the university that rarifies its mission as the distillation of culture, while
repressing and occluding its historical truth: that the Irish profes-
sionals it turns out are destined to do the Empire's dirty work, either
administering Ireland's own oppression in the civil service, executing Britain's project in India, or slaving in England's industrial slums
("Hynes was two years in Liverpool and he says the same. A frightful
hole he said it was. Nothing but midwifery cases. Half a crown
cases" [P 216]). Stephen's theory thus fails to swallow up the environment (and with it the novel) which maintains an indigestible residual resistance to the narration's aestheticizing rhetoric. The dialectical fracture survives across the narrative, as resonances of the
Philistines' unlovely prose clang especially harshly against Davin's
mellifluous Celtic burr that mystifies Irish woman—"She was half
undressed as if she was going to bed when I knocked and she had her
hair hanging; and I thought by her figure and by something in the
look of her eyes that she must be carrying a child" (P 182). The
young peasant woman, so pregnant with aesthetic signification for
Stephen ("a batlike soul waking to the consciousness of itself in
darkness and secrecy and loneliness" [P 183]), will become one of
the half crown midwifery cases the university medicals dread in an
Irish country practice.

Stephen's theory, throughout, creates for the text of *Portrait* a self-
problematization that makes it "paraesthetic," in David Carroll's
sense of a "critical approach to aesthetics for which art is a question
not a given" (xiv). We see this most readily in one of Stephen's
most extraordinary heuristic moves, the introduction of an example
whose representational confusions and absurdities prise open the
very questions of the inside and outside of art that his theory pretends to settle:

> A girl got into a hansom a few days ago, he went on, in London.
> She was on her way to meet her mother whom she had not seen
> for many years. At the corner of a street the shaft of a lorry shiv-
> ered the window of the hansom in the shape of a star. A long fine
> needle of the shivered glass pierced her heart. She died on the in-
> stant. The reporter called it a tragic death. It is not. (P 205)

Stephen's transformation of a putative newspaper report of a London traffic accident into an aestheticized discourse that betrays a patent hyperaestheticism ("A long fine needle of the shivered glass pierced her heart") sets aside the ostensible Aristotelian issue of the tragic and draws pointed attention to itself. Stephen's theory is pressing its argument with a self-reflexive parable of a romance of writing, a collision of industrial lorry and hansom cab, of East End and West End that dissolves their genres (of gritty naturalism and aristocratic comedy) into a Wildean fairy tale. The "incident" puts industrial pen ("the shaft of a lorry") on a friable glass surface ("shivered the window of the hansom in the shape of a star") to produce a starry text that breaks the heart of a young girl about to be reunited with her long-lost mother. The newspaper account of a traffic accident has borrowed the tropes of a spindle that creates a hundred year sleep, or a sliver of snow in the eye that turns a heart to ice. "Life we must accept as we see it before our eyes," Joyce wrote in "Drama and Life," "men and women as we meet them in the real world, not as we apprehend them in the world of faery" (CW 45). Wilde, author of such fairy tales as "The Star-Child" and "The Happy Prince," wrote "The final revelation is that Lying, the telling of beautiful untrue things, is the proper aim of Art" (CWOW 992). Joyce—using art's figuration of woman—performs, I believe, a paraesthetic maneuver when he replaces the naturalistic death of a girl in *Stephen Hero* (Isabel dying from the poverty of her environment soaked into her body) with the theoretical exemplum of a fairy tale of a girl who dies when her heart is pierced by a star. The practice of this sort of lying is demonstrated again in the way he transforms into a trope of aesthetic apprehension the physiological trauma known prosaically as the heart attack: "The instant wherein that supreme quality of beauty, the clear radiance of the esthetic image, is apprehended luminously by the mind . . . is the luminous silent stasis of esthetic pleasure, a spiritual state very like to that cardiac condition which the Italian physiologist Luigi Galvani, using a phrase almost as beautiful as Shelley's, called the enchantment of the heart" (P 213).

While Peter Buerger's critique of art is useful for identifying that what art lies about is its function rather than its content, Theodor Adorno's theory of aesthetics is useful for identifying an aspect of the metaphysics of Stephen's aesthetics that implicates it in lying. Specifically, Stephen's concept of "epiphany" as the "sudden spiritual manifestation, whether in the vulgarity of speech or of gesture or in a memorable phase of the mind itself" (SH 211) is not so different from the "plus" or "surplus" that Adorno finds as the source for art's transcendent quality—"Nature's beauty consists in appearing to say more than she is. Now the idea behind art is to wrest this 'plus' from its contingent setting in nature, appropriating nature's appearance and making it determinate, which means among other things negating its unreality" (Adorno 116). Stephen strives to apprehend that "surplus" in the world around him, and he fashions an ocular metaphor, the trope of the narrowed focus, into the imago of his vision: "Imagine my glimpses at that clock as the gropings of a spiritual eye which seeks to adjust its vision to an exact focus. The moment the focus is reached the object is epiphanised. It is just in this epiphany that I find the third, the supreme quality of beauty" (SH 211). But Stephen's formulation is as significant for what it leaves out as for what it posits. The moment of exact focus that epiphanizes the object is also the moment of greatest blurring of all that surrounds it, the moment of occlusion of all that lacks the "plus" or the "surplus"—that is, lacks an unreality to be made real. Stephen's theory is therefore simultaneously an anatomy of the privileged gaze, and an unarticulated demonstration of its occlusivity, the expulsion of materialism—what Wilde in his essay, in a rhetoric that attempts to demoralize the moral trope—calls "lying." Wilde comes closer to the truth of art than Stephen does, because he names art's occlusivity at the same time that he insists upon it, and thereby embeds his theory of art in its own immanent critique. Adorno writes:

> Plato's criticism of art is not convincing because he overlooked the fact that art negates the literal reality of its material content, arguing instead that such content understood literally reveals art's mendacity. In Plato the sublimation of the concept into the idea goes hand in hand with philistine blindness for the central aspect of art: form. Despite everything, Plato is correct in putting his finger on the lie of art. This is an indelible blemish; there is no guarantee anywhere that art will keep its objective promise. That is why every theory of art must also be critical of art. (123)

The critical lack in Stephen's theory exposed by the submerged effect of Wilde's concession of art's lying in his essay, is a paraesthetic component that would let Stephen's theory problematize itself politically. It is the novel as a whole—what in *Portrait* is "outside" of Stephen's theory—that supplies the paraesthetic elements that problematize its form.

But Joyce complicates the intertextual and paraesthetic function of Wilde, by having Wilde's essay surface again in "Telemachus."

Portrait's theory of aesthetics was a moment of entry for Stephen into the Wildean text, as Stephen steps out of history and into Wilde's aesthetics essay to reenact it with Lynch; in "Telemachus" Stephen steps out of Wildean theory and into Wilde's history, assuming his role as court jester to the British, his wit pimped to dazzle Haines with his aphorisms. But what we see is not so much Stephen become Wilde, but Stephen cynically appropriating Wilde's ideas and style as a self-critical role, a concession that Wilde's aestheticism lied about its own colonial role, and a determination that if Stephen is doomed to play Wilde, he will play him with a difference, he will act out Wilde's lying as lying. Stephen retrieves the political residue of art's lying when he transforms Wilde's words into colonial coin to be cunningly inserted into imperialistic cultural exchange. Mulligan conjures up the ghost of Wilde ("If Wilde were only alive to see you!" [U 1:143]) only to have him witness his own robbery, the spectacle of Stephen deftly stealing Wilde's aphorism from "The Decay of Lying" ("I can quite understand your objection to art being treated as a mirror. You think it would reduce genius to the position of a cracked looking-glass," [CWOW 982]) by turning it into a symbol of Irish art as the "cracked lookingglass of a servant" (U 1: 147). Stephen does not reveal the source of his aphorism to Mulligan, and Mulligan does not guess that it comes from Wilde; together they proceed to market the lie of the filched epigram to the British Haines, the dapper Oxford student in scarf and tennis shirt who flashes a silver cigarette case encrusted with a green gem: "Cracked lookingglass of a servant! Tell that to the oxy chap downstairs and touch him for a guinea. He's stinking with money and thinks you're not a gentleman. His old fellow made his tin by selling jalap to Zulus or some bloody swindle or other" (U 1:154). Haines's academic program is the study of the Gaelic language and of Irish folklore, the intellectual variant of his father's third world imperialism, the Oxford plunder of Irish culture. By passing Haines a purloined Irish aphorism, a forged cheque, as it were, Stephen merely makes the Sassenach's plunder of Irish culture redundant. "I intend to make a collection of your sayings if you will let me," Haines tells Stephen. "That one about the cracked lookingglass of a servant being the symbol of Irish art is deuced good" (U 1:480).

But Stephen, of course, alters Wilde's epigram slightly but significantly: Cyril's notion that mimetic art, or realism, would make genius a cracked lookingglass is altered by Stephen to make Irish art specifically the cracked lookinglass of a *servant*. Stephen thereby politicizes Wilde's figure by transforming it into a colonial trope: Irish art as a mirror fractured by the abuse of an imperial culture and reflecting back to the Irish people their subjection and oppression. Haines, as collector of Irish wit is so taken by its cleverness and value as entertainment, that he fails to penetrate it, and therefore fails to see himself in Stephen's trope as the imperial oppressor, caught in the mirror of the text that reflects him as the exploitive, patronizing, overweening Sassenach shamelessly picking the brains of his hosts. Joyce further carefully embeds the purloined epigram into a narrative of a literally purloined mirror—"I pinched it out of the skivvy's room, Buck Mulligan said" (U 1:138)—in order to add to the political spiral the further twists of class and sexual predation. In a parabolic reversal of the stereotype of the thieving servant, Mulligan enacts a figure of the thieving master ("He who stealeth from the poor lendeth to the Lord. Thus spake Zarathustra" [U 1:727]): the Irish Ascendancy stealing from its poor, its peasant and servant classes. They steal from them not only their livelihood and dignity, but also their power of self-recognition, their ability to see themselves and their oppression in an art of their own. Joyce further invokes the image of sexual predation—the servant's ugliness as defense against rape and seduction—to historicize, as he does throughout his *oeuvre*, the figure of colonial subjection as that of the poor woman: the old milkwoman obliged to become patient creditor to carousing students, the washerwoman wracking her body to keep her son in tennis flannels, and the slavey in "Two Gallants" made to yield a gold coin to pay her seducer's debts. By insisting on the material specificity of poor old or ugly women, Joyce demythologizes and repoliticizes the trope of Ireland as a Poor Old Woman.

The twist Stephen gives Wilde's aphorism is in one sense a pure rhetorical twist, a shift of trope from genius to servant as the depth of reflected art. But it is nonetheless a philosophical gesture directed against Wilde, transforming Wilde's aphorism into its own anathema, into the antithesis of aestheticism's expulsion of materialism from the domain of art. Stephen thus takes sides against Wilde in his quarrel with naturalism. In "The Decay of Lying," Wilde expels materialism from the domain of art, but not the domain of history or ethics. He concedes that Zola tells the truth, but indicts him on the ground of art, "But his work is entirely wrong from beginning to end, and wrong not on the ground of morals, but on the ground of art. From any ethical standpoint it is just what it should be. The author is perfectly truthful, and describes things exactly as they happen" (CWOW 974). Clearly Wilde's quarrel with naturalism stakes less a political position (his "Soul of Man under Socialism" urges reform by utilitarian means aimed at individualism) than a representational problematic that holds the rhetoric of naturalism, the forms of its figurations, as of insufficiently exteriorized artifice to achieve the hyperaesthetic effects Wilde desires. "Art begins with abstract decoration, with purely imaginative and pleasurable work dealing with what is unreal and non-existent. This is the first stage" (CWOW 978). Wilde consequently transforms social class into an aesthetic code on the basis of its relation to the material. He makes the aristocracy a figure of art because it is ornamental, because aristocrats as a class cultivate unreality and artifice in order to suppress the truth of the social costs their privileged existence represents. To Wilde the aristocracy embodies a surplus of unreality crucial to art that social or political analysis would destroy: "if a writer insists upon analysing the upper classes, he might just as well write of match-girls and costermongers at once" (CWOW 975). On this principle Wilde's aestheticism expels the lower classes—because their uncompromising foregrounding of material reality and its subjectivized internalizations in suffering makes them ugly. "In literature we require distinction, charm, beauty and imaginative power. We don't want to be harrowed and disgusted with an account of the doings of the lower orders" (CWOW 974).

Wilde himself never betrayed this faith—even in the "The Ballad of Reading Gaol" written under the inspiration of Her Majesty's Government, as a waggish judge is said to have said (OW 532). Indeed, given time, Wilde would have falsified even that poem of prison life and execution into a more aestheticist untruth—"He would celebrate liberty instead of prison, joy instead of sorrow, kissing instead of hanging" (OW 571). Wilde's personal extremity causes no defection to either realism or naturalism as he maintains a regime of discursive separation between art and history that consigns his plight to the latter. Refusing to speak the truth of his fate in Art, Wilde told it to the *Daily Chronicle* in a letter on prison reform in which he does not flinch from harrowing and disgusting readers with tales of the ravages of prisoners by diarrhoea (which had whittled his own frame from 190 pounds to 168 in a matter of months) and the indescribable degradation and misery produced by subhuman sanitation—"In old days each cell was provided with a form of latrine. These latrines have now been suppressed. They exist no longer. A small tin vessel is supplied to each prisoner instead. . . . A man suffering from diarrhoea is consequently placed in a position so loathsome that it is unnecessary to dwell on it" (CWOW 966). Wilde's "history" doubles realism's art, as Wilde repeats in journalism Ibsen's denunciation of pathogenic drainage conditions in *An Enemy of the People*—the very problem play that triggers stinging ridicule from Stephen's audience after he reads his Ibsen paper in

Stephen Hero: "Mr Magee said he did not know as much about Ibsen as Mr Daedalus did—nor did he want to know anything about him—but he knew that one of his plays was about the sanitary condition of a bathing-place. If this was drama he did not see why some Dublin Shakespeare should not pen an immortal work dealing with the new Main Drainage Scheme of the Dublin Corporation" (SH 102). Later in *Stephen Hero*, the text reiterates this facetious proposal more seriously when the *Evening Telegraph* juxtaposes drainage and literature as indifferent agenda items:

> *Nationalist Meeting at Ballinrobe.*
> *Important Speeches.*
> *Main Drainage Scheme.*
> *Breezy Discussion.*
> *Death of a Well-known Solicitor*
> *Mad Cow at Cabra,*
> *Literature &.*   *(SH 221)*

"I suppose you consider literature the most important thing there?" Cranly asks Stephen.

Joyce problematizes Wildean aestheticism's sharp excision of social waste—the products of a culture's drains, prisons, and slums—as a hypoaesthetic refuse of art relegated to the realm of sociology, ethics, and politics. ("Aesthetics are higher than ethics. They belong to a more spiritual sphere. . . . Even a colour-sense is more important, in the development of the individual, than a sense of right and wrong" ["The Critic as Artist" CWOW 1058]). Wilde's theory and practice of separating the laurel leaves and diarrhoea that intersected his social condition as an artist in history, reflect diverse rationalizations for the marginalization of naturalism (the onus of science, the charge of sensationalism, the pathology of cloacal obsession) in the critical discourse of the late nineteenth century. Joyce's challenge to this aestheticist problematic is impelled, I believe, by his understanding that art's relationship to its own exteriorization—its boundedness and closure within the social realm, is radically implicated in its possible role in progressive socio-political transformation. Wilde fails, as Irish artist, to provide Joyce with a viable aesthetic theory or praxis in the face of a modernity that, at the dawn of the twentieth century, is capable of murdering its aesthetes. Insofar as the Wildean separation of idealism and materialism continues to theoretically cleave the ideology of Irish literary movements, the young Joyce pictures himself regarded as immersed in the prophylactic sewer of naturalism in "The Holy Office":

> But all these men of whom I speak
> Make me the sewer of their clique.
> That they may dream their dreamy dreams
> I carry off their filthy streams   (CW 151)

"The Holy Office," written in 1904 when he was just twenty-two, is Joyce's first satirical resistance to his Calibanization as an Irish artist that was to be repeated in response to various of his publications throughout his career. He returned to it again, retrieving all of its cloacal imagery in order to subject an ideologically elitist modernism to a parodic naturalistic critique in "Shem the Penman," Book I Chapter 7 of *Finnegans Wake*.

CHAPTER FOUR

"Shem the Penman": Joyce's Tenemental Text

WHEN STEPHEN LOOKS in Mulligan's cracked mirror, he sees a figure of the artist that would harrow Wilde's ghost ("The rage of Caliban at not seeing his face in a mirror, he said. If Wilde were only alive to see you!" [U 1:143]). It is as though the lookingglass of the servant is still inhabited by her illfavored visage, to deform the artist's own: "Hair on end. As he and others see me. Who chose this face for me. This dogsbody to rid of vermin" [U 1:136]). But when Stephen has seen this dogsbody before, in *Portrait*—"A louse crawled over the nape of his neck . . . The life of his body, illclad, illfed, louseeaten, made him close his eyelids in a sudden spasm of despair" (P 233)— he transformed it by an act of intellectual and aesthetic magic into a sublime thing, turning his lice, and his squalid body, into a fallen angel and falling stars. "Yes; and it was not darkness that fell from the air. It was brightness—*Brightness falls from the air*" (P 234). In "Shem the Penman" the vermin return to take possession of the artist (and the text) again, proliferating their species and sites of infestation, and assuming verbal form as clichés that infest the narrative: "the foxtrotting fleas, the lieabed lice . . . the buzz in his braintree . . . the tickle of his tail . . . the rats in his garret, the bats in his belfry, the budgerigars and bumbosolom" (FW 180.18).

Finnegans Wake's "Shem the Penman," composed by Joyce in the wake of the controversial reception of *Ulysses* in the mid 1920's, revisits the problematic of artistic autonomy through the trope of self-reflexivity and self-portraiture in whose name he stepped into modernism with *A Portrait of the Artist as a Young Man*. He now abandons aesthetic theory for reasons that David Carroll's introduction to Foucault makes compellingly clear when he relates the trope of the infinite regress of mirrors, the *mise en abyme* of art, to ideological maneuvers that lead artistic self-reflexivity, and contemporary theory grounded in its rhetoric, to negate history:

For these reasons, the *mise en abyme* has largely been considered a tool of formalist critics used to ensure the purity of the literary and to exclude the extra-literary from having any significant impact on literary texts. In other words, in contemporary theory, the *mise en abyme* has almost always been the sign of literary or aesthetic closure and a denial of the impact of the historical, socio-political, and philosophical contexts of literature and art. (54)

"Shem the Penman" exteriorizes the history of modernism—and specifically modernism's relation to Irish art and artist—by way of entry through Mulligan's cracked mirror. The servant's crack, as sign of poverty and class, contaminates Mulligan's attempts to confine poetic history to the polished and gleaming hall of mirrors in which Wilde captures it in the famous preface to his parable of the representational separability of art and life in *The Picture of Dorian Gray* ("The nineteenth century dislike of Realism is the rage of Caliban seeing his own face in a glass. The nineteenth century dislike of Romanticism is the rage of Caliban not seeing his own face in a glass" [CWOW 17]). Mulligan's gesture, however Wildean, is an aggressive gesture, as he flourishes his critical mirror into the face of the Irish artist along with Wilde's Shakespearean trope that makes the full and empty mirrors of realism and romanticism the *mise en abyme* of art determined to interiorize (and conversely de-exteriorize) its own history. By calibanizing Stephen, Mulligan foregrounds the sectarian hostilities that rived the ecumenical pretensions of the largely Protestant Irish revival (Potts), and whose imperfectly repressed racism and class prejudice erupts through a veneer of Oxford impudence and high spirits. "Mulligan's remark and the manner of Stephen's response to it recall those centuries of cultural imperialism which had stamped on English minds an indelible image of native Irish primitiveness," L. H. Platt writes (78).

Joyce—whose 1907 essay "Ireland, Island of Saints and Sages" refutes this barbaric stereotype with excessive and vehement pedantry—was to endure its recrudescence again at the hands of his English modernist critics, as Patrick Parrinder has forcefully argued. In a reprise of language virtually drawn from Joyce's own 1907 satirical broadside, "The Holy Office," his modernist contemporaries attacked Joyce with a consistency of argument that suggests a sameness of prejudice among Joyce's critics at different times and in different artistic circles. In his essay on Joyce's reception (and rejection) in England, Parrinder cites Wells ("Mr Joyce has a cloacal obses-

sion" [156]), Pound ("obsessions arseoreial, cloacal" [157]), Wyndham Lewis ("So rich was its delivery, its pent-up outpouring so vehement, that it will remain, eternally cathartic, a monument like a
record diarrhoea" ([160]), and Rebecca West ("a great man who is
entirely without taste" [162]) as heaping on him an excremental
abuse. Joyce himself could not have said it better—"Myself unto
myself will give/ This name, Katharsis-Purgative" (CW 149). But
Parrinder's careful attention to a code of class disdain in this cloacal
imagery, a semaphoring of the old prejudice of people thinking Joyce
is not "a gentleman," draws attention to the much larger issue
of the relationship between modernism's obsession with *form* and
modernist notions of class. Parrinder's conclusion, that Joyce was
subjected to rank Bloomsbury prejudice against his class, breeding,
and culture that were finally bound up with the sectarian aspect of
his Irishness, explains as well why Joyce's characterization of how he
was treated by both Irish revivalists (who were largely wealthy Irish
Protestants), and the English Protestants who led Anglo-modernism,
is so strikingly imbricated.

But what is at stake here is the larger issue of the relationship
between the inside and outside of art: that is, that aesthetic *form* at
its most formalistic, in modernism, becomes visible here as historicized, and as determined by art's exterior, by non-aesthetic contingencies of historical crisis, by social and intellectual change, by class
and prestige. The historicizing of modernistic formalism requires a
complex narrative to which disparate critics are making converging
contributions at the present time. Consequently what we think of
as the Paterian *ascesis* of modernistic form, to borrow Richard Poirier's phrase, the emphasis on discipline, precision, control, and impersonality in writing that is, as Pound wished, "austere, direct, free
from emotional slither" (*Literary Essays* 12), is becoming dismantled as an ethical performance in the interest of being recontextual-
ized as part of an aestheticist legacy with a historically conservative
function. For Pater, Poirier argues, the logic for *ascesis* might have
anticipated Eliot's own austerity—"Rigor and self-restraint in the
use of language are especially necessary, so it is implied, in a situation where there is an admitted and not unwelcomed collapse of cultural institutions" (22). The precursers of modernist aestheticism—
Pater using discipline to conserve a self in the face of the death of
God, Arnold using cultural quality to stave off the effects of mass
education—preempt the modernist forging of an ethic and a practice
of disciplined form in the face of the threat of anarchy and futility
in the early twentieth century. Poirier would lead Pater directly to
Joycean aestheticism, but Seamus Deane inserts into this narrative

the cultural deformation that colonialism exercised on English and Irish literary relations.

Deane argues for an intricate spiral in Matthew Arnold's figuration of the Irish artist. If, as Platt claims, there is a tradition of simian figuration of the Irish in British thought ("The Catholics of Ireland were 'more like tribes of squalid apes than human beings'" [79]), then Arnold transforms the Irish trope from Caliban to Ariel, by replacing with reflectiveness and other-worldliness a type that had formerly been thought coarse, brutalized, irrational, corporeal, and rebellious. The sublimation of savagery into romantic wildness, a change whose origins Deane finds in Arnold's *Irish Essays*, gives the Irish nationalist movement the idealistic mythology that eventually emerges as Yeats' "legend of the poetic Celt" (12). But Deane finds in Arnold's Irishman less a figure of specific colonial history than a value-laden construct representing the "other" of the English middle-class commercialism and Philistinism Arnold sought to combat. "For him the Celts were the lost poetry of Saxon morality. The consequence of the fusion of these two races would be an escape from the confusion of history. This can now seem nothing more than an absurdly naive use of racial theory to glamorize (by pretending to solve) the unlovely and brutalized relationship between Ireland and England" (14). It is this poetical, mystical Celt, beneath whose mummeries and hypocrisies Joyce exposes the crass materialists, "Mammon's countless servitors," against which he pits himself in "The Holy Office." But it is also his own Icarean version of this Arnoldian figure of chivalric intellect (Deane 15)—whose precursor to Eliot and Joyce Poirier locates in Pater—that Joyce historically and critically dismantles as an ideologically intersected construct in "Shem the Penman." Joyce's recalibanization of the artist—enacting Pound's grim prognosis of the modern age when he writes in "Hugh Selwyn Mauberley" that "Caliban casts out Ariel"—requires a historical recontextualization that makes reference to the social ideology of Joyce's contemporary cultural and artistic institutions. By reappropriating in the figure of Caliban the Shakespearean topos of the colony ("The *Sea Venture* comes home from Bermudas and the play Renan admired is written with Patsy Caliban, our American cousin" [U 9:755]), Joyce cleaves the Irish revival's self-mythologizing into contradictory components (poetic Celt and urban brute) that expose the national, class, religious, and racial divisions deforming the Empire's literary history right up into the twentieth century.

Hugh Kenner consolidates Joyce with modernism by joining his anti-aestheticism to the tradition of Flaubert and Pound: "It may be helpful to remark that Joyce is in this respect like Pound, an artist of the Flaubertian kind; his Stephen Dedalus is a parody of himself, not an artist but an aesthete, at length mercilessly ridiculed in *Finnegans Wake*" ("Mauberley" 43). But the resulting personae and masks, what Kenner calls "homeomorphs" (*Pound Era* 34), ultimately violate in Joyce's Wakean apparition the ends of objectivity and impersonality that they serve in the heteroglossia of high modernism. It is tempting to construe the complex self-parody and mock-confessionalism of "Shem the Penman" as a belated twin of Pound's "Hugh Selwyn Mauberley" with its repudiation of efforts "to maintain 'the sublime' " and wring "lilies from the acorn." But the difference is that Pound's poem maintains itself as high art against the meretriciousness of modern culture, preserves its clean Flaubertian lines and neoclassical measure, while Joyce chooses, in "Shem the Penman," to shoot all the complex exfoliations of Stephen's aesthetic theory—epiphany, Thomistic *integritas, consonantia, claritas*, the classical temper, the static response, and above all, the Flaubertian impersonality of the narrative voice—to hell. In the end, "Shem the Penman" is not as close to "Mauberley" as it is to to "De Profundis," the text in which Wilde loses control and his aestheticist wit, distance, and charm perish as he blames his lover incident by incident, pound by pound, indignity by indignity, for his downfall. Atherton writes of *Finnegans Wake*, "The work of Wilde which is most quoted is *De Profundis*" (96). "De Profundis" is Wilde's embarrassment not only because it is the squalid story of art's genesis that no one wants to hear, but also because, while it repents his decadence, it refuses to maintain itself as lyrical "Envoi." Not only is Shem calibanized, but so is the text, thus disqualifying it from modernistic merit, and obliging it to internalize modernist attack.

In his introduction to the volume *James Joyce: New Perspectives*, Colin MacCabe writes "The portrait of Shem (FW: 169–195) is unflattering in the extreme" (36). Unflattering to whom? Clearly Joyce is not indulging either masochism or even self-parody as much as he performs a trangressive gesture in this writing, that—in an avant-garde spirit—violates and disrupts the compact art makes with its bourgeois public. Joyce's "Picture of Dorian Gray" is a mirror of the modernist establishment with a twice-cracked frame: it lets in the ruck of the Arnoldian Populace against which modernism offered to pit its formal bulwark, and it lets in the critical distemper with which the modernists greeted Joyce's fall from aesthetic grace and taste. "Shem the Penman" is in turn doubled by Joyce's own critical counterattack in *Our Exagmination* when he marshals his friends among the avant-garde moderns against his attackers, letting Eu-

gene Jolas take on Sean O'Faolain, and William Carlos Williams
thrash Rebecca West ("Rebecca West, on the other hand, has no idea
at all what literature is about. She speaks of transcendental tosh, of
Freud, of Beethoven's Fifth Symphony, of anything that comes into
her head, but she has not yet learned—though she professes to know
the difference between art and life . . . that writing is made of words"
[182]). But Joyce's own maneuver in "Shem the Penman" is less logopoetic than formalistically and aesthetically transgressive—a
mirror held up to the critical reception of Joyce's violation of modernist *ascesis.* The young Joyce on first reading Wilde's *Dorian Gray*
(in Italian) in 1906 already announces "Shem the Penman"'s prolep-
sis when he identifies both the problematic fissures in the Wildean
text's aestheticism ("It is not very difficult to read between the
lines") and supplies their legal reception, "I can imagine the capital
which Wilde's prosecuting counsel made out of certain parts of it"
(SL 96).

"Shem the Penman" functions as the nightmarish corrective to
Portrait's amnesia regarding the historical unfolding of the story of
modern art. Its considerable self-correcting ironies notwithstanding,
Portrait's formal beauty betrays it as the writing of modernism's
desire: modernism's favored version of itself as classical in form
and liberal—that is, inimical to a stultifying society—in politics.
Against this version, "Shem the Penman" would function as a critical gaze on modernism that exposes the elitism of its classical pretensions, the abhorrence of the masses behind its compulsion for
clean, dry, hard, clear language, and the obsession with force and
control behind its commitment to disciplined writing and taut form.
But by obliging itself to attack its own institutional foundation,
"Shem the Penman" must simultaneously turn against its own
status as art, and transform itself, by turning itself narratively, formally, and thematically inside out, into the sort of counterart that
is the aim of the avant-garde. By attacking both Shem *and* Shaun,
"Shem the Penman" desublimates the artist (the apotheosized Stephen of *Portrait*), desublimates the modernist critic (Pound, Lewis,
West, and his other tormentors), and desublimates itself—by turning itself into a parodic broadside, an exercise in slander, a piece of
vulgarity. Doubly vulgar, as the voice of a self-incriminating Philistinism attacking the Irish artist's plebeianism—the pot calling the
kettle black—"Shem the Penman" escapes the aestheticist *mise en
abyme* by foreclosing its pretensions as high art.

My strategy, in exploring "Shem the Penman" as an avant-garde
self-criticism of art, will focus on the text's heteroglossic polemic.
The many voices that together speak Shaun's malediction of Shem

include those of the modernists at their most unmodernistic. Shaun
parodies the mean-spirited snobbism of Wyndham Lewis' *Time and
Western Man*, Rebecca West's dithery fastidiousness in *The Strange
Necessity*, and the hilarious vituperations of Pound's unbridled epistolary play, which Lewis heard, unmistakably, in "Work in Progress." "He has evidently concluded that the epistolary style of Ezra
Pound should not be born to blush unseen," Lewis complains of
Joyce in *Time and Western Man*, "but should be made a more public
use of than Pound has done" (106). This heteroglossic chorus of
modernist criticism incriminates itself in "Shem the Penman" by
violating its most sacred modernist canons. Instead of the impersonality guaranteed by its masks and personae, it displays self-indulgent
subjectivity. Instead of the displaced feeling produced by the objective correlative, Shaun's polemic utters direct prejudice and blatant
ad hominem attacks. Instead of classical proportion and measure,
its prose expresses verbal excess and incontinence. The Flaubertian
obsession with *le mot juste* is replaced with the obsessional cliché
(McCormack), causing Lewis to complain that Joyce had "an intelligence so alive to purely verbal clichés that it hunts them like
fleas" (96). Modernism's restoration of metaphysical wit to the dis-
sociated personality is undone with broad irrationalism and vulgarity of humor. The polemic of "Shem the Penman" thus brings
together in one narrative utterance both the voices of Joyce's modernist critics, and the Philistine discourses Joyce's own aesthetic
modernism marginalized and discredited in his own earlier works.
As a result, "Shem the Penman" produces an effect of raveling, re-
weaving into itself numerous common voices from the earlier texts:
the earthiness and vulgarity of Lynch, the worldliness and commercialism of Bloom, the political prodding and propagandism of
McCann, the mimicry and malice of Simon Dedalus, the blasphemy
and mockery of Mulligan, and the personal hostility and judgmen-
talism of Cranly. In turn, Joyce is able to use "Shem the Penman" to
retroactively awaken in the earlier texts the articulation of their immanent critique. "Shem the Penman" speaks the Bakhtinian heteroglossia as a carnivalized discourse in the Joycean text (Kershner).

1. Cranly, Materialism, and Art

The voice most usefully isolated from this hostile clamor packed
into the vituperation of Shaun is that of Cranly, who is introduced
as a theorist of materialism in *Stephen Hero* ("Cranly's method in
argument was to reduce all things to their food values" [SH 208]).
Cranly plays a powerfully oppositional role to Stephen in *Stephen*

Hero, that is increasingly muted and suppressed in *Portrait* until he survives, like a ghostly Cheshire cat, in the memory of a smile ("Smile. Smile Cranly's smile" [U 9 : 21]) in *Ulysses.* But it is worthwhile unraveling Cranly's distinctive voice and values as those of a problematic counteraesthetical Philistinism to Stephen's aesthete. The Cranly of *Portrait* seems the scourge of the Philistine, directing his violence against the intellectually unanointed, fools like Moynihan ("A flaming bloody sugar, that's what he is!" [P 195]), Goggins ("Goggings, you're the flamingest dirty devil I ever met, do you know" [P 230]), Glynn ("A bloody ape . . . and a blasphemous bloody ape!" [P 235]), and Temple ("Temple, I declare to the living God if you say another word, do you know, to anybody on any subject I'll kill you *super spottum*" [P 200]). But besides formalizing Cranly's rustic idiom, changing his "d'ye know" from *Stephen Hero* to "do you know" in *Portrait,* and his "flamin' " to "flaming," *Portrait* also mutes Cranly's hostility to Stephen himself. *Portrait* alludes to Cranly's "listless silence, his harsh comments, the sudden intrusions of rude speech with which he had shattered so often Stephen's ardent wayward confessions" (P 232) but does not dramatize this behavior, unlike *Stephen Hero* which shows us Cranly's patent disdain and discourtesy toward his friend:

> Stephen stood on one of the steps of the porch but Cranly did not honour him with any kind of welcome. Stephen inserted a few phrases into the conversation but his presence was still unhonoured by Cranly. . . . Once he addressed Cranly directly but got no answer. (SH 137)

As a universal scourge, Cranly's role seems overdetermined. But the dialogical structures the texts create to problematize the role and function of art—for example, Lynch's pornological kineticism as comic foil to Stephen's sublime theory—urge us to focus Cranly's shifting dialectical possibilities as critic of the aesthete. While *Portrait* makes Cranly chiefly the paradoxically secular confessor, the conscience that reminds the artist of his social responsibilities to the institutions that give him community ("The church is not the stone building nor even the clergy and their dogmas. It is the whole mass of those born into it" [P 245]), the Cranly of *Stephen Hero* represents a much broader materialist secularism. His confessional function is therefore transmogrified in "Shem the Penman" into varieties of mock trial ("You see, chaps, it will trickle out" [FW 172.27]) and prosecution ("How is that for low, laities and gentlenuns?" [FW 177.8]) bordering on sadistic impropriety—"I advise you to conceal yourself, my little friend, as I have said a moment ago and put your hands in my hands and have a nightslong homely little confiteor about things" (FW 188.1). We are reminded that Stephen once "thrilled" to Cranly's touch, when forced to confess to his friend, "And you made me confess to you . . . as I have confessed to you so many other things" (P 247). The critical gravity of the confessorial Cranly has been abandoned in "Shem the Penman" in favor of pleasurable aggression marked with vulgar vehemence and plebeian accents, ("Can you beat it? Whawe! I say, can you bait it? Was there ever heard of such lowdown blackguardism?" [FW 180.30]). *Portrait*'s mock institutional overlay that makes of Cranly's dialogue a confession ("Yes, my child" [P 247]) is abandoned to let criticism float free, and attach itself to a shrewd but unlegitimated Philistinism.

Stephen, in *Stephen Hero*, recognizes Cranly's function as Philistinism pure and simple, a loutish and ignorant resistance to art— "He felt Cranly's hostility and he accused himself of having cheapened the eternal images of beauty" (SH 213). But the texts, I would argue, complicate Cranly's oppositional function, by identifying him with figures of production, to be sure, but without making his a 'vulgar materialism'—a preoccupation with, say, objects, or with production unrelated to the social totality of which it is a part. Rather the figure of Cranly, and his transmogrified voice in "Shem the Penman," appears implicitly to criticize art and the artist for ignoring the whole question of how the conditions of physical human survival, for the population as well as for the artist, are both effected and interpreted within their specific political and historical conditions. Joyce appears to conflate the Cranly of *Stephen Hero*, who wears "a very dirty yellow straw hat of the shape of an inverted bucket" (SH 113) with the silent, extruded butcher boy in *Portrait*, wearing Stephen's epiphanized basket "slung inverted on his head" (P 212). As a result of this conflation, Cranly's rustic and plebeian idiosyncrasies are more generally socialized, and the butcher boy's social mutism as disregarded witness to aesthetic theorizing is given an articulation in "Shem the Penman" that retains both a commercial and robust idiom without sacrificing a critical edge. Cranly's dream of owning a butcher shop in Dublin—"I often thought seriously . . . of opening a pork-shop, d'ye know . . . and putting *Kranliberg* or some German name, d'ye know, over the door . . . and makin' a flamin' fortune out of pig's meat" (SH 119) sharply nationalizes food production in the colonial situation, a matter to which Joyce gives ironic rather than historical attention when he turns Bloom's pork butcher on Dorset Street Upper from Michael Brunton into the Polish-

Jewish Dlugacz in "Calypso" (Gifford 70). But Cranly's wish seems to find its fulfillment (supplemented by the advertising skills of someone with Bloom's cattleman experience) in "Shem the Penman":

[Johns is a different butcher's. Next place you are up town pay him a visit. Or better still, come tobuy. You will enjoy cattlemen's spring meat . . . Fattens, kills, flays, hangs, draws, quarters and pieces . . .]. (FW 172.5)

The Wakean butcher, of course, adds a surplus of truth to his advertising ("kills, flays, hangs, draws, quarters") that restores the violence advertising normally suppresses: "What is home without Plumtree's Potted Meat? Incomplete. With it an abode of bliss" (U 17:597).

Vincent Cheng identifies this Johns, the butcher, as Shakespeare's father, John Shakespeare (134), a gloss that allows "Shem the Penman" to draw a much more significant connection between art and materialism. Indeed, by drawing attention to Shakespeare's commercial origin, to his father's livelihood as a butcher, it becomes clear that Cranly's materialist critical approach ("to reduce all things to their food values") is invested, along with his smile, in the Shakespeare lecture Stephen delivered to his Irish audience at the National Library. Stephen's aesthetic theory is surely modified by the notion that no less a figure than the Bard himself is grounded in a butcher boy's labor, perhaps having been cradled in a butcher boy's basket of the sort Stephen epiphanized. Thus Cranly's tutelage reshapes Stephen's retelling of Shakespearean history in a way that restores the elder Shakespeare's influence on his son: "Not for nothing was he a butcher's son, wielding the sledded poleaxe and spitting in his palms" (U 9:130). John Shakespeare, the butcher and commercial man, may well have lent his son political tropes as well as a shrewd head and inclination for business—"He was a rich country gentleman . . . with . . . a house in Ireland yard, a capitalist shareholder, a bill promoter, a tithefarmer" (U 9:710). Cranly's commercial spirit imprints itself on Stephen's materialist history of the Renaissance, that lets him recount the precise salaries and fortunes of the principals. Of Sir Walter Raleigh he says, "when they arrested him, had half a million francs on his back including a pair of fancy stays" (U 9:628), and of Ann Hathaway, "O, yes, mention there is. In the years when he was living richly in royal London to pay a debt she had to borrow forty shillings from her father's shepherd" (U 9:679). Stephen calls Elizabeth I the "gombeenwoman Eliza Tudor," (U 9:630) and notes she had "underlinen enough to vie with her of

Sheba." In his 1907 lecture at the Universita Popolare in Trieste ("Ireland, Island of Saints and Sages"), Joyce makes virtually the same point about Queen Victoria: "Once, it is true, when there was a horrible disaster in county Kerry which left most of the county without food or shelter, the queen, who held on tightly to her millions, sent the relief committee, which had already collected thousands of pounds from benefactors of all social classes, a royal grant in the total amount of ten pounds" (CW 164). Indeed, like Stephen himself, Joyce, too, is able to tote up fairly exact salaries for those who administer British rule in Ireland: "In Dublin alone, to take an example, the Lord Lieutenant receives a half-million francs a year. For each policeman, the Dublin citizens pay 3,500 francs a year (twice as much, I suppose, as a high school teacher receives in Italy), and the poor fellow who performs the duties of chief clerk of the city is forced to get along as well as he can on a miserable salary of six pounds sterling a day. The English critic is right, then, Ireland is poor, and moreover it is politically backward" (CW 167).

But it is Shakespeare himself whom Stephen draws most sharply as a gombeen man, a "tithefarmer" whose enterprises are repeatedly invested with Irish tropes ("a house in Ireland yard") in order to situate them within Empire, and to draw him as prototype of the Irish Ascendancy. Stephen measures Shakespeare's living with a pointed analogy—"he drew a salary equal to that of the lord chancellor of Ireland" (U 9:624), and implicates him proleptically in the sort of speculative food hoarding that made the Great Famine genocidal: "He drew Shylock out of his own long pocket. The son of a maltjobber and moneylender he was himself a cornjobber and moneylender, with ten tods of corn hoarded in the famine riots" (U 9:741). Mary Lowe-Evans writes of the potato blight of the 1840's, "The most salient feature of the Famine, and the one which placed it in the category of Foucault's bio-power, was its artificiality. Although the potato crop had failed, it was not the only crop in Ireland; rather, it was the only crop that could sustain the Irish year after year given the minimal amount of land allotted for their own use. The remainder of the land was dedicated to crops used to pay English landlords. Those crops remained healthy during the Famine." (16) She goes on to point out that lands from massive tenant evictions were converted to pasture. "Ireland was thereby transformed from granary to stockyard and dairy for Great Britain. . . . That produce—enough cattle, wheat, oats, and barley to feed twice the population of Ireland—was used to maintain the economic and physical health of England" (17). In his Trieste lecture, Joyce, too, blames England for Ireland's poverty: "Ireland is poor because English laws ruined the country's industries, especially the wool industry, because the neglect of the English government in the years of the potato famine allowed the best of the population to die from hunger, and because under the present administration, while Ireland is losing its population and crimes are almost non-existent, the judges receive the salary of a king, and governing officials and those in public service receive huge sums for doing little or nothing" (CW 167). Stephen's Shakespeare lecture, like Joyce's lecture at the Triestine university, is a deliberate interiorization of the imperial history of Irish colonialism into literary and poetic history.

Stephen's Shakespeare lecture in "Scylla and Charybdis" is, in many respects, "applied Cranly." Cranly's food value theory is introduced as a critical alternative to Stephen's aesthetics in *Stephen Hero* ("Cranly's method in argument was to reduce all things to their food values . . . and Stephen's conception of art fared very badly from such a method" [SH 208]). In *Portrait*, we learn it sometimes competes successfully with Stephen's aesthetic Thomism, even upstaging Stephen's first attempt to explicate his theory when "Cranly lost his temper and began to talk about Wicklow bacon":

—I remember, said Lynch. He told us about them flaming fat devils of pigs.
—Art, said Stephen, is the human disposition of sensible or intelligible matter for an esthetic end. You remember the pigs and forget that. You are a distressing pair, you and Cranly. (P 207)

But by *Ulysses* it seems that Cranly's influence has taken hold of Stephen and made possible a revisionary Irish criticism of the canonical English literary tradition. Inspired by both the pig-loving Cranly, and the butcher John Shakespeare, it is as though Stephen is able to revise his own "applied Aquinas" using the same porcine logic with which he corrects Best's faulty inferences—"Has the wrong sow by the lug" (U 9:390). Pigs versus art, theories of food value versus theories of aesthetics: these markers of the Philistine conflict with art are used in "Shem the Penman" to restore to the truism that man does not live by bread alone, the repressed caveat (that Joyce may have learned most forcefully from Hauptmann's *The Weavers*) that art might do well to concern itself with the ways man is obliged to live by bread all the same. Indeed, sometimes art lives by food production, as Joyce himself discovered when he published his very first piece of art, the story "The Sisters," in AE Russell's agricultural weekly, *The Irish Homestead*, which Stephen terms "The pigs' paper" (U 9:321).

The body, which is to *Portrait*'s Stephen pure form, is to Cranly, as to Bloom, a living organism whose sustenance depends, as its failures during the Great Famine appallingly dramatized, on the effective will and operation of political, economic, and social structures (Lowe-Evans). Cranly's materialism, which appears in *Stephen Hero* like a Satanic temptation to Stephen's idealism ("I regard that view of life as the abnormal view . . . It is monstrous because the seat of the spiritual principle of a man is not transferable to a material object" [SH 222]), is rehabilitated both in "Scylla and Charybdis" and in "Shem the Penman" in spite of its Philistinism. Cranly's sensible reply to Stephen's objection—"You cannot call that abnormal which everyone does" (SH 222), becomes the donnée of "Shem the Penman," in which Cranly's pig obsession merges with Shaun's aggressivity to produce for the artist an insulting antonomasia, "a certain gay young nobleman whimpering to the name of Low Swine" (FW 173.4). (Joyce changed "Low Bugger" to "Low Swine" in the fair copy manuscript [JA 47474–6].) But even in its most primitive application, as Shaun's criticism of what Shem eats ("Shem was a sham and a low sham and his lowness creeped out first via foodstuffs" [FW 170.25]), Cranly's food value theory serves not only to say, like Bloom in "Lestrygonians," that we are what we eat, but also makes visible the truth that food production, particularly for the Irish under British colonialism, is governed by ideologically masked operations and exploitations. Cranly's diet as Stephen notes it in *Portrait* ("he eats chiefly belly bacon and dried figs" [P 248]) is recollected in the earliest draft of Shaun's discourse for "Shem the Penman": "None of your . . . bloody beefsteaks or juicy legs of melting mutton or fat belly bacon or greasy gristly pigs' feet" (JA 332 47471b-50v). But Cranly's food value theory serves both aesthetic and critical ends in "Shem the Penman." On the one hand, Cranly's gourmandizing is transformed into a Philistine poetry, a rhapsodic gustatory and commercial paean whose stripping in Rose and O'Hanlon's paraphrase ("he swore that no natural-grown jungle pineapple ever tasted anything like the bits he forked out of a can" [103]) first alerted me to the robust energy of Shaun's Philistine prose ("he repeated in his botulism that no junglegrown pineapple ever smacked like the whoppers you shook out of Ananias' cans, Findlater and Gladstone's, Corner House, Englend" [FW 170.30]). Shem's pineapple pieces are "whoppers," plump and huge, not "bits," and they are mightily "shook"—not "forked"—out of their can. Cranly's appetite takes further lip-smacking, gourmandizing gusto in a speech engorged by mouthfuls of scrumptious, plump, alliterative words, "None of your inchthick blueblooded Balaclava fried-at-belief-stakes or juicejelly legs of the Grex's molten mutton or greasilygristly grunters' goupons or slice upon slab of luscious goosebosom with lump after load of plumpudding stuffing all aswim in a swamp of bogoakgravy for that greekenhearted yude!" (FW 170.32).

But, on the other hand, the attention to brand names at once Biblical (Ananias) and redundant (German: *Ananas*, pineapple), and to a commercial address (Findlater's) transposed from Dublin to London, interrogates the imperialist politics of commercial importation and trade. The fragile survival of Irish industry was historically threatened by foreign competition. George O'Brien writes, "From the time of the Union it was the deliberate policy of the British manufacturer to swamp the Irish market and to drive his Irish competitor out of business" (420). For this reason Joyce chooses addresses and brand names in his fiction with extreme care. In "Grace," for example, with its economic donnée, Joyce takes pains to give the originally Protestant Kernan a British employer, "the name of his firm with the address—London, E.C." (D 154). The drafts of "Shem the Penman" show that Joyce chose brand names in the *Wake* with careful deliberation. He eventually replaced Lazenby (JA 341 47471b-55) the London soupmaker (F. Lazenby & Son, Ltd. [Gifford 389]) who also makes a product preferred by Gerty's family ("they had stewed cockles and lettuce with Lazenby's salad dressing" [U 13: 313]) with Gibsen (FW 170.26) as the producer of tinned salmon, and he replaced Heinz (JA 341 47471b-55) as the canner of pineapple, although retaining the German name for pineapple (*Ananas*). Shaun applauds British commonwealth beef, "Rosbif of Old Zealand!" (FW 171.1)—which McHugh glosses as Fielding's "Oh! the roast beef of old England." Joyce also alerts us with references in Shaun's sumptuous verbal feast to the Crimean War—"inchthick blueblooded Balaclava fried-at-belief-stakes" (FW 170.33)—of the point Mary Lowe-Evans cited, that essential potato growing during the famine was sacrificed for the production of export beef to the British. (The reference to Balaclava was added to the fair copy [JA 47474-4 363]). At the same time, Shaun himself nationalizes food criticism when he accuses Shem of saying "he would far sooner muddle through the hash of lentils in Europe than meddle with Irrland's split little pea" (FW 171.5), and blames him for drinking European wine ("some sort of a rhubarbarous maundarin yellagreen funkleblue windigut diodying applejack squeezed from sour grapefruice" [FW 171.16]) rather than "honest brewbarrett beer" (FW 171.14). Shaun's food judgments signify all sorts of sometimes confused national and class allegiances—(he likes "blueblooded" steaks but dislikes the elitism of European alcohol, "rhubarbarous maundarin," the mandarin wine of Arnoldian

Barbarians). Indeed, his final prescription to cure Shem of his apocalyptic cultural nihilism and anarchism ("death with every disaster,
the dynamitisation of colleagues, the reducing of records to ashes,
the levelling of all customs by blazes" [FW 189.34]) is his famous
recipe for the plebeian *bricolage* of a new Irish stew (FW 190.3–190.9).

Joyce's emphasis on naming commercial establishments and their
addresses, and identifying food by its brand names, suggests that
Joyce from the beginning of his writing sought a more historically
grounded analysis of the relationship between art and commerce in
his work. The consequence of this practice was a direct confrontation with his own power to produce art, when his publisher George
Roberts—advised that he could be sued for libel by the businesses
whose establishments and products were named in *Dubliners*—
refused to publish. In "Gas from a Burner," Joyce has Roberts say,
"Shite and onions! Do you think I'll print/ The name of the Welling-
ton Monument,/ Sydney Parade and Sandymount tram,/ Downes's
cakeshop and Williams's jam?" (CW 244). Joyce experienced, then,
the power and will of commerce to control its own public representations, and to enlist the power of law to oppose Joyce's appropriation of its prerogative. Joyce creates advertising in his art that commerce can neither contort, control, nor purchase, and that therefore
functions as anti-advertising advertising, or pop-art with the politics
restored, like Warhol's Campbell soup cans embedded in a historical
context that more specifically identifies their role in the larger culture. "Shem the Penman" offers an updated reprise of Joyce's satirical broadsides about his own role as Irish artist that insert him into
a complex interplay between art and commerce. Shaun echoes and
redefines Joyce's own "Holy Office" when he resurrects an old prescription, first made by the English priest, Father Butt, in *Stephen
Hero* (SH 226), when he suggests to Mrs. Daedalus that her poet son
get himself a job in a brewery—"You let me tell you, with the ut-
most politeness . . . your birthwrong was, to fall in with Plan, as our
nationals should . . . and do a certain office . . . in a certain holy
office . . . during certain agonising office hours . . . so much a week
pro anno (Guinness's, may I remind, were just agulp for you . . .) and
do your little thruppenny bit" (FW 190.10).

2. Shem as *Bête Noire* of Modernism

Joyce's treatment of commerce glosses modernism's fear of Philistinism with an ideological analysis and an alternative poetic practice. While Pound and Eliot despise the commercial world's degradation of art with mass-produced commodities ("For two gross of

broken statues,/ For a few thousand battered books"), Joyce inte-grates a critique of commerce and its mass produced culture into his artistic discourse (Herr, Kershner). While Pound and Eliot reproduce in their poetry the ideological pathologies that the pressures of mass markets and credit capitalism stamp on middle class thinking—in the anti-semitic codes of Pound's Brennbaum and Eliot's Bleistein, for example (Froula)—Joyce, in "Nestor," "Cyclops" and "Shem the Penman" dramatizes anti-semitism's origin in commercial xenopho-bia, and its cultural function as the logical extension of Arnoldian racial typologies—for example, in Shaun's "greekenhearted yude" (FW 171.1). Joyce added this conflation of Arnold's Hellenism and Hebraism at a very late stage of composition, in the mid thirties when he marked the *transition* pages for the printing of *Finnegans Wake* (JA 474756–64v). Joyce seems, in "Shem the Penman," to have captured the terrific class contradictions that made the mod-ernists so enslaved, culturally, to the ideological class deformations and snobberies produced by that same commercial system they os-tensibly despised. Nowhere are these strains more baldly expressed than in Rebecca West's "strange necessity," which is quite specifi-cally a class conundrum with Joyce in the middle: the mystery of Joyce's artistic power against all her class resistances, and her trou-bling compulsion to assert his genius against his egregious deficien-cies of taste and breeding. Patrick Parrinder responds to West's tacit invitation by describing her stance with a commercial trope: "For who, Rebecca West seems to say, given access to Fortnum & Ma-son's and to the drawing-rooms of Riverside Drive, needs a genius with a mind like a Westland Row tenement?" (163). Bonnie Kime Scott's work in progress on Rebecca West promises to ameliorate this snobbism by stressing West's socialism against Parrinder's polemic.

But West's description of Joyce's mind as "furnished like a room in a Westland Row tenement in which there are a bedstead and a broken chair, on which there sits a great scholar and genius who falls over the bedstead whenever he gets up" (56), becomes a central trope in "Shem the Penman." By conflating Shem's mind, house, body, and writing into a single class trope, that of the slum, Joyce produces in the chapter the effects of what Patrick McGee calls an "ideology of style." The writing of the chapter—in its abandonment of modernistic scrupulosity and clarity—becomes itself tenemental, full of junk, filth, brokenness, and squalor. Codes of class, and their signification in figures of commercial and residential address, per-dure: "You brag of your brass castle or your tyled house in ballyfer-mont? Niggs, niggs and niggs again" (FW 183.4) Shaun tells Shem. The slum becomes the point of departure from which the narrative

launches the elaborately effluvient description that simultaneously
represents Shem's house, mind, and writing. This figurative edifice
will stink to the Anglo-Saxons ("Angles"), a prediction that might
have done for Joyce as well as Shem, "For this was a stinksome
inkenstink . . . Smatterafact, Angles aftanon browsing there thought
not Edam reeked more rare" (FW 183.7). The narrative then begins
the remarkable house inventory ("The warped flooring of the lair
and soundconducting walls thereof . . . were persianly literatured
with burst loveletters, telltale stories, stickyback snaps, doubtful
eggshells, bouchers, flints, borers, puffers") that restores to Joyce's
tenemental texts not only the extirpated butcher boys ("bouchers")
from Stephen's aesthetic theory and Shakespeare's imperial chronicles, but the rest of the material, bodily, social world which Stephen's theory elides and his epiphanic vision occludes. This catalogue of West's mental "furniture"—"writing the mystery of himsel
in furniture" (FW 184.9)—is not nearly as random as it seems. Indeed, its individual items—for example, the assorted bodily excretions that include seedy ejaculations, crocodile tears, blasphematory
spits, worms of snot, toothsome pickings, and tress clippings—are
all forms of decontextualized textual detritus from the early works
that can readily be restored to their owners: seedy ejaculations to
Stephen and Bloom; crocodile tears to Cranly and Father Ghezzi,
Stephen's Italian professor ("And could he repent? Yes, he could: and
cry two round rogue's tears, one from each eye" [P 249]); blasphematory spits to John Casey ("*Phth!* says I to her like that, right into
her eye" [P 37]) and Mulligan; worms of snot to Stephen; toothsome
pickings to the orts of figs in Cranly's teeth; and tress clippings to
Gerty MacDowell's split ends. "Shem the Penman" spits back at
Joyce's critics, the *Dreck* of his early texts, the offal, as it were, of
what West describes as "the dirty kitchen of his mean house" in
which Bloom gives Stephen "his gross and greasy best" (42).

Joyce's modernist critics, in troping his mind like a tenement, betray an embrace of naturalistic assumptions about the effects of environment on character that is, finally, at odds with the ostensible
liberalism of such representatives of the period's intelligentsia as
Bloomsbury. Raymond Williams' acute analysis of "the Bloomsbury
fraction" traces the imperfect adaptation of this group to the changing social dynamics produced by World War I and the loss of Empire.
His analysis of Leonard Woolf's self-representation in this group is
useful for identifying West's strained attempts to reconcile 'genius'
with squalor of class—"There is the very characteristic admission
and yet blurring of the two factors in success: 'family influence,'
'high level of . . . individual intelligence.' . . . Within each range, in

fact, the proportionate effect of class provenance, including family influence, and examined or demonstrated individual intelligence would need to be very precisely estimated" (161). Joyce's response to the strains of this problematic blurring, particularly as it issued in the fastidious charges of being underbred by the British women, Woolf and West, was to characterize it as a failed liberalism that makes of Shem a Barbarian social reject, "he had been toed out of all the schicker families of the klondykers from Pioupioureich, Swabspays . . . Pension Danubierhome and Barbaropolis" (FW 181.3). Indeed, liberalism broke down sufficiently in the modernist case against Joyce to betray a particular class rigidity that takes form as special distaste for fourflushing or social climbing. Wyndham Lewis, therefore, castigates in Joyce's *style* the mark of the *arriviste* or intellectual parvenu:

In this *quiet* 'Tell me, Mulligan'—(irish accent, please)—you have the soul of this small, pointless, oppressive character in its entirety. You wonder for some pages what can be the cause of this weighty inanition . . . You slowly find out what it is. *The hero is trying to be a gentleman!* That is the secret—nothing less, nothing more. The 'artist as a young man' has 'the real Oxford manner,' you are informed; and you eventually realize that his oppressive mannerisms have been due in the first instance to an attempt to produce the impression of 'an Oxford manner.'" (98)

Joyce, following the model of logocentric social desire dramatized by Flaubert in the plot of *Madame Bovary*, repeatedly transforms imitative style into various forms of internalized social mimicry in his writing—like the "classicisms" I will later discuss as affectations in Gerty MacDowell's narration.

But Joyce, I believe, quite deliberately internalizes as desire the role of the accent and the discursive social mark in class mobility, that George Bernard Shaw exteriorizes in the pedantry of Eliza Doolittle's language lessons in *Pygmalion*. In "Shem the Penman," then, Joyce burlesques Lewis' criticism by having Shaun accuse Shem, in precisely Lewis' terms, of mimicking a stage Englishman for social profit:

Yet the bumpersprinkler used to boast aloud alone to himself with a haccent on it when Mynfadher was a boer constructor and Hoy was a lexical student, parole, and corrected with the blackboard (trying to copy the stage Englesemen he broughts their

house down on, shouting: Bravure, surr Chorles! Letter purfect!
Culossal, Loose Wallor! Sprache! (FW 180.34–181.3)

Joyce further twists Lewis' version of Stephen's putative Oxford
imitation into a satirical portrait of Shem's "endlessly inartistic portraits of himself" sporting "a jucal inkome of one hundred and thirty-
two dranchmas per yard from Broken Hill stranded estate, Came-
breech mannings, cutting a great dash in a brandnew two guinea
dress suit and a burled hogsford hired for a Fursday evenin merry
pawty" (FW 182.18). Joyce originally drafted this description as "a
tiptop tenor voice, a ducal income of £20,000 a year derived from
landed property, Oxford manners, morals and [sic], a brandnew
3 guinea evening suit for a party" (JA 47471b-61v). The hammed up
Oxford "haccent" and Cambridge "mannings" of "Fursday" and
"pawty"—which are especially fine—were added later. Another re-
textualization of a nationally marked linguistic exchange occurs in
a passage that describes Shem's brutalization after an Oxford football match ("All Saints beat Belial" [FW 175.5], that is, All Souls
College versus Balliol). Both Trevor Williams and Seamus Deane
have commented on the political contamination of Irish school
sports, Williams noting the Anglicizing of Clongowes with the importation of cricket (316), and Deane the paramilitary overtones of
many school sports ("Liberalism" 16). Here Shem is described as an
Irish football being kicked down the streets of Goldsmith's sweet
Auburn; Atherton writes of Joyce's use of Goldsmith, "It is the first
line of *The Traveller*: 'Remote, unfriended, solitary, slow,' which
Joyce is using (in 56.20–56.30) to reply to Wyndham Lewis's attack
on him in *Time and Western Man*" (97). The passage recalls Davin's
account to Stephen of the Buttevant match in *Portrait*:

> One hailcannon night . . . he was therefore treated with what
> closely resembled parsonal violence, being soggert all unsuspect-
> ingly through the deserted village of Tumblin-on-the-Leafy from
> Mr Vanhomrigh's house at 81 bis Mabbot's Mall as far as Green
> Patch . . . by rival teams of slowspiers counter quicklimers who
> finally, as rahilly they had been deteened out rawther laetich,
> thought, busnis hits busnis, they had better be streaking for
> home after their Auborne-to-Auborne. (FW 174.21)

Davin's detention after the match is transformed back into a parody
of the marketplace accent on "detained" in the speech of Father Butt
(of the "tundish") whom Stephen thinks of as "a poor Englishman
in Ireland" (P 189)—"*I hope I am not detaining you.—Not in the*

least, said the dean politely" (P 188). In the first typescript for "Shem
the Penman" (JA 47174–26) Joyce hammed up this discourse with
an exaggerated Oxford accent, "as rahilly they had been deteened
out rawther laetich" (FW 174.29).

But Joyce goes much further than his critics when he uses "Shem
the Penman" to interrogate the effects of *Deklassierung* and dena-
tionalization on young expatriates on the Continent during the
teens and twenties. "Shem the Penman," then, can be read as the
Joycean version of Stein and Hemingway's "lost generation" that
brings into the prewar and postwar era of Modernism the alienations
of exile thematized in the earlier works (for example, in Stephen's
cynical account of his Paris sojourn in "Proteus"), and thus assimilates modernist *Angst* to the historical dispossessions of the Irish
émigré. If we compare Stephen's memory of the exiled Irish revolutionary Kevin Egan in Paris, with Rebecca West's genteel account of
her Parisian promenade in *Strange Necessity*, the aesthetic and stylistic dissonances, organized largely around issues of class, gender,
and culture, become dramatically focused. Strolling from Sylvia
Beach's bookstore near the Odéon to the Boulevard St. Germain,
West thinks of *Pomes Penyeach* as she smiles "up into the clean
French light" (13), and thinks of *Ulysses* on her way to the dress-
maker on the Rue de Rivoli where she buys a black lace dress. "I
had been to a milliner's shop which the head *vendeuse* of a famous
house had just started as her own venture and had ordered three
hats" (51). Of Kevin Egan, Stephen remembers, "In gay Paree he
hides, Egan of Paris, unsought by any save by me. Making his day's
stations, the dingy printingcase, his three taverns, the Montmartre
lair he sleeps short night in, *rue de la Goutte-d'Or*, damascened
with flyblown faces of the gone. Loveless, landless, wifeless" (U 3:
249). These are dramatically different views of cosmopolitanism,
and Shem's version in the *Wake*, like that of the accused Stephen in
Stephen Hero ("Mr Daedalus was himself a renegade from the Nationalist ranks: he professed cosmopolitism. But a man that was of
all countries was of no country—you must first have a nation before
you have art" [SH 103]), makes of the stateless, peripatetic, polyglot
Irishman an indeterminate, uprooted hybrid abused as *"canaille"*
(FW 173.2).

In "Shem the Penman" Joyce particularly mocks or parodies the
mockery of an apoliticalism that at the time of World War I ("the
grand germogall allstar bout was harrily the rage between our wel-
tingtoms extraordinary and our pettythicks the marshalaisy and Irish
eyes of welcome were smiling daggers down their backs" [FW 176.20])
made his confused national situation as an Irishman with a British

passport residing in a disputed Italian Austro-Hungarian city, and his polyglot Berlitz skills, political liabilities as marks of disengagement. Shem is ridiculed for servile linguistic adaptation:

> the accomplished washout always used to rub shoulders with the last speaker and clasp shakers . . . and agree to every word as soon as half uttered, command me!, your servant, good, I revere you, how, my seer? be drinking that! quite truth, gratias, I'm yoush, see wha'm hearing? also goods, please it, me sure?, be filling this!, quiso, you said it, apasafello, muchas grassyass. (FW 174.8–174.15)

The chapter extends this criticism in a more historically focused way to a parody, in Shem's cowardice, of Joyce's own suspect nonpartisanship at the time of the First World War: "the cull disliked anything anyway approaching a plain straightforward standup or knockdown row" (FW 174.5). Joyce is making here a larger point about the problematic position of artists, but especially the Irish, who were noncombatants during World War I. (Yeats' "An Irish Airman Foresees his Death," of course, speaks of the soldier, "Those that I fight I do not hate,/ Those that I guard I do not love" [55]). Shem's escape to his "inkbattle house," where "he collapsed carefully under a bedtick from Schwitzer's" (FW 176.34) remembers not only Stephen hiding under the cowl of his blanket (perhaps indeed from Switzer's department store, as the commercially minded Shaun would note) wanting to shut out the world after writing the villanelle, but also Joyce's flight to asylum in Switzerland at the onset of each of the world wars. Shem's artistic engagement at the time of World War I is characterized as "hemiparalysed by the tong warfare and all the shemozzle" (FW 177.5). Joyce allows that his Shemian self "never had the common baalamb's pluck to stir out and about the compound" unlike others, men and women alike, who went "on educated feet, plinkity plonk, across the sevenspan ponte *dei colori* set up over the slop after the war-to-end war" (FW 178.23). In a curious shift, Joyce changed a much more graphic earlier image of the intelligentsia picking its way through the carnage of World War I, "everyone else of the city throng, slashers and sliced alike, waded on his daily bonafide avocations while the fairer sex on their usual quest for higher things went stonestepping across the human bridge set up over the slop by Messrs a charitable government" (JA 47474–8 367) to the more abstract rainbow bridge "sevenspan ponte *dei colori*" but also the more pointed reference to World War I as the "war-to-end war." Joyce may be glossing Eliot's "Waste Land" here, with its trope of the death bridge, "A crowd flowed over London Bridge, so many,/ I had not thought death had undone so many." In a double-sided critique of artistic engagement with World War I, Joyce here indicts himself as cowardly lamb in safe asylum, and indicts other modernists for pursuing the higher avocations of art amid war's carnage. It is a long way from Joyce's boast in "The Holy Office" ("Where they have crouched and crawled and prayed/ I stand the self-doomed, unafraid" [CW 152]), and the heroicizing of the martyred artist has been desublimated and repoliticalized to restore to early twentieth-century artistic reception and criticism, particularly for the Irish artist within the Anglo-modernist literary establishment, the intersecting ideologies of class and nationalism.

In Shem's persecution Joyce replaces mythologies of artistic martyrdom with layers of overdetermined historical typologies that re-politicalize literary history. "Shem the Penman" is Wildean Realism—the artist forced to see himself seen not in heroic fantasies of desire ("I flash my antlers on the air" [CW 152]) but as crouching and crawling beast, as Caliban, as patronized plebeian, "Again there was a hope that people, looking on him with the contemp of the contempibles, after first gaving him a roll in the dirt, might pity and forgive him, if properly deloused, but the pleb was born a Quicklow and sank alowing till he stank out of sight" (FW 174.36). Raymond Williams characterizes Bloomsbury's social conscience in terms that analyze such a "'concern for the underdog.' For what has most carefully to be defined is the specific association of what are really quite unchanged class feelings—a persistent sense of a quite clear line between an upper and a lower class—with very strong and effective feelings of sympathy with the lower class as victims" (155). Joyce in "Shem the Penman" assimilates the Irish artist to this lower class whose treatment by modernism reflects Jameson's sense of "that heroic fascism of the 1920's for which the so-called 'masses' and their standardised city life had become the very symbol of everything degraded about modern life" ("Ulysses and History" 134). Joyce represents the Irish artist as such a "pleb," regarded lunatic in his ambitions (delivered in his cups "while drinking heavily of spirits" [FW 177.18]) to outrun the hounds of the great English literary tradition, Shakespeare, Dickens, Thackeray, and Scott, and beard the literary lions at Lyons tea shop in London by telling them that he plans to rival Shakespeare:

> that he was avoopf (parn me!) aware of no other shaggspick, other Shakhisbeard, either prexactly unlike his polar andthisishis or procisely the seem as woops (parn!) as what he fancied or guessed

the sames as he was himself and that, greet scoot, duckings and
thuggery, though he was foxed fux to fux like a bunnyboy rodger
with all the teashop lionses of Lumdrum hivanhoesed up ga-
gainst him . . . he would wipe alley english spooker, multaphon-
iaksically spuking, off the face of the erse. (FW 177.31–178.7)

The trope of the hunt is Wilde's, Joyce's ("I flash my antlers on the
air"), and Joyce's on Wilde: "When he got out of prison, thugs urged
on by the noble Marquis of Queensbury were waiting in ambush for
him. He was hunted from house to house as dogs hunt a rabbit"
(CW 203)—or "a bunnyboy rodger" (FW 177.36). The prose—slurring,
lurching, and bumping into its own words, "(parn me!) . . . (parn!)"—
burlesques West's image of Joyce's mind falling over his bedstead and
bumping into his broken chair, on his way to overtake Shakespeare.
But Joyce's writing in "Shem the Penman" is not itself poetic slumming—of the sort Eliot indulges with, say, the Cockney pub talk in
"The Waste Land"; it is rather parody and exaggeration of the class
contempt implicit in modernism's representations of such slumming.
     Through the crack in modern art's self-reflexive mirror, the rep-
resentational *mise en abyme* is ruptured, and "Shem the Penman"
lets the manifold implications of genius seeing its reflection in the
likeness of a servant seep through as the historical and materialist
residue of modernism. As self-portrait of the artist, Shem's vilifica-
tion incorporates Joyce's modernist reception, as I have tried to argue, using Lewis and West as representatives, and thereby internalizes a critique of Joyce's own contemporary literary history in the
thirties. "Shem the Penman" is the historical countertext to modernism's theorizing and revaluation, in its criticism, of literary history. At the same time, "Shem the Penman," revisits Joyce's tale of
artistic production, and the history he earlier (1912) separated from
his serious art and consigned to the broadside and to commerce (pen-
ning "Gas from a Burner" on the back of his *Dubliners* contract
with Maunsel and Co.) he now internalizes, in the wake of a Continental avant-garde tradition, in his poetic text. Thus the material
history of artistic production is penned, with "Shem the Penman,"
on the back of *Dubliners, Portrait,* and *Ulysses*—texts that eventually were awarded varying degrees of modernist canonization. "Shem
the Penman" restores the myth of Stephen's Icarean exile to a material history that recounts the effect of censorship on artistic sustenance and productive capability:

His costive Satan's antimonian manganese limolitmious nature
never needed such an alcove so, when Robber and Mumsell, the

pulpic dictators, on the nudgment of their legal advisers, Messrs
Codex and Podex, and under his own benefiction of their pastor
Father Flammeus Falconer, boycotted him of all muttonsuet
candles and romeruled stationery for any purpose, he winged
away on a wildgoup's chase across the kathartic ocean and made
synthetic ink and sensitive paper for his own end out of his wit's
waste. (FW 184.36)

The word "boycott"—which Joyce emphasizes by underlining it on
one of the first pages he ever drafted for this chapter, *"boycotted*, local publicans refuse to supply books, papers, ink, foolscap"
(JA 47471b-50 331)—was given to the world by Irish political history, its eponym Captain Boycott, an Ascendancy land agent tar-
geted by Parnell's strategy for dealing with enforcers of involuntary
evictions. Its ironic use here by the publishing establishment against
the poor artist, dispossessing him of the material means of literary
production, reflects the curious retrospective perversity of Irish his-
tories (particularly those published in Ulster) that still refer to Boycott as the Land League's "victim." Brendan Lehane's *The Companion Guide to Ireland,* a very popular contemporary tourist guidebook,
describes Boycott as victimized by Land League agitation: "Boycott
and his master offered ten per cent, then twenty per cent, and when
this was refused began forceful evictions. A few days before, at En-
nis, Parnell had made new proposals for dealing with any evictor;
isolate him 'as if he was a leper of old.' Overnight Boycott was a
lonely outpost of the Ascendancy. His crops were neglected, as were
all his animals, his mail, his laundry. No shop would sell to him or
his wife. But he stood his ground, and when his stand was publicised
found support in many quarters" (353). Lehane reports that the historical episode had a happy ending. "A year later the agitation had
died down and Boycott returned. The most revealing and least known
part of the story is that this time he stayed and soon after found a
popularity he had never known before" (354). The notorious image
of Shem as the artist who writes on his own body with his own
excrement is actually politicized in the chapter, to serve as trope
of material extremity produced for the artist by the nexus of law and
commerce in the early twentieth century. Indeed, the text regularly
mentions Joyce's writing as under the mark of censorship or prosecution, from *Dubliners'*s "pollute stoties . . . the ligatureliablous
effects of foul clay in little clots" (FW 186.21) to his "usylessly unreadable Blue Book of Eccles, *éditions de ténèbres* (even yet sighs
the Most Different, Dr. Pointdejenk, authorised bowdler and censor,
it can't be repeated!)" (FW 179.26). The text inscribes the problem

of textual obscenity into its historical system, and Shem's copro-
graphic *Aeneid* ("Then, pious Eneas . . . shall produce nichthemeri-
cally from his unheavenly body a no uncertain quantity of obscene
matter not protected by copriright in the United Stars of Ourania"
[FW 185.27]) will be vulnerable to American censorship and piracy,
like Joyce's *Ulysses*.

Joyce couples the two parts of his own material history—the inability to earn because of censorship and publishing misadventure,
and the generous patronage he was ever accused of abusing—into
the seemingly contradictory figure of Shem as indigent wastrel. The
result is a revisionary reading of artistic practice as idealistic, that
translates the artist's strategy from silence, cunning, and exile, into
its material version of guilty dependence ("he fell heavily and locally
into debit" [FW 172.16]), profligacy ("you squandered among under-
lings the overload of your extravagance" [FW 193.1]), and manipulative poormouthing:

> Malingerer in luxury, collector general, what has Your Lowness
> done in the mealtime with all the hamilkcars of cooked vege-
> tables, the hatfuls of stewed fruit, the suitcases of coddled ales,
> the Parish funds, me schamer, man, that you kittycoaxed so flex-
> ibly out of charitable butteries by yowling heavy with a hollow
> voice drop of your horrible awful poverty of mind. (192.5)

At the same time that he invokes here the accusations of fraud lev-
ied against Parnell for misusing the Paris funds, Joyce gives voice
also to the tacit reproaches of Harriet Shaw Weaver and Sylvia Beach
for his own abuse of "Paris funds" ("to give you your pound of plati-
num and a thousand thongs a year" [192.16]) wasted on expensive
taste in food, wine, and restaurants, while he never ceased to plead
hardship and poverty. He recounts other patronage as well: "Where
is that little alimony nestegg against our predictable rainy day?"
(FW 192.32) probably refers to his support from Robert McAlmon,
nicknamed "Robert McAlimony" because the money with which he
underwrote his publishing ventures had been bestowed on him as
"alimony" by Bryher Ellermann.

With "Shem the Penman" Joyce puts closure on the artistic self-
reflexion for which *Portrait* became the chief emblem in modern
literature. By obliging genius to see itself in the likeness of a servant,
and to see itself *seen* in the likeness of a servant, Joyce prises open
the contradictions in modern art's aspirations to serve as latter-day
vanguard of liberalism. The hope that its artists can lead an adversary culture that staves off anarchy and futility with a chivalry of

intellect is challenged in *Finnegans Wake* by portraying the artist as ineluctably inscribed with history, bearing the scars of class and colonialism whose materialist imprint on his sensibility will leave its mark on poetic production, form, and reception. "Shem the Penman" foregrounds modernism's sensitivity to the marks the artist's specific history—money, education, nationality, breeding—etch on qualities of control in the handling of language that tend to be coded as "taste" and "style." Rebecca West identifies them as "two colossal finger-prints left by literary incompetence" and "an insensitivity about the spirit" that leads Joyce "wildly astray even while he is still loyal to the classicism" (28). But in subjecting to reflection and critique modernism's own tacit class assumptions, "Shem the Penman" is also raveling and reweaving the earlier Joycean portraits of the artist in a way that pulls his earlier inscriptions of materialist analyses of culture and society forward into a more explicitly dialectical relation to the earlier aestheticism. In Shaun's vilifications of Shem, Joyce has the butcher boy take issue with the art of the plebeian tricked out as an aesthete. "Shem the Penman" greatly exceeds any personal counterattack against Joyce's critics, or any purely local exercise of *ressentiment*. In its scurrilous form as a libellous broadside it defaces the modern artist's ideologically favored portrait, as well as that of his critics, in an avant-garde gesture that self-destructively makes the text itself a nemesis of the modernist establishment. The experimentalism of the *Wake* text can therefore be seen to be something other than autotelic, something other than a pure gesture of linguistic freedom proclaiming its autonomy from all but self-referential and logopoetic ends. Instead, I believe, it executes a gesture of social responsibility by opening itself, and the earlier Joycean texts, to the analysis of those aspects of its author's literary history that can properly be termed, in their economic, social, and national implications, as "political."

My own closure to this series of essays on the artist will enact the text's own gesture at the end of "Shem the Penman." First, the shift in person, from third, to second, to first, lets Shem, the now beleaguered aesthete, speak a *mea culpa* on his own behalf in a way that sharply marks the difference from the Shaunian prose, and thus brings their dialectical relation into very clear focus. Shem regressively retreats to the English canon, speaking his remorse not as Hamlet but in the more calibanized voice of Richard III—"My fault, his fault, a kingship through a fault!" (FW 193.31). Shaun's robust colloquial speech is transformed back into poetic writing that attempts to recuperate the authority of the canonical body of sacred books: Shakespeare, the Bible ("Pariah, cannibal Cain, I who oathily forswore the

womb that bore you and the paps I sometimes sucked" [FW 193.32]),
and the Mass ("*Domine vopiscus!*" [FW 193.31]). The text is transforming itself back into high art, restoring to the artist romantic
self-sublimations—"you alone, windblasted tree of the knowledge
of beautiful andevil, ay, clothed upon with the metuor and shim-
mering like the horescens, astroglodynamonologos" (FW 194.14)—
and cloaking its confession in the beauty of a formal *de profundis*
never written by Wilde: "to me unseen blusher in an obscene coal-
hole . . . dweller in the downandoutermost where voice only of the
dead may come" (FW 194.17). But a second textual gesture (which I
will follow with my next section of this study on "The Women")
interrupts this first. Narratively, Shem's voice returns to Stephen's
moment of confession to Cranly at the end of *Portrait,* and to Mulligan at the beginning of *Ulysses,* when he concedes that he has violated *amor matris,* that he has killed his mother. At the end of Shem's
confession, the mother's voice erupts in his speech, speaks from the
dead in a homely, working class idiom, reproaches him with her
banishment—"where voice only of the dead may come, because ye
left from me, because ye laughed on me, because, O me lonly son,
ye are forgetting me!" (FW 194.20). Indeed, Stephen, Shem, and all
the artist sons of modernism have always been forgetting the mother.
But not Joyce, who remembers her at the last and who closes his
oeuvre, the end of *Finnegans Wake,* with her poetic homely words.
This has been Joyce's project all along: to stage the suppression of
the voices that art silences, that modernism derided or despised, and
that, at last, in *Finnegans Wake,* break through the silence and make
themselves heard once more in their discredited vernacular forms as
gossip ("bab's baby walks at seven months" [FW 194.24], news
("stud stoned before a racecourseful" [FW 194.25]), fashion ("four-
tiered skirts are up, mesdames, while Parimiknie wears popular short
legs" [FW 194.27]), and the poetry not of Shakespearean iambic pen-
tameters telling the history of England's imperial legitimations and
illegitimations, but the poetic lilting brogue of old Irishwomen making the most magical vernacular music of all, "happy as the day is
wet, babbling, bubbling, chattering to herself, deloothering the fields
on their elbows leaning with the sloothering slide of her, giddy-
gaddy, grannyma, gossipaceous Anna Livia. He lifts the lifewand and
the dumb speak" (FW 195.1).

PART 2
The Women

CHAPTER FIVE

"Who Killed Julia Morkan?": The Gender Politics of Art in "The Dead"

A Joycean joke that isn't funny:
Question: Who killed Julia Morkan?
Answer: The pope.

I. Stifled Back Answers

Although the first sentence of "The Dead" tells us that "Lily, the caretaker's daughter, was literally run off her feet" (D 175), Lily does not complain about her lot. Indeed, that is why she gets on so well with her mistresses, as we learn a little later; "But Lily seldom made a mistake in the orders so that she got on well with her three mistresses. They were fussy, that was all. But the only thing they would not stand was back answers" (D 176). If we decode the bourgeois agenda of the narrative voice[1] at this moment, its intention to offer a politically complacent representation of the Morkans and therefore to neutralize the master-servant relationship at the outset as benign, then we can read in this description of Lily as a pleasing domestic fixture its suppressed truth: the orders are scrupulously checked to make sure that Lily does not steal,[2] and she is valued because she has stifled her "back answers" and does not protest the exacting demands made on her by the fussy ladies, even when she is asked to do too much, when she is run off her feet. The narration of "The Dead," promoting the Philistine ideals of the beautiful, the good, and the true (Adorno 138) in its representation of bourgeois society, successfully stifles a series of back answers that it cannot prevent from erupting in the text. Back answers repeatedly disrupt the pretty picture of prosperous and happy domesticity, of social harmony, and of refined culture in the story with a repressed force that lets them echo in our ears even after they have been silenced by a gold coin, or an after-dinner speech, or a change of topic—"The men that is now is only all palaver and what they can get out of you" (D 178), "West Briton!" (D 190), "There's a nice husband for you, Mrs Malins" (D 191), "And if I were in Julia's place I'd tell that Father Healy straight up to his face . . . " (D 195), "And why couldn't he have a voice too . . . Is it because he's only a black?" (D 198).

Joyce dramatizes in "The Dead" the politics of art's determination
to conceal its own politically oppressive functions by raveling a primary narrative text, Gabriel's story told in what we might call the
audible or "loud" text, with a largely silent but disruptive feminist
countertext.

Joyce uses Gabriel's altercation with Miss Ivors to raise the central question of the text: whether or not art serves a political function. The moment is cleverly double for while the couple's words
concern the politics of nationalism, their engagement, as intellectual and social equals, concerns the politics of gender:

> He wanted to say that literature was above politics. But they
> were friends of many years' standing and their careers had been
> parallel, first at the University and then as teachers: he could not
> risk a grandiose phrase with her. He continued blinking his eyes
> and trying to smile and murmered lamely that he saw nothing
> political in writing reviews of books. (D 188)

Interpretations of "The Dead" have traditionally assumed that Gabriel is right, and that on the basis of Joyce's quarrels with the propagandistic aims of the Irish revival he too would have held art
above politics. But this critical stance colludes with the story's endorsement of an ideology that holds nationalism to be more properly
or "literally" political than feminism—and that makes Miss Ivors'
"West Briton!" the only back answer taken seriously in, and by, the
story. But Joyce's politics in "The Dead" are not literalized into the
form of a polemic, but are rather implicit in the scepticism that
the text creates in us toward the "grandiose" phrases and ideological
assumptions of its own aestheticist narrative. We must be especially
careful, like the women in "The Dead," not to be seduced by the
story's exceptionally beautiful prose, for its lyrical narrative voice is
not "innocent" but rather produces a fair share of male palaver. It
effectively promotes a cultural ideology that is especially inimical
to the female subject and to the female artist, and Joyce nudges us
repeatedly to think against the ideological grain of the narration
by genderizing ourselves not merely as subjectively female, but
as politically feminist, as resisting readers, critics, and sceptics of
the text.

"The Dead," composed while Joyce was writing *Stephen Hero*,
internalizes the submerged socially critical influence of Ibsen, who
is here overtly replaced by Browning as he will be replaced by Byron
in *Portrait*, but who nonetheless functions as the critical leaven that
ferments the sweet optimistic narration in which Gabriel's story is

told. "The Dead" is Joyce's inverted *Doll's House*—"The purpose of *The Doll's House* . . . was the emancipation of women" (Power 35)—the husband's version of Ibsen's plot of a New Year's party that ends in a ruinous marital exchange. The wife's revolt is less activist but psychologically subtler in Joyce's version, as she takes revenge for a denied trip to Galway by revisiting it spiritually and romantically in a way that displaces her husband forever from the passional center of her life, and marginalizes him in his own self-image. Joyce further shifts the locus of feminist critique from the institutions of law and economics to those of art and culture. He can thereby dramatize male hegemony over art and culture as tacit denial of just that power, and as faith in the apoliticism of an art exposed not by a cumulative historical political women's movement, but by a series of disruptive, stifled, choked, female outbursts and protests. Joyce thereby imbricates not only a series of analogous political problems in the story (national self-figurations, artistic and cultural desires and idealizations, bourgeois patriarchalism and parochialism, etc.), but a series of generic functions as well. Following Ibsen's own generic reversions and play, Joyce overlaps drama and fiction in "The Dead" (while interpolating painting, picture, sculpture, and music as other intertexted arts) by giving the narration itself, the story's "telling," a performative function. I will therefore treat the narration of "The Dead" as a *mise en scene* of artistic patriarchy—and will therefore urge the reader sceptical of Gabriel's romanticizing infantilization of his wife to be equally sceptical of the narrator's romanticizing infantilization of the story, and particularly of the story's treatment of the marginalized Morkan women. Not only is Gabriel Conroy Joyce's Torvald Helmer, but the narration, the story itself as narrated, is Joyce's Torvald Helmer. Ibsen is the intertextual tool—personified in my reading by what I've called the stifled back answer—by which both can be critically penetrated and ideologically dismantled. If this imputes more political and feminist acumen to Ibsen than has traditionally been allowed, reference to Joan Templeton's 1989 *PMLA* article, in which she persuasively argues that Ibsen was systematically defanged by his male critics, suggests that it is the critical perception of Ibsen that needs to be revised.

By being largely female, the back answers in "The Dead" suggest that Joyce uses the politics of gender to conduct his self-critique of art in the story. But he does this by having the story's art replicate the problems of sexual politics in society by twisting its plot in such a way that the ubiquitous oppression of woman is both blatant and discounted, unmistakable and invisible at the same time. The narrative maneuvers its emphasis in such a way that Irish nationalist political issues eclipse sexual politics, and the story's donnée emerges as the tragedy of the would-be male artist, his failure of sensibility and its recuperation, rather than the tragedy of the would-be female artist, her silencing, protest, and silencing yet again by art itself. Art's self-critique requires Joyce to dramatize that art's representation of woman is inherently oppressive, and thereby obliges him to specularize his own role as male artist for the purpose of critique:

> He stood still in the gloom of the hall, trying to catch the air that the voice was singing and gazing up at his wife. There was grace and mystery in her attitude as if she were a symbol of something. He asked himself what is a woman standing on the stairs in the shadow, listening to distant music, a symbol of. (D 210)

In this superb staging of the aestheticizing act, Joyce displays his acute awareness that in their genderized form, in the male artist's representation of the female, the politics of representation are expressed in doubly brutal gestures of occlusion, oppression, and exploitation: doubly brutal, because these acts are masked as love. The very form of Gabriel's gesture toward woman—the rhetorical question ("He asked himself what is a woman . . . a symbol of") that proclaims its disinterest in what woman is in favor of parading its own profundity—masks artistic conceit as gyneolatry. The generality of the question implies an answer of indeterminacy and overdetermination, that woman is a symbol of anything and everything man wants her to represent—except her own sense of who or what she is. By staging Gabriel's thoughts in this way, the text of "The Dead" offers a silent second answer, a tacit back answer, to Gabriel's rhetorical question: that when woman is transformed into a symbol by man, woman becomes a symbol of her social decontextualization, her silencing, the occlusion of her suffering, the suppression of her feeling.

To give us purchase on the irony or internal self-criticism of "The Dead," Joyce first manipulates Gabriel's literary influences. Notwithstanding Gabriel's interest in literature and especially in Continental language, and presumably art, it is not Ibsen but the English Browning he touts. Yet Joyce pairs Browning and Ibsen, I believe, to ironize the romantic climax of the story. Joyce uses Browning's "My Last Duchess" against Ibsen's *Doll's House* in a way that deromanticizes Gabriel's balcony scene with Gretta on the stair to reveal the oppressive sexual and aesthetic politics that propel it. To examine these oppressive maneuvers both in love and in art more minutely, I will resort to a modification of the psychoanalytic theories of Jacques Lacan and the aesthetic theories of Theodor Adorno—strange bedfellows, perhaps, but useful for linking the problem of desire to the problem of representation. My overall thesis will be to argue that Joyce uses the events of "The Dead" to dramatize that art is not above politics at all, but that, on the contrary, art is produced by, and embodies, the social conditions of class, gender, age, and race relations. He then doubles this insight by having the narrative voice of the story act out the same disavowals of art's oppressiveness that the characters themselves act out in "The Dead." The feminist strategy I impute to Joyce is therefore less a politically correct representation of woman, than a representation of the occlusional practices that contort the representation of the female according to the ideological requirements of a patriarchal agenda. I further reckon Joyce's feminist strategy as a "cost," or at least a "risk," to his own art. The young Joyce was learning through the painful experience of rejection and censorship that it was his aesthetic effects, his lyricism, his romanticism, but not his social critique, that would earn him publication and acclaim. In "The Dead" and in *Portrait* he polishes these effects to a commercially marketable gloss, but not without covertly ironizing his lyrical language to let us see it as an exquisite form with a hypocritical soul: a paradigm for establishment aestheticism.

2. The Woman as *objet d'art*

Joyce weaves Browning and Ibsen as intertexts into Gabriel's romancing of his wife in "The Dead," because he finds in these writers a grasp of the brutalization that the idealization of female beauty can produce and conceal. By overdetermining his intertexts Joyce can generalize the argument, that the female is aestheticized in the service of a disavowed violence, and that male discourse in tribute to female beauty must be scrutinized critically as symptom and mask of murder and rape.

Joyce carefully weaves variations of a phrase that alludes to Browning in and out of Gabriel's thoughts and the narration, "He repeated to himself a phrase he had written in his review: *One feels that one is listening to a thought-tormented music*" (D 192). The text's obsession with the phrase, like Gabriel's, is with its quotability, the aesthetic ring that demands reiteration and repetition. Indeed, Gabriel rhetorically asks permission from himself to borrow part of it for his speech—"we are living in a sceptical and, if I may use the phrase, a thought-tormented age" (D 203)—and saves the rest for the title and description of the mental portrait he paints, frames, and titles, of his wife. "He asked himself what is a woman standing on the stairs in the shadow, listening to distant music, a symbol of. If he were a painter he would paint her in that attitude. . . . *Distant Music* he would call the picture if he were a painter" (D 210). But the distant music that Gabriel hears is, according to the narrator, the quotability of his own prose, the lyricism of the rhetorical question (*Is it because there is no word tender enough to be your name* [D 214]) with which Gabriel, like Joyce himself in a letter of 26 September 1904 (SL 31), graced his love letters to his wife, "Like distant music these words that he had written years before were borne towards him from the past" (D 214). Gabriel's wife is occluded and displaced in his memory by the grandiose phrases he can risk with this unsceptical woman, and he caresses his own words in his mind in a masturbatory gesture initiated by his caress of the written form of his own name upon the heliotrope envelope sent him by Gretta ("A heliotrope envelope was lying beside his breakfast-cup and he was caressing it with his hand" [D 213]).

By carefully focusing our attention on Gabriel's self-displaying discourse in relation to Browning, Joyce sets up an implicit analogy between Gabriel's presentation of Gretta as a painting called *Distant Music*, and Browning's dramatic monologue in "My Last Duchess."[3] The analogy produces the theme of marriage as a connoisseurship of a female *objet d'art*, an appreciation of female beauty that resents the life and living feeling of the subject, and therefore proceeds to murder the living woman in order that she might perdure as she is desired, as pure representation, as "as if" alive rather than "as" alive, "That's my last Duchess painted on the wall,/ Looking as if she were alive." But not only is the woman displaced by a painting in Browning's poem: the painting is displaced by the perverse discourse of the Duke of Ferrara—perverse because it disavows the horror of what it narrates by masking itself as art history.

The Gothic elements of Browning's poem are tempered in Gabriel's aesthetic appreciation of his wife by the mediation of the bourgeois intertext of Ibsen's *Doll's House*. "A woman was standing near the top of the first flight . . . . It was his wife" (D 209). That Gabriel appears, or pretends, not to recognize his wife immediately as she stands at the top of the stair, that he is excited by her in her guise as a beautiful and mysterious stranger, recalls Torvald's strange seduction fantasy of Nora:

Do you realize—when I'm out at a party like this with you—do you know why I talk to you so little, and keep such a distance away . . . It's because I'm imagining then that you're my secret darling, my secret young bride-to-be, and that no one suspects there's anything between us. (Ibsen 183)

Gabriel, upon the couple's arrival at the Gresham after the party, has a similar elopement fantasy about his wife—"as they stood at the hotel door, he felt that they had escaped from their lives and duties, escaped from home and friends and run away together with wild and radiant hearts to a new adventure" (D 215). The painful irony of both Gabriel and Torvald's erotic fantasies is, of course, their hidden truth: their wives *are* mysterious strangers with great secrets of their own, and these men scarcely know the women with whom they live in such intimacy. Furthermore, it is precisely the secrets that animate the women, making them remote and strange, that excite the men. This produces the double horror—the man's excitation by the female's hidden pain inciting him to contemplate her seduction and rape—that ends each of these aborted conjugal encounters. Torvald is excited by the wild desperation of Nora's tarantella, a desperation of which he is the unwitting cause, and his erotic stimulation by his wife's suicidal dance of death is macabre. His anger when the distraught wife rebuffs his seduction—an anger shadowed by conjugal enforcement ("You will, won't you? Aren't I your husband—?" [183])—is enacted also by Gabriel, "A dull anger began to gather again at the back of his mind and the dull fires of his lust began to glow angrily in his veins" (D 218). Ruth Bauerle's paper and essay first drew my attention to the sinister threat of mate rape hanging over this romantic scene, as she argues that Gabriel unwittingly begins to act out for Gretta the date rape in *The Lass of Aughrim* (*New Alliances* 118).

Both Ibsen and Joyce make of the irony of aesthetic creativity a political point. Torvald and Gabriel are excited by what eludes them in their wives, by what is mysterious and strange in the women, and both impute this mysteriousness and strangeness to their own imaginations, their own powers of aesthetic and erotic sensibility. They imagine themselves Pygmalion, as it were, creating the objects of their own lust. Both imagine their wives weak and helpless in order to create gallant poses for themselves, and thereby discount the women's great strength. "She seemed to him so frail that he longed to defend her against something and then to be alone with her" (D 213), Gabriel thinks of the woman who had nursed a disapproving and ungrateful mother-in-law through her dying illness. Torvald likewise pledges to Nora, who successfully and secretly secured a life-saving therapy for his critical illness while contending with the terminus of her first pregnancy and the death of her father, "You know what, Nora—time and again I've wished you were in some terrible danger, just so I could stake my life and soul and everything, for your sake" (186). She has done just that for him, while he ignominiously abandons her in the face of a real threat.

Both Ibsen and Joyce transform this fatuity of husbands into a poignant irony. The men *do* create the mysteriousness of their wives—not with art, but with a rigorous social and personal suppression. Both Torvald and Gabriel, ashamed for different reasons of their provincial wives, go to enormous lengths to alienate them from their origins, isolate them from families and friends, and silence their memories and feelings. Through this suppression, they make their wives strangers to their husbands, and estrange the women from themselves. Ibsen makes a careful point of dramatizing that Torvald knows nothing of Mrs. Linde while Dr. Rank instantly greets her as Nora's old friend—"Torvald loves me beyond words, and, as he puts it, he'd like to keep me all to himself. For a long time he'd almost be jealous if I even mentioned any of my old friends back home. So of course I dropped that" (157). Gretta's little dance of joy at the prospect of a trip to Galway ("His wife clasped her hands excitedly and gave a little jump") suggests that she has not returned to her home since her marriage—"'O, do go, Gabriel, she cried. I'd love to see Galway again" (D 191). Gabriel's coldness toward her home might explain Gretta's secrecy about Michael Furey as the result of his own interdiction. Gabriel's desire to control Gretta's memory and attention serves the interest of suppressing the social reality of their marriage and their lives in order that the idealized forms of a socially stripped union, like the fantasy encounter of Torvald and his mystery bride, might be distilled from their lives. "He longed to recall to her those moments, to make her forget the years of their dull existence together and remember only their moments of ecstasy. . . . Their children, his writing, her household cares had not quenched all their souls' tender fire" (D 213). The glimpses we get of these household cares at the beginning of the story is one of petty paternal tyrannies masked as solicitude and practiced on the bodies of wife and children: "what with green shades for Tom's eyes at night and making him do the dumb-bells, and forcing Eva to eat the stirabout. The poor child! And she simply hates the sight of it! . . . O, but you'll never guess what he makes me wear now!" (D 180). Gabriel's forcing his family to eat and wear and do what he prescribes is anticipated in Torvald Helmer's infantilizing ban on macaroons for Nora. Indeed, Gretta's playful joke about Gabriel's solicitude, "The next thing he'll buy me will be a diving suit" (D 180), nicely pinpoints Gabriel's strategy of making his family feel as though the world in which they live is an alien and dangerous element from which only his prescribed devices and appliances will save them. Both Ibsen and Joyce create female protagonists who bear enormous family responsibilities, who nurse sick and dying friends and relatives, who bear and raise children with coercive interference from their fathers, who repress their own identities and society of origin in order to maintain their husbands' social standings, who are obliged to endure a variety of personal interdictions and domestic prohibitions, patronized in private and sometimes insulted in public, and who, it is hinted, may be subjected to the enforcement of unwanted conjugal duties. These are women with complex and oppressive social realities first produced, then disavowed, by their husbands before the men can love them. The representational logic of this situation is that, like the Duke of Ferrara, who is happiest praising the beauty of a murdered bride, these bourgeois husbands are ultimately most excited by their double power to oppress but disavow their oppression of the female. This is the perversity of uxorious bourgeois love.

3. Woman as the Other Woman

In the critique of bourgeois love and marriage he conducts in "The Dead," Joyce, like Ibsen, was careful to choose a happy, prosperous family with a model *paterfamilias* at its head. Gabriel is the antipode to the shiftless, brutal, or ineffective family men who people Joyce's texts: the senior Dedalus, Martin Cunningham, Jack Power, Paddy Dignam, Farrington, little Chandler, and so on. Like Ibsen, Joyce chose a best-case bourgeois scenario to expose inherent problems in conjugal sexuality and love. Joyce goes on to elaborate Ibsen's social analysis by giving it an aesthetic dimension, by transforming love into aesthetic creation, and by critiquing the homologous oppressions that constitute both. To provide a theoretical explanation for these twin pathologies whose symptom is idealization in love and art, I find especially useful a modification of the theories of Jacques Lacan[4] and Theodor Adorno—two writers with different philosophical etiologies who nonetheless share a common antiessentialism and a perception that idealization is the product of complex perceptual structures. These structures—displacements, repressions, extrusions, and the like, that produce sexual desire or the concept of beauty—give to love and beauty political mechanisms and political ends.

Lacan retrieves from Freud the startling implication of an inherent pathology in human sexuality—"Freud, as we know, went so far as to suggest a disturbance of human sexuality, not of a contingent, but of an essential kind" (*Écrits* 281)—that derives from the role that the fear of castration plays in the original perception of sexual difference. The child learns the difference between male and female by making a fatal perceptual error, by imagining that the female is castrated, with the consequence that sexual identity is evermore fraught with anxiety and danger. "There is an antimony, here," Lacan writes of the unconscious castration complex, "that is internal to the assumption by man (*Mensch*) of his sex: why must he assume the attributes of that sex only through a threat—the threat, indeed, of their privation" (*Écrits* 281). The consequence of this perilous construction of sexual identity is that even in adult love relations, men and women find the pursuit of desire, the pursuit of the significance and recognition that is at stake in the sexual relationship, elusive except by a series of complex symbolic maneuvers. For women, especially, what Lacan calls "the demand for love," and which more closely resembles being nurtured, having the emotional security of knowing that one's physical needs will be supplied, being treasured as a valued and cherished object—that is, relations more proper to the parent-child relation—are easier to achieve than recognition and significance as a subject. Nora is a perfect example of a woman whose relationship to her husband is patterned on such a model of "demand for love," and Ibsen shrewdly metaphorizes precisely this aspect of it in the child and doll house tropes. Nora's desire for prestige and recognition from her husband is deferred until "the wonderful" is to happen, until she can lay before her husband her heroism on his behalf, her sacrifice of honor and risk of safety, that will coerce his respect. Gretta enjoys a similar oppressive and infantile nurturance without recognition in her marriage.

Because the man fails to find in the woman the significance that would allow him to give her his recognition, he will, according to Lacan, seek for it in other women—

> If, in effect, the man finds satisfaction for his demand for love in the relation with the woman, in as much as the signifier of the phallus constitutes her as giving in love what she does not have—conversely, his own desire for the phallus will make its signifier emerge in its persistent divergence towards 'another woman' who

may signify this phallus in various ways, either as a virgin or as a prostitute. (*Écrits* 290)

In respectable bourgeois men like Torvald or Gabriel, where adultery is prohibited, this divergence toward the other woman takes the form of transforming the wife herself into another woman, into the stranger or the bride. Lacan, however, points out that since male anatomy does not exempt men from the anxiety of castration, the love of woman for man likewise produces a displacement. "Yet it should not be thought that the sort of infidelity that would appear to be constitutive of the male function is proper to it. For if one looks more closely, the same redoubling is to be found in the woman, except that the Other of Love as such, that is to say, in so far as he is deprived of what he gives, finds it difficult to see himself in the retreat in which he is substituted for the being of the very man whose attributes she cherishes" (*Écrits* 290). Both Nora and Gretta fail to find in their husbands a freedom from anxiety in the face of the other that would give the men a mastery worthy of the women's recognition. Torvald's obsession with his respectability, his prestige, his authority, his rage at Krogstad's failure to proffer him a formal titular address, this enthrallment to the other has its counterpart in Gabriel's extreme social nervousness which expresses itself in a series of bodily tics, a blinking of his restless eyes, adjustments of his tie, playing with cuffs, flicking at boots—a fear of disapproval even by those he considers his social inferiors. This ontological slavishness in the social realm prevents the woman from granting the man mastery except as "another man," either literally another man, as in the case of Gretta, or to an idealized version of the man, as in the case of Nora. The Torvald Nora worships is not her human and socially real husband, the cowardly petty martinet who bullies her at home and his colleagues at work, but a man of sterling nobility and integrity—who does not, in fact, exist. It is only when Torvald fails to live up to Nora's idealization, when he makes his discrepancy from her ideal of him unmistakable, that he produces her *anagnorisis*, her moment of self-recognition and truth, that causes her to leave him and to reclaim herself as a signifier. Joyce also makes Gretta love an idealization of the man, but in a cruel gender twist, he permits the woman the sort of divergence usually practiced by the man. Gretta presumably "loves" her husband as a "generous person," that is, she is grateful to him for his nurturance, but she reserves her desire, her recognition, for the virginal male, Michael Furey, the idealist who achieves metaphysical mastery over her by his willingness to risk life.[5] Joyce beautifully draws the parallel between the husband who aborts the very endangerment from which he fantasizes heroically rescuing his wife, by making her, and himself, wear galoshes, while her tubercular lover stood in the rain mourning the loss of his love— "I think he died for me" (D 220). Gabriel, seeing himself as he imagines Gretta seeing him, sees himself striving to surmount his social anxieties and perils, "a pennyboy for his aunts, a nervous well-meaning sentimentalist, orating to vulgarians and idealising his own clownish lusts, the pitiable fatuous fellow," (D 220) ever teetering on the brink of symbolic castration while the social caste of the boy from the gasworks is rendered nugatory by a fatal gesture that may have taught Gretta to enshrine an ideal memory of him, while marrying a man with enough sense to wear galoshes in the rain.

4. Songs, Romance, and the Social Real

The displacements and divergences that constitute the subtle symbolic power plays behind the social drama in bourgeois love and sexuality, also constitute a subtle aesthetic politics in the realm of beauty and representation. Adorno argues that the appreciation of beauty requires both the negation of the ugly, and the realization of that negation: the ugly is both banished from beauty and necessary (as banished) to it. This concept is useful, particularly if the ugly is more precisely conceptualized as the particular, the material, the social real, to understanding the gender implications of Joyce's representational strategy in "The Dead." The aesthetic "truth" of the Joycean text is simultaneously a political "truth" for it must be sought in the way the beautiful displaces the ugly, the way art displaces social reality, and the way male creativity displaces female labor. Because love and art share a homologous infrastructural repression, a similar idealism produced by the disavowal and repression of the social real, and because both practice a kind of essentialism, a conceptual faith in love or beauty as intrinsic to the subject and object, rather than as a historical and social product, love and art mirror each other in a reciprocal mimesis in "The Dead."

The figure who unwittingly exemplifies the victimization of this bourgeois essentialism of love and art is, I will suggest, Julia Morkan. She is marginalized in the periphery of the story as an infantilic, toddling, moribund old maid, robbed of a unique identity by her relational title as "Aunt Julia" and by being invariably treated as a twin or a triplet with sister and niece. Yet she is, I will argue, perhaps the truest and greatest artist in "The Dead," whose art has been suppressed, and ultimately extinguished, on purely gender grounds, to a mimic and functional female labor. And her sister Kate's "back answer" on behalf of Julia Morkan is stifled not only by their patronizing niece and nephew, by Mary Jane impatient with her aunts' peeving and their old fashioned ways, and by Gabriel who considers his aunts merely "two ignorant old women" (D 192), but by the narration itself, that notwithstanding the nice little things it says about them at the beginning, also treats them as two ignorant old women. Yet Joyce embeds in "The Dead" itself a kind of shadow text, the ghost of a counternarrative that provides a "back answer" or articulation of Julia's grievances, a complaint necessary for the critique of the social function of art in the story to be heard.

On the Morkans' wall Gabriel notices two pictures of scenes from Shakespeare's plays that serve to foreshadow two intertextual moments at the climax of the story. When Gabriel watches Gretta listening on the stair, both will mentally enact the balcony scene from *Romeo and Juliet*, while the song Gretta hears and remembers, *The Lass of Aughrim*, repeats a version of the theme of infanticide or murdered innocence, "my babe lies cold . . . ," the infant killed by exposure to prevent it from claiming a noble or royal birthright, like the murdered princes in the Tower. However it is more than a symbolic adumbration that these pictures accomplish. They function also to exemplify the bourgeois domestication of tragedy, the use of an art whose violence is neutralized as its ugliness is expelled to become "kitsch" in Adorno's sense of purified beauty whose expulsion of the ugly makes itself ugly (71). Shakespeare serves, in bourgeois homes, to adorn and enhance property rather than to communicate his violent message:

A picture of the balcony scene in *Romeo and Juliet* hung there and beside it was a picture of the two murdered princes in the Tower which Aunt Julia had worked in red, blue and brown wools when she was a girl. Probably in the school they had gone to as girls that kind of work had been taught, for one year his mother had worked for him as a birthday present a waistcoat of purple tabinet, with little foxes' heads upon it, lined with brown satin and having round mulberry buttons. (D 186)

Woman's relation to art is here historicized as a product of education, and is defined as essentially *reproductive* rather than productive—Shakespeare "worked" in wools, mindlessly copied without comprehension of his textual or poetic meaning, reduced to cultural pretension or kitsch as home decor. Even Gabriel's mother, for all of her ambition and family pride, is a mere family "brains *carrier*" (emphasis mine), according to her sister (D 186), a producer of intellectual sons, and of distaff adornments for them, such as the embroidered waistcoat.[6]

It is these domesticated versions of Shakespearean romance that Gabriel and Gretta both enact when their emotional passions are stirred. As Gabriel looks up at Gretta standing atop the stair, he silently plays the balcony scene with her, only first veiling his Juliet's face ("He could not see her face") in order to preserve the illusion of her beauty. The artistic act requires the suppression of the social particularity of the model ("A woman was standing . . . ") and the particularity of the face, its age, the specificity of its features, the inscription of fatigue or sadness. When the apparition of Gretta is dispelled, Gabriel must reconceptualize her in a series of gentle negatives, as a tempered version of the expelled ugly, the real—"She had no longer any grace of attitude" (D 213)—like Gretta's half-open mouth in sleep, or the adumbrated snore in her deep drawn breath, "He did not like to say even to himself that her face was no longer beautiful but he knew that it was no longer the face for which Michael Furey had braved death" (D 222).

Gabriel plays *Romeo and Juliet* with Gretta for the joy of producing the lyricism of the poetic language that his vision of her stimulates, a poetry of stars and sunlight and singing birds and the warm touch of a glove—"he was placing a ticket inside the warm palm of her glove" Gabriel's narrator has him remember (D 213), in echo of Romeo's "O, that I were a glove upon that hand / That I might touch that cheek!" (II.2). But as Gabriel produces musical love lyrics under the spell of his Juliet, his Juliet is spinning her own version of *Romeo and Juliet* in her imagination, that she plays back to him in their bedroom in the Gresham. Only her Romeo is Michael Furey standing under the dripping tree that is the synecdoche of the Capulet orchard, throwing gravel at Gretta's window to protest their fatal separation. Gretta grasps in *Romeo and Juliet* not the lyricism of the language but the idealism of the gestures, of lovers willing to die for love.

Gretta's version of *Romeo and Juliet* is curiously inspired by the ballad narrative of *The Lass of Aughrim* that is, in a sense, an anti-*Romeo and Juliet*. Romeo braving Juliet's hostile home to declare his love has a sinister mirror in Lord Gregory raping the lass in the sanctuary of her own home—

Oh Gregory, don't you remember,
In my father's hall.

When you had your will of me?
And that was the worst of all.[7]

The nobleman's brutal violation of hospitality is cruelly iterated in his refusal to give the girl and her babe admission on a cold and rainy night. Finally, Lord Gregory's demand of a password to challenge the woman's identity ("Oh if you be the lass of Aughrim/ As I suppose you not to be/ Come tell me the last token/ Between you and me") refigures the treatment of the wife as stranger, the man's transformation of his woman into another woman, here too for the purpose of disavowing the social real in order to elude responsibility for woman's oppression. This discursive strategy within the ballad re-iterates the double oppression, the discursive violence of the disavowal of violence that I have pointed to earlier in Browning's Duke.

In its structure of an alternating male disavowal of sexual preda-tion and a female "back answer," the girl's complaint of having been exploited, the ballad of *The Lass of Aughrim* recapitulates in melo-dramatic form the scene between Gabriel and Lily in the pantry at the beginning of the story. Joyce borrows Ibsen's technique of using a small unremarked moment in the play to indicate that hidden behind the bourgeois tragedy, and repressed and discredited by it, lie the far more egregious sufferings and oppressions of the ser-vant class. While Ibsen's audience, actors, and critics transformed into censorship their shock at Nora's abandoning her children, they failed to bring similar outrage to Ibsen's depiction of servants quite routinely deprived of illegitimate offspring.[8] Joyce makes the story of Lily, then, a similarly unremarked and unremarkable gap or ab-sence in "The Dead." The male critics largely ignore this gap by treating Lily as Gabriel treats Gretta, wondering what she is a sym-bol of, and deciding that she must be the Easter Lily (Torchiana 253). In suppressing Lily's social reality as a servant, critics collude with the narration's promoting of Lily's willing sufferance, her stifled back answers. Thus her "back answer" to Gabriel is all the more remark-able, and invites us to explore the circumstantial context that links Lily subtly, proleptically, to the Lass of Aughrim, and Gabriel, by implication, to the cruel Lord Gregory. Lily's labor at the party takes the form of an isolated service as valet to the gentlemen arriving at the party. Alone in the pantry with her employers' nephew, helping him off with his coat, she is not unreasonable to interpret his pleas-ant allusion to her marriagability as a favorable comment on her sexual maturation. The narrative voice prods us to think of Lily as a little hysterical in construing Gabriel's pleasantries as a sexual ad-

vance, but the narrative events by no means totally preclude a repressed sexual interest as Gabriel's motive. "He looked up at the
pantry ceiling, which was shaking with the stamping and shuffling
of feet on the floor above, listened for a moment to the piano and
then glanced at the girl, who was folding his overcoat carefully at
the end of a shelf" (D 177). One could infer from this sequence of
ocular gestures that Gabriel ventures upon a flirtation with Lily
only after assuring himself that goings-on in the pantry would not
be heard over the noise of dancing and piano upstairs. If so, then we
have here a possible answer to his later question, "He wondered at
his riot of emotions of an hour before. From what had it proceeded?"
(D 222). It may have been the surprise of Lily's slim prettiness that
inspired his lust, its frustration later displaced onto the more sexually tractable wife. Gabriel's romanticizing of Gretta might thus be
construed as having far more cynically hypocritical depths than we
imagined, and his great repentant gesture, excoriating himself for
romanticizing his clownish lusts, a cowardly cover for intentions
variously adulterous, exploitive, and insincere. The narrative leaves
as a gap just exactly what has happened to Lily, although we are
prodded to infer that she has been sweet-talked into seduction by
some young man, and has suffered either the onset of pregnancy or
abandonment in consequence. The narrative, too, sweet-talks and
abandons her, treating her essentially as a decorative fixture at the
party, without inquiring further into her social reality. Only her
"back answer" disrupts the narration's seductive fatuities, as it disrupts Gabriel's.

   The Lass of Aughrim, like the narration of "The Dead," is art: and
art does not speak the truth of social reality. The ballad gives pleasure in its discursive form, its poetry, its play upon the ambiguous
credibility of the lord and lass in dialogue, and the horror of the
situation, the female with her infant left homeless in the rain, is
assimilated as a melodramatic type to the Celtic romanticism of the
song. No wonder, then, that Gretta's remembered version of the ballad, both as sung and as enacted by Michael Furey, abandoned and
pleading for admittance, like the lass in the rain, and eventually lying cold like the babe in the arms of her memory, shares the romanticism of a disavowed violence. For Gretta's lyrical story with its
romantic donnée ("So she had had that romance in her life: a man
had died for her sake" [D 222]) conceals a picture of depressed and
futile life in the west of Ireland, of young people apprenticed to unwholesome jobs ("a seventeen-year old Catholic probably shoveled
coal to be heated for coal-gas," Torchiana speculates, [241]) or sent
away to schools away from home, to suffer aborted ambitions ("He

was going to study singing only for his health"[D 221]) and inadequate medical care. Concealed are the poverty and wasted lives not reflected in Molly Ivors' Gaelic League romanticizing of the West of Ireland, with its educational linguistic field trips to the Aran Isles. In the story, Miss Ivors' political anti-colonialism too fails to recuperate the social real.

5. The Silencing of Female Art

The actual performance of *The Lass of Aughrim* that inspires the twin internalized balcony scenes of the Conroys is itself, however, narrated in a strangely dual way, almost as *langue* and *parole*, functioning as an ideal form in its conceptual power and effects on the memories of the Conroys, and yet presented in its socially contextualized and material quality in the present real. As an artistic performance, it is a failure: "The song seemed to be in the old Irish tonality and the singer seemed uncertain both of his words and of his voice" (D 210). The text invites us to ask why this performance occurs at all, why does the celebrated Bartell D'Arcy ("All Dublin is raving about him" [D 184]), who resists all night the importunities of Mary Jane and Gretta to perform ("He's full of conceit, I think" [D 191]), sing a song he scarcely knows, to a virtually empty hall, when his voice is hoarse from a cold? Clearly this man who once kissed Molly Bloom on the choir stair, sang it to please Miss O'Callaghan—a song about seduction pressed into service as a serenade to seduction. We can only speculate about its success, as he and Miss O'Callaghan go riding off together in the horse-drawn cab after leaving the Conroys off at the Gresham, but it is possible that he will have had better romantic luck with his song than Gabriel does with the serenade he and Gretta inadvertently overhear.

Yet the text, elevating the badly sung performance of *The Lass of Aughrim* to a climactic and emotionally affective and effective moment in the story, conversely discredits another musical performance whose splendor even the narrator concedes. The narrator and the assembled company, who had earlier barely listened to Mary Jane's academy piece, listen attentively to Julia Morkan's performance of *Arrayed for the Bridal*, and the narrator pays her the extraordinary compliment, "To follow the voice, without looking at the singer's face, was to feel and share the excitement of swift and secure flight" (D 193). The narrative voice nearly lets itself get carried away for a moment, although, in a telling gesture, the narration has closed its eyes, separating sound and sight, ear and eye, precisely in order to separate the female voice and face respectively into the beautiful and the ugly. But because the narration "sees" her largely through Gabriel's eyes, sees her as old and moribund ("Poor Aunt Julia! She, too, would soon be a shade. . . . He had caught that haggard look upon her face for a moment when she was singing *Arrayed for the Bridal*" [D 222]), the text colludes with dismissing Julia as insignificant and depreciating her art. Moments after having waxed nearly ecstatic over her singing—"To follow the voice . . . was to feel and share the excitement of swift and secure flight"—the narration begins to ambiguate her highly enthusiastic reception ("Gabriel applauded loudly with all the others at the close of the song and loud applause was borne in from the invisible supper-table" [D 193]) by remarking that the applause "sounded so genuine," implying either that it wasn't or that Julia was sceptical about its sincerity. Further, Julia's most fulsome praise comes from the two men who are treated as a comical or clownish pair by the narration, and Freddy Malins's immense, sincere praise "I never heard you sing so well, never . . . I never heard your voice sound so fresh and so . . . so clear and fresh, never" is cancelled by Browne's facetious, "Miss Julia Morkan, my latest discovery!" [D 193]. Why should the applause not be sincere, and why should praise of Julia's singing be undermined when there is absolutely nothing in the text to contradict the narrative account of her singing as absolutely superb? I will argue that the company at the party will not let a homely old woman be a great artist, and neither will the text. The narration, caught off guard and surprised by Julia's singing, blurts out its honestly thrilled appraisal, as does the company in its long applause. But the praise is almost instantly qualified and retracted by everyone but Freddy as soon as its implications for the social real are grasped: that the people and narrative voice might need to stop patronizing Julia, might need to revise all their prejudices and stereotypes and give her esteem as the supreme artist among them.

The extent to which this deliberate suppression of the possibility that Julia produced a singing of extraordinary beauty, a musical triumph, is carried over into the male criticism of the text, can be seen most dramatically in what was perhaps the most vexing of the deliberate textual misrepresentations in John Huston's film version of "The Dead." The film renders Julia's performance of *Arrayed for the Bridal* as pathetically dreadful and painfully embarrassing, though Huston seemed to find her pathos "sad." The film's representation deliberately violates and contradicts the clear and unequivocal direction of Joyce's text on how Julia's song is sung: "Her voice, strong and clear in tone, attacked with great spirit the runs which embellish the air and though she sang very rapidly she did not miss even the smallest of the grace notes" (D 193). In the film, her voice is made thin, cracking, and quavery, and Julia sings neither in tempo nor in tune. Furthermore, the film destroyed an opportunity that the text does not possess: of demonstrating that *Arrayed for the Bridal* is a fiendishly difficult piece whose singing is an operatic *tour de force*. Compared to the simple and miniscule range of the ballad tonality of *The Lass of Aughrim*, Julia tackles a major operatic challenge, and the film could have dramatized what the text implies but suppresses: that as a genuine musical talent Julia is probably far superior to the celebrated Bartell d'Arcy. I urge sceptics to listen to the New Hutchinson Family Singers' performance of *Arrayed for the Bridal* (a song adapted by George Linley from the melody *"Son vergin vezzosa"* in Bellini's opera *I Puritani*) and ask themselves whether a performance of this song, which requires a coloratura soprano of extraordinary range and flexibility, sung very rapidly and accurately in a strong clear voice, would not represent an impressive achievement. And, as if he wanted to ensure that this point not be missed, Joyce corroborates it in *Ulysses*, using the judgment of a man who does know professional singing, and who has heard her sing: Leopold Bloom. *"There is not in this wide world a vallee,"* Bloom remembers, "Great song of Julia Morkan's. Kept her voice up to the very last. Pupil of Michael Balfe's, wasn't she?" (U 8:416). But the Huston film blatantly ignores the narrative descriptions of Julia Morkan's musical performance as stunning, and Bartell D'Arcy's as miserable, and reverses them to make them conform to the very gender stereotypes with respect to art that the text goes to pains to discredit. So do readers and critics let the text's retroactive scepticism influence them into depreciating Julia's talent. We wonder instead what Julia and her song are a symbol of, letting ourselves be diverted by the incongruity of its bridal motif to her aged spinsterhood,[9] without heeding either the artistic significance of her performance, or the political significance of its silencing.

Joyce's text, as art, reproduces the social ideology that devalues female talent and depreciates female art. But Joyce inscribes into the oppressive discourse of his narration a "back answer" that will be stifled, to be sure, but that at least manages to write in the clearest, most factual, historical terms the formal institutionalization of the abolition of female art. The beauty of Julia's voice is professionally silenced by a simple, authoritative act of patriarchal gender privilege: Pope Pius X's pronouncement on 22 November 1903, in *Motu Proprio*, that the singing of church music constituted a liturgical function for which women were ineligible and that henceforth soprano and alto voices must be produced by young boys (Reichert,

Senn, Zimmer 269). The date of this edict is significant, not only because it allows Torchiana to date the story's events as occurring in early January of 1904 (Torchiana argues for Wednesday, 6 January 1904 [225]), but because it further invites us to speculate that Julia Morkan is a perverse martyr to art, killed by sex discrimination, the victim of a species of ecclesiastical murder. I don't claim to be able to "prove" a causal link between the church edict of November 1903 and Julia Morkan's death by 16 June 1904—that is, within months of the papal destruction of her career. But I believe the text does prod us to interrogate a "lie" the narration tells us right in the beginning, when it claims "Julia, though she was quite grey, was still the leading soprano in Adam and Eve's" (D 176). Kate Morkan will contradict this statement in her bitter complaint about Julia's papal ouster from the choir ("it's not at all honourable for the pope to turn out the women out of the choirs that have slaved there all their lives and put little whipper-snappers of boys over their heads" [D 194]), and if Julia sings in the choir at all any more, it is certainly not as its lead soprano.[10] The opening narration of the story then conceals that this particular Morkan Christmas party will be different from all the others because it follows within weeks of a trauma whose dimensions for the Morkan sisters include something like personal, professional, theological, and economic violence. Julia's ouster, by papal edict, on the basis of her sex and without regard to either her talent or her service, from the church choir after thirty years of service, may well account for what is 'wrong' with her throughout the story: the dark shadows in her flaccid face, the haggard look, the way she is 'out of it' throughout the evening. The pre-Christmas ouster may also give Julia's performance of *Arrayed for the Bridal* on the evening of the party a particularly poignant significance: it may have been her last, a swan song of particular humiliation, as stripped of her artistic profession she is degraded back to amateur status and relegated to parlor performance. The debasement inflicted on her by a Church she has so faithfully served is particularly cruel in light of the possibility that, trained by Michael Balfe—perhaps Ireland's most famous musical figure—she sacrificed the promise of having her rare coloratura soprano make her a *prima donna* like the one in Mr. Browne's story, whose carriage was unyoked by the gallery boys of the old Royal and pulled through the streets of Dublin. Instead of the concert stage where she belonged—she herself meekly owns that "Thirty years ago I hadn't a bad voice as voices go"—Julia Morkan seems to have ended up "slaving there in that choir night and day, night and day. Six o'clock on Christmas morning! And all for what?" (D 194), her talent wasted in marginalized and unappreciated musical labor. "I often told Julia, said Aunt Kate emphatically, that she was simply thrown away in that choir" (D 194), and so the Morkan sisters are left with a pompous nephew who considers them ignorant old women, and a spineless niece who nearly publicly insults her aunts in the interest of toadying to her clients.

Kate Morkan's protest of the pope's politically oppressive act, and her outrage at the injustice inflicted on her sister are, I believe, Joyce's equivalent to Nora's discursive assumption of selfhood in Ibsen's *Doll's House*. But the narration takes its cue from the brutally patronizing Mary Jane, who stifles Kate's "back answer" as an infantile tantrum ("when we are hungry we are all very quarrelsome" [D 195]), and treats the whole episode as silly. If the narration tries to conceal from the reader an important truth about the oppression of the female artist, Joyce nonetheless gives Kate Morkan a moment of outraged voice, whose immediate stifling should attract our notice and concern and serve as our wedge for forcing a larger critique of the narration. The pope's patent injustice to her sister, to women, shakes Kate Morkan to the point of heresy: "I suppose it is for the good of the Church if the pope does it. But it's not just, Mary Jane, and it's not right" (D 194). Kate virtually challenges papal infallibility (announced by the First Vatican Council in 1870, less than thirty-five years before) with this protest, and her heresy alarms Mary Jane sufficiently to shame her aunt into silence by reminding her that she is "giving scandal" to the Protestant Mr. Browne. Joyce—who according to Groden's chronology in the *Archive* wrote "The Dead" in 1907, and began the writing of *A Portrait of the Artist as a Young Man* in September of the same year—is aware, I believe, that he is drawing here a highly ironic parallel between two artists thwarted by religion in pursuit of their artistic vocations. He semaphores the adolescent boy's traumas at the hands of the Church—pandy-batted as a child, terrorized by a retreat sermon, upbraided for heresy in class and beaten by his friends for defending Byron—into a spiritual oppression of epic proportions, culminating in a heroic and dramatic *Non Serviam* at the novel's end. Stephen's "back answers" are treated very differently from those of women. "The Dead"'s version of an ecclesiastical oppression much more pointed and tragic in its effects—an arbitrary and unconscionable act that nullifies a lifetime of devotion and labor, that treats Julia's sacrifice and dedication of a great talent to God and his Church as a female impertinence, that deprives an aging single woman of her livelihood—is treated as a comic triviality, and the spiritual mutiny it precipitates in her sister's heart is treated as a childish tantrum.[11]

Joyce was not blind to the cruel irony he has his texts produce, nor to the difficulty of driving it home to his readers against the grain of a disavowing narration. Knowing that we are likely to follow the text's collusion in dismissing Aunt Julia and Aunt Kate as comic relief to Gabriel's *angsts*, Joyce devises a second maneuver to repeat and reinforce the political point the sisters dramatize, when he has Freddy Malins rise to the defense of the negro chieftain at the *Gaiety*. The scholarly problems of legitimating Freddy's critical judgment are so vexed—it is difficult to establish whether G. H. Elliott, the presumed singer referred to, is either a tenor or black[12]—that I think it best to judge Freddy's argument on its abstract merits rather than to put it to historical proof. Should Freddy be considered wrong in his aesthetic impartiality that first acknowledges the beauty of an old woman's singing, and later decries the injustice of barring black singers from the legitimate operatic stage on the basis of race? "And why couldn't he have a voice too? asked Freddy Malins sharply. Is it because he's only a black?" (D 198). Why, indeed? Freddy's protest against racial discrimination is not so easily dismissed by either the company or the reader as his protest against gender and age discrimination—practices that seem to have been far better internalized and naturalized in his society. But it, too, is stifled, and Mary Jane, leading her protesting aunts to the dinner table, where their distaff domestic responsibilities will divert them from their political grievances, and leading Freddy Malins' conversation back to "legitimate opera," from which the illegitimate voices of black singers are banished, leads the narration, too, back to essentialist notions of art that aspire to stifle political protests.

Joyce understands perfectly, I believe, that art reproduces political ideology and social relations. He also understands, I believe, that it is establishment art's first aim to disavow just this fact about itself, in order to disavow its reproduction of social oppressions. By eschewing using his art polemically to criticize social oppressiveness, Joyce is able to critique art's own oppressive practices. He has his text, on the one hand, maintain implicit faith in an essentialist aesthetics—a faith that art is above politics—while disrupting it with incidents that show that art is the product of social forces that operate on the same principles of privilege and exclusion that categories such as gender, race, class, and age produce in other areas of social and cultural life. By inscribing in his disavowing narration a series of linked and analogous "back answers" or protests that trouble the text and cause it to stifle them in collusion with characters who do the same, Joyce stages art's censorship of its own oppressiveness.

CHAPTER SIX

Narration under a Blindfold:
Reading the "Patch" of "Clay"

"CLAY" WILL BE A "patch" of *Joyce's Web* that I will explore as a text that functions like a bandaged wound, a blindfold to prevent painful seeing, a futile piece of mending that tries but fails to fool people into believing there is no tear. The trope of the "patch" is meant also to conjure up the emblem of genteel poverty, the attempt to bridge the gap between class circumstance and class desire, as discursive attempt to claim possession of the virtues and values—if not the material resources—of the middle class. I will use "Clay" then as an ur-patch that is subsequently raveled and rewoven in Joyce's later texts. "Nausicaa" will rework all of its major features: the Homeric laundry, the old maid, the children's play, the illusory courtship, the concealed deformity, the oscillation between display and blindness, the mimic discourse and the gestured pantomime—all these elements of "Clay" are revisited and reworked in "Nausicaa." *Finnegans Wake* again ravels "Clay," splitting the laundry and the children's games into two contiguous chapters, "Anna Livia Plurabelle" (I.8) and "The Mime of Mick, Nick, and the Maggies" (II.1) that deepen "Clay"'s wounds and fissures and retrieve from its silences much that it elides: the labor of the washerwomen and the lot of children. The "patch" as symptom of ruptured self-knowledge—whether as ideological screen hiding the truth of selfhood socially oppressed, or as Lacanian prattle concealing the truth of psychic sexual wounds—is troped as the eye-patch, with which Joyce in later life became painfully familiar, the blindfold or "bandage" which protects the injured ontological eye. These interwoven chapters of old maid, washerwomen, and children tend to be marked discursively by the applications and removals of epistemological blindfolds—making readers, like Maria, oscillate between groping in the dark or painful "seeing." Joyce still has the trope explicitly in mind when he drafts "The Mime of Mick, Nick, and the Maggies": the very first sketch of the chapter is titled "Blindman's Buff" and later

describes "⊏ blindfold.□.X vident." (JA 47482 a.2). By the writing
of the "Mime" Joyce is still raveling the children's game of "Clay,"
and this incessant and never-ending raveling presses Joyce's most
sophisticated narrative and generic experiments into service as ideological critique, in order to dramatically implicate discourse as a
tool of social power and control.

"Clay" is a "deceptively" simple little story by design: its narrative self-deception attempts, and fails, to mislead the reader. But as
a special case of the blind leading the blind, "Clay" also offers the
multiple revelations that come with the restoration of sight: it allows us to see the blind spots in Maria's story, and in them, to see
ourselves as their cause, if not their instrument. Joyce displays a
surprising philosophical and technical maturity in this very early
work, whose object is, I believe, to dramatize the powerful workings
of desire in human discourse and human lives. In "Clay" this desire,
whatever its etiology, must contend with the symbolic valorizations
that attach to socially constructed categories of inclusion and exclusion: class, gender, age, and normative figurations of the body. The
perfect protagonist for this purpose is indeed *the old maid:* a figure
who seems to lack everything and therefore embodies total desire, a
desire for the recognition and prestige that would let a poor old
woman without family, wealth, or social standing maintain her human status in paralytic Dublin, and that would let her story be cred-
ited by those who hear it. "Clay" will attempt to mislead the reader,
and it fails when we become deaf, as it were, and start seeing.

In addition to its textual functions, the narrational manipulations
of "Clay" produce extra-textual effects as well. Let me demonstrate.
In developing an allegory of Maria as "the Poor Old Woman or Ireland herself," William York Tindall writes, "Shopkeepers conde-
scend to her; and when a British colonel is polite to her on the tram,
she loses her cake" (30). A British colonel? The narration tells us
only that "Maria thought he was a colonel-looking gentleman and
she reflected how much more polite he was than the young men
who simply stared straight before them" (D 102). Tindall has risen
to the narrative bait and has swallowed Maria's efforts to inflate the
bumptious attentions of a garrulous old drunk into the courtly devoirs of a gentleman of rank from the ruling class. He never questions, for example, what a British colonel in prerepublican Ireland
would be doing on the Drumcondra tram in mufti. This small mistake is quite unimportant in itself,[1] but it is symptomatic of a larger
impulse in the critical history of the story which, curiously, precisely mirrors Maria's own quest. Readers and critics of the story
can no more accept the possibility of Maria's insignificance than can

Maria herself. The impulse behind the critical tradition of "Clay," with its heavy emphasis on allegorizing Maria in some form—as either Witch or Blessed Virgin, for example—is therefore a curiously collusive response to the story's rhetorical aim of aggrandizing Maria. This allegorizing tendency extends beyond the boundaries of the story to a strain in Joyce criticism as a whole that Attridge and Ferrer call the "transcendentalist" approach to Joyce's fiction (5), and that they trace back to T. S. Eliot's influence as a critic of Joyce. The motives impelling its allegorizing strategies include the need to save modern fiction from charges of triviality, vulgarity, and nihilism, by assimilating it to larger symbolic orders and traditionally sanctioned systems of value. But behind its quasi-religious motivation, Eliot's transcendental aesthetics are impelled by a class ideology that equates the spiritual torpor of modernity with the material squalor of its masses. Joyce, however, explores in "Clay" the psychopolitics of one of the least significant members of such an urban mass.

The critical need to create significance out of pointlessness also shapes the readings that most of my students have been taught before they come to my classes: specifically, that the meaning of the story depends on interpreting the "clay" as "death"—as though this constituted some sort of punch line, some sort of illumination that makes sense of an otherwise meaningless joke. "Death" is, of course, a privileged figure in medieval allegory, and, in this interpretation, Maria's failure to perceive its prophetic beckoning through the symbols of the game makes her—all evidence of her sincere Catholic piety to the contrary—a kind of vain and foolish *Jedermann*. But the reading of "clay" as "death" is anomalous within the context of the story, for even if All Hallow Eve is the night the dead walk abroad in folk tradition,[2] thought of death is conspicuously absent both from the narration and from its representation of Maria's thoughts. When Joyce does want a story read through a tropology of "death" (as in "The Dead" or in "Hades"), he weaves a complex texture of incident and allusion to guide us to his meaning.

I will suggest a different way of reading "Clay" that takes its cue from the interpretive backfire that reveals at the heart of the desire for significance the operation of its lack. The critics' need to capitalize Maria, to transform her negative attributes into positive symbols—from poor old woman into Poor Old Woman, from witch-like into Witch, from virginal into Blessed Virgin—betray how little esteem the social construct of the ungarnished old maid is able to muster. It is not Joyce, I will argue, who promotes the old maid to metaphoric status as much as he explores her need, and her strategies, for promoting herself. These strategies are narrational and rhetorical, as "Clay" becomes her defense against her interiorization of all the derision and contempt that has been her traditional portion as a spinster in a country that in the century following the Great Famine "had the highest rate of unmarried men and women in the world" (Walzl 33; Lowe-Evans). To the extent it fails, the reader is implicated and functions as a critical actor in the story. Joyce dramatizes the social consequences and psychological costs of *feeling oneself designated as insignificant* as a repressive force that splits all the discursive elements of the story in two: the story's subject, its narrative mode, and its reader. Maria divides into two versions of herself (into admirable and pathetic, bourgeois and proletarian, Lady Bountiful and victim), the narration is split in two (into testimonial and exposé, prattle and pantomime, empty language and expressive silence), and the reader is split in two (into gullible narratee and cynical critic, flattered ear and penetrating gaze, consumer of realism and dupe of naturalism). This fractured discourse of "Clay" is produced by the interplay between the two senses of *significance* working through the text: *significance* as an experience of psychological importance or ontological prestige, and *significance* as the linguistic or semiological meaning produced by modes of signification. It is the exigencies of the first (Maria's need to be significant) that brings about the manipulations of the second, as though the text were trying to control its own meaning because its interpretation *mattered* to Maria.

At this point it is necessary to emphasize two theoretical points about the nature of desire that help to account for the curious "social" function of the narration of "Clay" and for the phantasmal nature of the narrative voice. In metaphysical terms, desire is always born out of an imaginary lack, and desire is therefore always desire for recognition.[3] Maria's lacks are imaginary because, like everyone, as an organism she is a plenum, she has everything sufficient for life, and the things she lacks (marriage, wealth, class, beauty) exist only symbolically, in the significance they have for her: a significance itself grounded in their desirability to others. Maria is victimized by class and gender ideology, and it is in the way sexual attributes become socially codified and significant—the way the difference between male and female, sexually active and celibate, fertile and barren, for example, becomes ontologically as well as semiotically significant within the symbolic order of her society—that Maria, as old maid, is made especially to suffer. *Of course* being an unmarried, childless, and virginal woman doesn't make Maria intrinsically less valuable. But it does endow her, in her social world, with a negative prestige whose consequences are encoded even in something as trivial as a card game that treats the Old Maid as the nightmare image of undesirability, whose visitation is greeted with dread and disgust as though she could spread her own negativity, her status as loser, to all she touches. It is, in fact, a different children's game that Maria plays in "Clay": a game of divination that foretells the future life of young virgins (JJ 158), a future whose state-of-life symbols (ring and prayer book, for example) express the semiology of sexually marked and unmarked states. Maria's inappropriate inclusion in the game—she is, after all, an adult and already has a life—betrays the way a sexually unmarked life, a life negatively marked as virginal, is treated by her society as a life perpetually deferred.

The symptoms the old maid's lacks produce are therefore not solitary brooding and depression, but social strategies designed to capture significance by winning the approval of the "other." This theoretical background helps to shape a more precise explanation for the sense we have, that although "Clay" is narrated in the third person, it is *really* Maria speaking. I would formulate it this way: narrative speech in "Clay" is, for the most part, uttered in the language of Maria's desire; it is Maria's desire speaking. And because it is the function of the narration to restore significance to Maria, it preserves the triangular structure of an eavesdropped conversation: the narrative voice of "Clay" describes Maria as she would like to catch someone speaking about her to someone else. Expressed differently, the narration is putatively directed toward us, to tell us about Maria, but its true beneficiary is Maria herself, whose prestige is certified by being "recognized" by objective and anonymous "others." This imaginary social function of the narration is demonstrated with an explicit and literate double in "A Little Cloud" (a story with which "Clay" was conjoined in its earliest draft as "Christmas Eve") in which Chandler imagines flattering reviews of verses he has yet to write—"He began to invent sentences and phrases from the notices which his book would get. '*Mr Chandler has the gift of easy and graceful verse*'" (D 74). "Clay"'s narration has its analogue in Chandler's invention of flattering "English critics" for his hypothetical writing. The personification of "Clay"'s narrative voice, if we were to construct a "narrator" from these functions, would produce an impossible social hybrid—a creature that is simultaneously Maria's social superior (like the authoritative and eloquent Protestant matron) and her metaphysical inferior (as loyally committed to her admiration and protection as the "vassals and serfs" of her song). This is why the narration is ultimately so counterproductive on its errand of desire. It is as though Maria sends us an inadequate signifier to extol her merits: a servant in the penetrable disguise of master. It is not the narrator, but her paltry stratagem itself, that betrays Maria's ontological plight.

Some of the distinctive features of "Clay"'s narration can now be explained in terms of its function of gratifying Maria's desire for recognition. Its rhetoric is shaped to restore to Maria, discursively, everything that might seem to constitute a social "lack" for her—beauty, husband, children, home, wealth, status—albeit with the qualifications and feints of psychological realism. Restored, these things remain as imaginary as when they were "lacks," but they allow Maria to feel *as though* she possessed them, as though she enjoyed the security of wealth ("how much better it was to be independent and to have your own money in your pocket" [D 102]) and the affection of a family ("he had wanted her to go and live with them" [D 100]); as though she had emotional, if not biological, children ("but Maria is my proper mother" [D 100]) and enough attractiveness for her purposes ("she found it a nice tidy little body" [D 101]). The effect of these restorations is to create a version of Maria's condition that she presumably would like to believe, although the narration does not ultimately succeed in making it tenable. According to this, Maria is a well-bred, middle-class, maiden lady living on a small but independent income from a job that earns her the respect of co-workers and superiors. Though unmarried, and, of course, childless, she enjoys the affection of a surrogate family that had once employed her more as a governess than as a domestic, and that still cherishes her as a favorite sort of godmother who visits them laden with gifts. This version of Maria's life is contradicted by a second, repressed version that is never articulated in the narrative speech, but must be read in the narrative silences, ruptures, and evasions that lie between the lines, or in the margins of the text, so to speak, and that constitute the smudged and effaced portions of the "Clay" palimpsest. According to this second, unconscious version which she "knows" but does not "recognize," Maria works long hours for meager pay as a scullion in a laundry for reformed prostitutes who make her the butt of their jokes. She is ignored and patronized by everyone, including the family whose slavey she once was, and from whom she succeeds in extorting only a minimal and ritualized tolerance by manipulating their guilt and pity. These two versions are intrinsically related, and it is important to remember that they are both psychically *authored* (but not *authorized*) by Maria. The first, positive version functions to replace and abolish the second, whose "truth" about her insignificance Maria finds intolerable. It fails in spite of the inestimable advantage of being articulated in speech. Maria's fears can utter the negative version of her life, her paranoid "truth," only in silent semiologies: a wince, a blush, a lost object, a moment of forgetfulness, a mistake. "Clay"'s narration becomes a psychological *mise en scène* in which desire is attacked from within.

The drama that transpires within the narrative speech of "Clay" inevitably triggers a hermeneutical drama that fragments and conflicts the reader. Although I will reify this reader as "we" in my discussion of the story, I intend the plural to encompass not only the collectivity of actual readers, but also the multiplicity of roles that the "reader" as a fictional construct of the story embodies: such roles as the gullible narratee, the skeptical critic, the self-reflexive meta-reader. "Clay" also utilizes, I believe, the extent to which the reader has been historically constructed by novelistic convention. "Clay"'s narratee, for example, the putative listener who believes that Maria's life is simple, but good and admirable, embodies the ideology of a docile consumer of nineteenth-century narrative conventions. This interpretation reflects the fiction of Victorian fiction: that mousy governesses and plain dependents, the Jane Eyres and Esther Summersons, can become the heroes of their lives and stories by their everyday acts and virtues—a fiction cruelly subverted by Flaubert in "Un Coeur Simple." But as discrepancies mount between what is said and what is shown, the reader is transformed into a critical gaze, hostile to Maria's desire in its determination to see her not as she wishes to be seen, but *as she wishes not to be seen.* This vision corresponds to the aims and methods of naturalism, as it exposes beneath bourgeois desire and delusion the occluded squalor and humiliation in the lives of the poor. Where the reader as narratee hears the testimonials of Maria's admiring co-workers, for example, the reader as critic sees old prostitutes amuse themselves at her expense. But Joyce ultimately subjects even this naturalistic "truth" to a final interrogative twist that causes the text to reflect the reader's smug superiority like a mirror. In the end, the reader of "Clay" is read by the text.

The reader's collusions and defections from the narrative agenda are partly conditioned by the authority (and its erosion) of the narrative voice. "Clay" could not be narrated in the first person, by Maria herself, because if Maria is really as insignificant as she (unconsciously) believes, we would undoubtedly dismiss her flattering version of herself as empty boasting or wishful thinking. Furthermore, the narration engenders doubt as to whether Maria could speak for herself. She is, after all, quoted directly only in her reactive speech, as affirming or disclaiming the statements of others, "*Yes, my dear,*" and "*No, my dear.*" We don't know if her elided "actual" speech would possess the refinement of accent and diction required to convey the favorable impression that is its object. It makes sense, therefore, to imagine Maria implicitly inventing, or wishing she could invent, a spokesperson who will speak *for* her (while pretending to speak *of* her) in the ways she cannot speak for herself. This narrator (the fictitious embodiment of this invented or wished-for narrative voice) must therefore be rendered respectable, and to this end an important strategy in the arsenal of desire is produced: imitation. The narrative voice probably does not speak in the language of Maria's actual class—whose diction can't be verified from the text—but in the idiom of someone mimicking the accents of respectable bourgeois folks, like the matron of the *Dublin by Lamplight* laundry—"so genteel." In this, the narration of "Clay" operates precisely on Hugh Kenner's "Uncle Charles Principle" insofar as "'The Uncle Charles Principle' entails writing about someone much as that someone would choose to be written about" (*Joyce's Voices* 21). The gentility of Maria's attitudes and opinions—with its optimistic accentuation of the positive ("she found it a nice tidy little body" [D 101]) and its polite circumlocutions ("how easy it was to know a gentleman even when he has a drop taken" [D 103])—represents, if not the language of the bourgeoisie, then Maria's notion of both the sentiment and the phrasing of proper middle class speech. Maria's speech and "Clay"'s narration are symptomatic of what Marcuse called "affirmative culture": a society that lets art compensate its shortcomings. R. B. Kershner writes of this language "If 'Counterparts' is a paradigm of linguistic aggression, 'Clay' is the model of affirmative appeasement" (105).

The narrative voice further buttresses its credibility by producing documentation of Maria's prestige in the form of testimonials from witnesses in all strata of her world. Strategically clustered at the beginning of the narration, in order to create a favorable first impression, these testimonials are curiously self-canceling because each tribute to Maria appears to depend on pushing aside an unpleasant reality in her world. One of the laundry women, for example, will certify Maria's influence and moral persuasion in language that inflates Maria's diplomatic skill by setting it in an implied climate of bullying and violence—"And Ginger Mooney was always saying what she wouldn't do to the dummy who had charge of the irons if it wasn't for Maria" (D 99). The cook illustrates Maria's domestic skill by replacing with an aesthetic image ("the cook said you could see yourself in the big copper boilers" [D 99]) the grim visage of Maria's drudgery as she scours and scrubs the pots

to make them shiny. But the most prestigious testimonial comes
from a witness in authority whose commendation is quoted verba-
tim—"One day the matron had said to her:—Maria, you are a veritable peace-maker!" (99). Maria's peace-making, the estimation of
the matron, and the matron's fine vocabulary—"veritable"—are all
paraded here, and any remaining skeptics are offered additional cor-
roboration—"And the sub-matron and two of the Board ladies had
heard the compliment" (D 99). But not only does this lavish praise
for Maria's intervention paradoxically draw attention to the chronic
quarrelling and dissension that seem to necessitate it: later narrative
events sharply dispute these claims for its success by dramatizing
just the opposite. Maria's meddling into the Donnelly brothers'
quarrel nearly kindles a marital fight. We may hear of her peace-
making, but we see these efforts prolong and multiply discord.

This complimentary prattle becomes exposed as empty words
about the self that fill the space of Maria's insecurities as soon as we
confront the censored blanks in the narrative discourse. The first of
these occurs when a string of pleasantries about the *Dublin by
Lamplight* laundry is punctured by a curious complaint: "There was
one thing she didn't like and that was the tracts on the walls; but
the matron was such a nice person to deal with, so genteel" (D 100).
The text creates a series of related enigmas about the laundry: that
it has a puzzling religious and institutional character rather than a
more logical commercial nature, and that pious Maria is inexplicably offended by a religious text on its walls. This informational
gap clearly defines the story's narratee as a *naïf* who will be im-
pressed by the elegant Ballsbridge address, but whose ignorance
about the precise nature of *Dublin by Lamplight* can be exploited
to Maria's good account. Groping for an explanation, the puzzle
about Maria's complaint diverts the narratee's attention from the
nature of the laundry and draws it to the only difference that seems
to signify: the sectarian difference between Catholic and Protestant.
The complaint is interpreted as another of Maria's virtues, a theological virtue, no less, in the form of her Catholic orthodoxy af-
fronted by Protestant bible-thumping. Only the reader armed with
the knowledge that *Dublin by Lamplight* was a charitable institution for reformed prostitutes (Beck 204) can foil this narrative stratagem and discover what it conceals: that Maria knows the kind of
place that is her home, that the tracts on the walls are a constant
reminder of that fact—even if she could overlook the vulgarity and
the violence of the women, and that anyone who visits her at the
laundry finds its status as a laundered whorehouse advertised on its

walls. It is worth noting the skill of the narrative voice in keeping the true nature of the laundry a secret, and its cunning in remarking, but disguising, Maria's discomfort with it.

If we explore the semiotics of Maria's complaint just a little further, however, its structure as a censored blank comes into even clearer focus. The laundry's scandal—the sexual promiscuity whose abolition is its premise—is communicated to us through a series of displaced negations or effacements. The narrator transforms us, in a sense, into a myopic or blind person, confronted by a wall we cannot see that contains writing we cannot read—although we are given to understand that it is there. The blindfold motif is thus introduced as a structure of reading before it becomes thematized in the children's game later in the story, the children's game set in Drumcondra, famous (as Torchiana tells us [160]) for housing St. Joseph's Asylum for the Blind. If we could read the tract on the wall of the laundry (as Klaus Reichert, Fritz Senn, and Dieter Zimmer hypothetically read the motto of *Dublin by Lamplight* laundry: 2 Timothy, 2:26, "that they may recover themselves from the snare of the devil, to whose will they are held captive" [253; my translation]) we would find in the text only the erasure of the vice, the bleaching of the stain, as it were, in the exhortation to reform that is its message. But we, as readers, are given to read all of this only through the disapproval in Maria's eye as she gazes at walls we do not see.

The transitional passages that relate Maria's journey from Ballsbridge to Drumcondra reflect an apparent narrational shift to accommodate a changing ontological perspective of Maria. The laundry and the Donnelly home represent sheltered interior spaces in which Maria appears to be socially encoded in flattering and affectionate terms as valued co-worker and dear family friend. But her journey thrusts Maria—anonymously and without credentials—into an outer world of crowded trams and frenetic shoppers in which she must make her way existentially, without the help of flattering testimonials. The narrative voice is obliged to adopt a seemingly existential mode in this section, relying on description as much as on interpretation, and reporting action as much as attitude. This makes the manipulation of the reader's favorable response more difficult—a problem that produces a set of self-correcting narrative maneuvers. The narration really only *seems* more objective in this section, and while this lends it a particularly credible sound, it exerts itself no less in Maria's service. Whenever the narration cannot quite prevent us from catching glimpses of unflattering external perceptions of Maria, our attention is quickly diverted from the potentially critical eyes of strangers to Maria's laudable mental apparatus. For example, the determined objectivity of the report "The tram was full and she had to sit on the little stool at the end of the car, facing all the people, with her toes barely touching the floor" (D 102), risks implying that the passengers might have found her pathetic sitting there "facing all the people," like a child on a dunce stool, and that she might have felt her conspicuous shortness ("her toes barely touching the floor") uncomfortably exposed. But the eyes of the strangers are occluded by a deft narrative move into Maria's mind, where we find no painful self-consciousness whatsoever as she busily tends her affairs ("She arranged in her mind all she was going to do"), cheers herself with happy anticipation, and weaves concern over the Donnelly boys' fraternal quarrel into home-spun philosophy: "but such was life" (D 102).

It is not until we see Maria hopelessly dithering about between the two cake shops that we begin to suspect flaws and distractions in her putative mental composure. If she already "arranged in her mind all she was going to do" on the tram, why does she only begin to tackle her major decision of the evening, what treat to buy the Donnelly parents, when she has already finished her shopping in Downes' cake-shop? Standing outside the shop she begins her deliberations from scratch, "Then she thought what else would she buy: she wanted to buy something really nice. They would be sure to have plenty of apples and nuts. It was hard to know what to buy and all she could think of was cake" (D 102). *Of course* all she could think of was cake—having just come out of a cake-shop after a protracted wait! A series of revisionist questions suggest themselves at this point. Was Maria distracted in her planning on the tram by the critical stare of the other passengers? Was it really the scanty icing on the Downes' plumcakes that prompts her to visit another shop or is it her embarrassment and annoyance at having to re-enter a shop that had served her rather tardily only moments before? Once she decides on plumcake, why does she vacillate so much in the Henry Street store that she earns a smart prod from the clerk? The narrative voice mentions only the stylish saleslady and Maria in the shop, but it does not actually say that they are alone. Is the shop crowded with people who look on testily while Maria takes forever making her decision? I ask these questions to draw attention to the incompleteness and illogicality of what is narrated. The narrator's assertion of Maria's composure is often at odds with the depictions of her nervous and disorganized behavior—and the reader must decide whether to trust the narrative speech or the narrated gestures. However, notwithstanding the gaps that invite the investigation of the increasingly skeptical reader, the narrative voice still ably pro-

tects Maria from exposure at this point—covering even her self-
betraying blush at the clerk's sarcastic wedding reference with an
elaborate courtship anecdote as the narration continues on the
Drumcondra tram.

If the revisionist reading of the shopping incidents are initiated
entirely by the critical reader, the narration itself offers an initial
version of what happened on the Drumcondra tram that is subsequently revised in a way that exposes the first account—so flattering to Maria—to have functioned as a "lie." We are given an anecdote of gallantry that mitigates the sense we may have received
earlier—through Maria's defensiveness ("she didn't want any ring or
man either" [D 101]) and the revealing blush at the clerk's offer of
wedding cake—that she suffers from a painful and humiliating
sense of unmarriagability. But the small vignette on the tram portrays Maria as not only pleasing enough to still attract the attentions of a distinguished ("colonel-looking") gentleman, but as capable of entertaining his courtesies with perfectly well-bred ease and
aplomb, "favoured him with demure nods and hems" . . . "thanked
him and bowed" (D 103). His tipsy-ness is mentioned only as a
trivial afterthought embedded in an exoneration—"she thought
how easy it was to know a gentleman even when he has a drop
taken" (D 103). But later, when the forgotten plumcake is missed,
we receive a different version of Maria's reaction, one that the narrative voice had, in fact, concealed from us—"Maria, remembering
how confused the gentleman with the greyish moustache had made
her, coloured with shame and vexation" (D 103). This "confusion,"
and the blush of remembrance it evokes, bears witness to a riot of
hopeful, painful, uncontrollable feeling that erupts in Maria at every
mention of the subject of marriage—a subject one had assumed was
long ago serenely settled as outside her realm of plausible possibilities. We are now invited to recognize that the narrative prose, with
its genteel accents, had been giving us the romantic distortions of
Maria's desire: the wish to see in a fat, flushed, old drunk, a courtly
gentleman whose military bearing is a metonymic expansion of a
grey moustache, and whose social imbibing ("when he has a drop
taken") a synecdochic contraction of intemperate swilling.

It is important to ask why the narrative voice would tell us the
"truth" about Maria's encounter with the colonel-looking gentleman—namely, that he aroused "confused" feelings in Maria—after
having troubled to conceal or censor just that fact in the first place.
The answer is that the narration does not technically "lie" in the
sense of deliberately concealing a known fact, but rather exhibits
the "blind spot" that is the epistemological consequence of desire:

that as we look for a glorified image of ourselves in the admiring eye of the other, we fail to see ourselves as we are at that moment, as seekers of glorified self-reflections in others' eyes. As the language of her desire, Maria's narration is doomed to fail in its attempt to direct and control how others see her precisely because it has such a "blind spot" and cannot, therefore, entirely manipulate the truth about herself—or itself. Her narration cannot see itself as a language of desire, as it were: it cannot see the insecurities and fears that are its source. The forgotten plumcake catches both Maria and her narrative voice off-guard, and causes the narrative voice, shaken by Maria's discomposure, to blurt out a series of damaging revelations: Maria's hidden excitement on the tram, her urgent need to trade scant resources for good will ("At the thought of the failure of her little surprise and of the two and fourpence she had thrown away for nothing she nearly cried outright" [D 104]), and her bad manners in moments of stress ("Then she asked all the children had any of them eaten it—by mistake, of course" [D 103]). Preoccupied as it is with soothing Maria's distress, the narrative voice that earlier said too little now says, perhaps inadvertently, too much—"the children all said no and looked as if they did not like to eat cakes if they were to be accused of stealing" [D 103]). This is an important and prescient observation because it supplies the children's motive for their subsequent trick-or-treat-like reprisal against Maria. But the narration obscures its significance by immediately shifting attention away from the injured feelings of the children (who receive no apology from Maria and no sympathy from the narrative voice) and onto the attention lavished on Maria, who is plied with stout, nuts, and entertaining anecdotes—ostensibly to distract her from her loss. The narrative agenda here is clearly to establish Maria's privileged status in the Donnelly household, as it previously established Maria's privileged status in the laundry. The shadowy children, whose unspecified number, gender, and names indicate both Maria's and the narrator's lack of interest in them, are repressed like unpleasant thoughts and behave accordingly. They erupt in unexpected places and in devious ways, and although we never clearly see them there, their grievance is behind the disturbance in the game that causes the narration to falter and nearly fragment, although it recovers without exposing Maria: "Maria understood that it was wrong that time and so she had to do it over again: and this time she got the prayer-book" [D 105]. I will argue later (in Chapter 9) that the children's chapters in *Finnegans Wake*, particularly "The Mime of Mick, Nick, and the Maggies," function as ideological reparation to these repressed and elided children, retrieving their games along with their subjectivities, and ultimately along with their own oppressive and occluded social realities (Norris, "Heliotrope").

There are such sizable gaps in the narration of the game, that the reader is obliged to reconstruct through elaborate inference both a scenario of what happens on the level of plot, as well as an interpretation of what it means. Yet critics who plunge into this task without interrogating the reason for the gaps, and questioning the function they serve in supplementing the narrative, risk being manipulated into narrative collusion. For example, Warren Beck, whose excellent reading of "Clay" I much admire, nonetheless perfectly duplicates the narrator's function of protecting Maria when he construes the game's disturbance as an elaborate protection of Maria (212–214). His reconstruction—that Mrs. Donnelly protects Maria from the shock of receiving the ill omen of "death within the coming year"—begs many questions. If "clay" is a traditional symbolic object in the game, then surely it has been chosen, and survived, by players in previous years and is neither taken seriously nor feared? Why must Maria, who is neither ill nor seemingly concerned with her mortality, be protected from the omen on this particular occasion? If the "clay" is a traditional figure in the game, why doesn't Maria recognize it in the "soft wet substance" she touches and note, with satisfaction, Mrs. Donnelly's kindness in sparing her its meaning? There is nothing in Beck's explanation that the narrative voice, at least, could not report to us explicitly.

I would argue that the narrative fracture of this episode makes sense only if there is something to hide, from Maria, and from us, if we are to be maintained as appreciative narratees. I believe that the narration supresses the causal link between the lost plumcake and the sabotaged game, a link in which the maligned children's reprisal takes the form of a trick that is itself an eruption of the "truth" of the children's true feelings; had it worked, it would have forced further, involuntary, self-betrayals from Maria. The children are coerced into providing involuntary testimonials to Maria's generosity ("Mrs Donnelly said it was too good of her to bring such a big bag of cakes and made all the children say:—Thanks, Maria" [D 103]) and are prevented from expressing their obvious dislike of her except through the veil of ambiguity. While the narrator nudges us to interpret "*O, here's Maria!*" as a joyful welcome, we can, in retrospect, hear in it the inaudible expletives and qualifications of resigned hostility and displeased surprise, as in "*O god, here's Maria already.*" The prank with the garden dirt serves to express and gratify the Donnelly children's aggression toward Maria with minimal risk to themselves: it is perpetrated by the older next-door girls (presum-

ably immune to punishment from the Donnelly parents) and it is a
trick that cunningly mitigates the pranksters' blame by manipulating the victim's own imagination to inflict the shock and repulsion
that are its harm. For it strikes me as curious, if the "clay" is a symbolic object in the game, that Maria guesses neither its meaning *nor
the nature of its substance.*[4] It seems clear to me that Maria is subjected to a much more primitive, conventional, universal childish
trick: a trick that depends on making the victim mistake a neutral
and benign substance (spaghetti, mushroom soup, Baby Ruth bars,
in its American versions) for a repulsive, usually excretory material
(worms, vomit, feces, etc.). The point of the children's joke, I believe,
is to make prim, "genteel" Maria recoil in shock and disgust at the
mistaken sensation of touching "excrement"—only to reveal to her,
upon removal of the blindfold, the harmless garden dirt. The embarrassment would be self-inflicted: the victim would be betrayed by
her own "dirty" mind. Joyce could readily have gotten the idea for
such a trick as a version of traditional Hallow Eve games and charms
from Nora, who played them as a girl in Galway. Mary O'Holleran,
Nora's girlhood pal, describes a somewhat similar game and trick:

> We had a party one Holly eve night My father used to make
> games for us such as cross sticks hanging from the ceiling there
> would be an apple on one stick soap on the other and a lighted
> candle on the other stick our eyes would be covered so we could
> not see and my father would spin the sticks around and we
> would bite at the apple my father would put the soap in Noras
> mouth the house would be in roars of laughter while Nora would
> be getting the soap out of her mouth. (JJ 158)

The remarkable thing about this trick in "Clay," of course, is not
only that it fails—that Maria doesn't get it—but that a trick, as
such, is never mentioned in the story at all, meaning that the narrative voice doesn't "get it" either:

> They led her up to the table amid laughing and joking and she
> put her hand out in the air as she was told to do. She moved her
> hand about here and there in the air and descended on one of the
> saucers. She felt a soft wet substance with her fingers and was
> surprised that nobody spoke or took off her bandage. There was a
> pause for a few seconds; and then a great deal of scuffling and
> whispering. Somebody said something about the garden, and at
> last Mrs Donnelly said something very cross to one of the next-
> door girls and told her to throw it out at once: that was no play.

> Maria understood that it was wrong that time and so she had to
> do it over again: and this time she got the prayer-book. (D 105)

This is narration under a blindfold. Like Maria's literal blindfold or
"bandage," the gap in the narration—the narrative voice's failure to
explain to us what really happened—represents, metaphorically, the
"blind spot" that marks the site of Maria's psychic wound, her
imaginary lacks and fears. For at issue here is more than the simple
repression in Maria's failure to make the connection between garden
dirt and excrement. She dare not recognize the trick itself, that a
trick has been played on her: that she is an object of ridicule, the
butt of jokes, a person without sufficient authority to restrain the
pranks of malicious youngsters. What is censored by the narration
is the *significance* of what happens—and that significance is the
demonstration (once more) of Maria's fear of utter *insignificance*.
What Maria fears is not the touch of excrement on her fingers, but
the recognition that her only "family"—like the rest of the world—
treats her like shit. This explains as well why the word "clay" never
appears in the story except as its title. The "soft wet substance" in
the narrative is never named because the very ambiguity of its identity is fraught with such cruel danger to Maria's ego. The naming of
the story poses a similar crux, a similar danger; the chosen title,
"Clay," therefore promises an interpretation of Maria's life that preserves complex registers of truth-telling and lying. For the narration
of "Clay" is "clay"—in the sense that it is a polite circumlocution
that eradicates the dirt and squalor of Maria's life, and thereby rep-
licates her own efforts as a slavey. "Clay" names and exhibits the
work of a rhetorical scullion.

Maria's song, her third task in the triadic fairy tale structure of the
story, marks—like her earlier efforts of the gift and the game—an
unsuccessful social ritual, a failed attempt to govern her symbolic
relationships with others to her better advantage. Once again, there
is ambiguity in the request that she sing, and we suspect that perhaps the family asks Maria to sing less because it gives them pleasure ("Mrs Donnelly bade the children be quiet and listen to Maria's
song" [D 105]) than because it is an effective way to get rid of her, to
hint that she has overstayed her welcome—"At last the children
grew tired and sleepy and Joe asked Maria would she not sing some
little song before she went" (D 105). Maria responds on two levels
to the double meanings of this request. Consciously, she fulfills the
conventions of parlor performance by acting like a demure girl,
feigning reluctance to extort coaxing ("*Do, please, Maria!*" [D 105])
and delivering her song with blushing modesty. Unconsciously, she

answers this extrusion from the Donnelly "family" with a song of exile—a song written in language of desire even more explicit than "Clay." Maria chooses a song from an opera, *The Bohemian Girl*,[5] that is itself a nearly perfect example of the infantile wish fantasy Freud called the "family romance"—the child's fantasy that its parents are really imposters, and that its "true" parents are royalty or aristocrats to whom it will one day be restored. The prescience of Bunn's princess, abducted in infancy by gypsies but still able to divine her true estate (*"I dreamt that I dwelt in marble halls / With vassals and serfs at my side"* [D 106]) nicely mirrors Maria's own implied sense of class displacement, of being trapped in a class below that compatible with her breeding and sensibility ("she knew that Mooney meant well though, of course, she had the notions of a common woman" [D 101]). The song—another version of Maria's desire expressed in the borrowed language of the superior class—is such a perfect analogue to the narration of "Clay," that Maria's lapsus—her omission of the verse depicting courtship and a marriage proposal—seems almost superfluous. But Joyce uses the specifically romantic content of Maria's repression (suitors, husband, love) to carefully focus the sexual etiology of her inferiority complex, and to make it clear that it is not poverty alone, but the negative symbolic value of being an old maid and being unloved, that robs her of significance. Because the performance of the song operates on several semiological levels, it requires a complex act of decoding—and it is not clear, from the text, whether Joe listens to the song or to the singer. Does he hear the pathos of her own plight in Maria's song and weep for her, or—made maudlin by an excess of stout—is he moved to tears by the pain of the Bohemian Girl ("What's Hecuba to him, or he to Hecuba, / That he should weep for her?" [*Hamlet*, II:2]) while he remains deaf to Maria's song of exile and longing?

When "Clay" ends—fittingly, with blindness and lost objects— what has been accomplished? "Clay" remains a hypothetical speech act, Maria's story as no one will ever tell it, as she could not tell it herself even, but as it might be imagined being told. For Maria, the story, far from remedying her lacks, has multiplied them—but not until they have passed through the detour of a flattering lie. But is the story, in its residual meaning, merely an exhibition of a pointless life, or is it the exhibition of the failure of Maria's denial of its pointlessness? It may seem to come to the same thing: but in the difference between a judgment (that Maria's life is pointless) and her failed resistance to that judgment is lodged that attitudinal half-turn away from Maria and toward the critic who does the judging. By producing Maria's interpretation, we are implicated in her estimation (offering it as narratee, withdrawing it as critic) and, consequently, implicated in her victimization. The naturalistic "truth" of her poverty and isolation, that we uncover by seeing "through" the narrative agenda, makes her life hard enough. But what disturbs her contentment with her lot and ruins the efficacy of a kind of Ibsenite "life lie" are the insecurities produced by her fears of the estimation and interpretation of the "other." In her insecurities, in her fears, we should see our own "evil eye" as readers, encoded as we are within the story as the washerwomen, the shopkeepers, the young men on the tram, the children, and Society ("with a big ess," as Gerty MacDowell would say). It is we, as critical and perceptive readers, who create the pressures that necessitate Maria's defensive maneuvers in inventing her story.

I was myself prodded to make a self-reflexive turn beyond my naturalistic reading of "Clay" by students who stubbornly refused to let me get away with an elision necessary to sustain my reading of the story: what about the narrator describing Maria (a mythical three times, no less) in the unmistakably stereotyped features of a witch—"the tip of her nose nearly met the tip of her chin" (D 101, 105)? This is indeed a problem, because surely the narrative voice does not flatter Maria here. Yet the voice and context in which the narration delivers these descriptions is very revealing of a kind of necessary concession fronted with the best possible "face," as it were, that one finds elsewhere in the story. Following the initial description of the kitchen, with its flattering signs of Maria's industry in its cleanliness, coziness, and orderliness, we receive a no-nonsense description of Maria's physical appearance: "Maria was a very, very small person indeed but she had a very long nose and a very long chin." (D 99) The bluntness and plain objectivity of this sentence is as eloquent in *what it does not say* as in what it does say. Neither the narrative voice, nor any character in the story, ever says or is described as thinking that Maria is plain or homely, deformed or grotesque-looking, hideous or witch-like. Such interpretations are produced strictly by the inference of the reader and are therefore hermeneutical, not rhetorical, products of the text. Indeed, the rhetoric of the description softens its sense in subtle ways. The description of Maria's stature, while quite emphatic in its "very, very small . . . indeed," nonetheless averts and replaces more evaluative judgments that would interpret her size as an abnormality or deformity and identify Maria as a dwarf or midget. Also by calling attention to her size and body first, as though they were her salient feature, the more damaging information about her facial physiognomy is rendered less conspicuous; the curious syntax, with the "but" serving as a possible qualification ("Maria was a very, very small person indeed but she had a very long nose and a very long chin") could even be read as a compensatory tribute, as though Maria's childish height were effectively countered by distinctive, well-marked adult features. I am suggesting here only that the narrative voice appears to *try* to put a good face on Maria's face—not that it succeeds in convincing us.

During the tea (D 101), Maria twice produces the famous laugh in which "the tip of her nose nearly met the tip of her chin"—a laugh repeated a third time later at the Donnelly house, just as she is blindfolded for the game. The common feature of each of these occasions is that they represent moments of extraordinarily heightened—but uncomfortably ambiguous—attention to Maria: she is told she is sure to get the ring; a toast is drunk to her health with clattering tea mugs; the children insist on blindfolding her for the game. Is Maria being singled out for affectionate tribute, or is she being pressed into service—as dwarves and midgets historically were—as jester and fool? If the latter, does the narrative voice strategically use an uncharacteristically unflattering image of Maria— "the tip of her nose nearly met the tip of her chin"—to divert our attention from much more painful revelations? Does this rhetorical maneuver turn Maria from tormented buffoon into indulgent good sport ("she knew that Mooney meant well, though, of course . . .") and mask as jolly heartiness her grimace of pain? Does Lizzie Fleming twit and goad Maria nearly to tears about the ring, obliging the narrative voice to gallantly mask Maria's face at that painful moment with a most genteel turn of phrase—"when she laughed her greygreen eyes sparkled with disappointed shyness" (D 101)? The narration has here produced another highly ambiguous scene whose possible interpretations hold the extremes of estimation for Maria: was the tea entertaining, was Maria made much of by people who love her, and did she express her pleasure in a grimace of hilarity, or was it a frequent ritual of cruel humiliation in which the aging prostitutes mock Maria's unlosable virginity?

Maria never sees that "the tip of her nose nearly met the tip of her chin" because it is, ironically, her most public gesture: her response to uncomfortable moments in the limelight when, perhaps terrified of the extreme exposure, she loses altogether her ability to compose herself into a controlled form. When she later looks at herself in the mirror, in the privacy of her room, she doesn't see her face at all but only her body, as it looked when it was young and when, perhaps, its size was less conspicuous, and she serenely approves what she sees—"In spite of its years she found it a nice tidy little body." If the narration shows us only Maria's contented acceptance of her appearance, and records no negative reaction on its own part, or on the part of any character in the story, to Maria's very long nose and very long chin—then why would a reader infer she is ugly and witch-like? With such a question the story turns itself to the reader like a mirror: a turn announced in the opening paragraph of the story when "the cook said you could see yourself in the big copper boilers" (D 99) and invited us to inspect our own visage in Maria's efforts to scour away the squalor of her life. Why do readers think Maria is ugly? Because we possess, if our place in the symbolic order of our culture is a safe distance from its margins, a hermeneutical touch as poisonous as that of any witch who ever turned prince into toad. We take minute anatomical deviations—a few inches in height, a few centimeters extra on a nose or a chin, and—pouf!—we construct a witch-like hag that we expel from possibilities of desirability or estimation. "Clay" tricks us with the same trick the children try to play on Maria. It offers us a benign, neutral substance—a woman, just a woman—and we recoil with cries, or at least thoughts, of "witch!" as surely as we would recoil with cries of "shit!" from the harmless garden soil. "Clay" reads the reader when it implicitly asks "Which is the witch?"

CHAPTER SEVEN

The Work Song of the Washerwomen in "Anna Livia Plurabelle"

JOYCE'S "ANNA LIVIA PLURABELLE" reverses the forcible dissociation of art from manual labor that Max Horkheimer and Theodor Adorno find figured in Odysseus' stratagem in the sailors' encounter with the sirens in their *Dialectic of Enlightenment* (34). The sirens' song loses its efficacy for the deafened sailors who labor in silence. The art overheard by Odysseus, the man who dominates the scene by depriving himself of the ability to work in order to attend the song, is an impotent art voided of its power. But the washerwomen who pour forth the lyricism of the ALP chapter in *Finnegans Wake* sing a seductive sirens' song that is nonetheless coterminous with their labor, beginning with their washing, conditioned and shaped by the motion and rhythms of their scrubbing, and ending when it is done. "Anna Livia Plurabelle" is a work song, with the women's labor of washing figuratively and socially inscribed in the lyrical, vulgar, idiomatic, robust speech produced within the social conditions and social relations of their work. It is a song that asks us to listen—not like Odysseus with his hands tied, impotent to act on the sirens' song; nor like his sailors with their ears stuffed with wadding ("It's that irrawaddyng I've stoke in my aars" [FW 214.9])—that is, not like scholars too preoccupied poring over maps and atlases looking for the Irrawaddy and the Aare to hear the beauty of their song. Instead, I believe, Joyce asks us to listen with proletarian interest, like sailors with unsealed ears, who hear in the beauty of the text's lyricism a work song of the kind rarely heard in high art, that they can recognize as their own. This is neither a song of denial, like Walt Disney's little miners whistling while they work, nor a song of protest, like that of Hauptmann's weavers. Nor is it modernist poetry reclaiming the modern wasteland from the masses whose materialism and Philistinism is thought to have spiritually destroyed the land. "Anna Livia Plurabelle" is the song of a collective but specific figure of those masses, two washerwomen, encoded in a still-humanized social space, obtruding their essential experience, the speech of their labor, into poetry's privileged discourse.

The strange self-contradictory nature of the beautiful and the ugly in woman and language in this chapter makes the text emblematic of the aesthetic conundrum of representing the modern world whose optimistic romantic resolution in nineteenth-century aestheticism—the Baudelairean enterprise of finding flowers in evil, gold in mud—can no longer be held immune from ideological critique. Ellmann's innocence in ascribing a strategy of unproblematical fusion of the beautiful and the ugly to Joyce (JJ 6) begs too many questions that in the current climate of interrogating modernistic ideology must be addressed. I will argue that Ellmann's dialectical explanation for the doubled nature of Anna Livia Plurabelle ("The river is lovely and filthy; Dublin is dear and dirty; so are the mind and body. In theory we grant these combinations, but in practice seem to hold the units apart. Joyce never does" [JJ 6]) elides Joyce's complex intertextual revisionary gestures, his widening of the fissures of "Clay" to retrieve the speech and feelings of the repressed washerwomen, his possible embrace of Samuel Butler's radical use of gender to produce a historical reversion of the *Odyssey*, and his retrieval of the hidden familial and social politics behind his female model's discomfort with his portrait. "When Livia Svevo heard that Joyce in *Finnegans Wake* was using her flowing hair as a symbol of the lovely river Liffey, she was flattered, but when she heard that in the river were two washerwomen scrubbing dirty linen, she was disgusted" (JJ 5), Ellmann reports, although it is not until Brenda Maddox fills in the subtext of this relationship, that Nora Joyce is doing Signora Svevo's ironing, that the class intersections of Joyce's complex female figure, and their political implications, become clear: the beauty of the lovely lady with the beautiful hair is striated with the labor of other women—like Joyce's wife—who launder and prepare her dress. I will elaborate this point at greater length later, but wish for the moment to observe that Joyce explores in "Anna Livia Plurabelle" what I would call "the *other* of the female *other*," the river as lovely woman first internalizing and then exteriorizing the labor of women of another class.

Woman plays the same role in the Joycean text as do his other signifiers: she represents a contradictory signifier that precludes our finding in her a single figure, a self-identity or entity that is identical to itself, and in this way embodies the otherness of language. Christine Van Boheemen has elegantly elaborated the metaphysical feminism of this textual practice in a formulation I have cited earlier—

"Joyce is not the only one to use the image of a woman to legitimize the inscription of the idea of ontological otherness within his text, thus fleshing out what is and can never be more than a trace, and using what should probably be termed a synecdoche (i.e., the image of half of mankind) as figure for a generally human, ontological condition which can only be approached in metaphor" (100). My own address to this concern will be to contend that Joycean woman does not simply represent otherness as the negation of presence in a way that allows her to stand, emblematically, for the way humanity cannot be represented as an ontological singularity. Rather, the Joycean female figure represents the intersection of desire and truth, a point that is situated in social perception and in social being, and that inevitably traps her in a contradictory double register of the kind I have already partially explored in "The Dead," where I tried to reconstruct the text's two Julia Morkans, toddling aunt and dazzling singer, as well as its two Gretta Conroys, mysterious beauty and bullied wife. ALP likewise constitutes such an intersected, indeterminate figure—desirable nymphet and rag-picking hag, clear rivulet and polluted harbor—her doubleness itself doubled by the prose that narrates her either in fluent lyricism or a vulgar brogue. These binaries are neither moral categories nor essentialist archetypes, but rather perceptual and hermeneutical expressions of the conflict between desire and knowledge in our relation to reality, that result in the indeterminacy of the representational act, as it attempts to commit woman to metaphor, picture, and genre.

Instead of epiphanizing and sublimating the ugly modern world, I will describe Joyce's strategy in reverse, as desublimation of aesthetic convention by restoring to art and poetry the social truth of those occluded by art, particularly the women occluded by art, the female figures whose labor negates art but underlies it in the most personal way: Stephen's mother ironing clothes in the kitchen while he reads her his paper on aesthetics, or putting his second-hand clothes in order that he may fly by his nets, or Nora Joyce taking in laundry to support the family during her husband's illness in Trieste. "Anna Livia Plurabelle" tries less to salvage beauty from labor and ugliness, than to have labor and ugliness assert themselves in art, the institutional site for discourses of beauty. Joyce remembers and memorializes the laboring speech of washerwomen in "Anna Livia Plurabelle" in a gesture that approximates Theodor Adorno's political mandate to art: "One of the basic human rights possessed by those who pick up the tab for the progress of civilization is the right to be remembered. Contrary to the affirmative totality of ideologies of emancipation, this right demands that the marks of humiliation be committed to remembrance in the form of *imagines.* Art must take up the cause of that which is branded ugly" (*Aesthetic Theory* 72). If Joyce seduces us with a poetry of woman as magical as a mountain stream, he does it to confront us with the poverty, isolation, and derision modern social life visits on poor laboring women, and that modernism's oppressive class ideology doubles with its poetic censure. The verbal female flooding of the washerwomen's prattle is politically fecund in the *Wake,* I would argue. Maud Ellmann finds its contrast in "The Waste Land": "When Mrs. Porter and her daughter wash their feet in soda water, the ceremony of innocence is drowned, and the baptismal rite becomes its own defilement" (104).

Using *desublimation,* then, the specific strategy Peter Buerger identifies with the self-critical capability of the historical avantgarde, Joyce in *Finnegans Wake* (I.8) turns back Stephen's recoil from the raggedy street hoyden selling flowers, the kitchengirls and pert factory workers, all the proletarian women whose disdain he gathers into the trope for his debasement of the Church when he calls it "the scullerymaid of christendom" (P 220). Stephen betrays the brutally abused and exploited women of Gerhart Hauptmann's dramas by transforming them into pre-Raphaelite wraiths—"The rainladen trees of the avenue evoked in him, as always, memories of the girls and women in the plays of Gerhart Hauptmann; and the memory of their pale sorrows and the fragrance falling from the wet branches mingled in a mood of quiet joy" (P 176). Stephen in his Thomistic phase reproduces the ideology of the Brotherhood's nostalgic aestheticism to occlude the industrial reality of nineteenth century women's lives with idealized and sublime female forms. He therefore finds on the strand not the social or psychological reality of a Gerty MacDowell, but a pre-Raphaelite version of Botticelli's Venus, a woman sublimated and apotheosized into the exquisite form of the wading bird-girl—"Her image had passed into his soul for ever and no word had broken the holy silence of his ecstasy" (P 172). Stephen finds in the stream woman-as-art; the washerwomen find in the stream woman-as-not-art.

The lovely bird girl is transformed by them into the caged bird of marital capture: "I heard he dug good tin with his doll, delvan first and duvlin after, when he raped her home, Sabrine asthore, in a parakeet's cage, by dredgerous lands and devious delts" (FW 197.20), and Stephen's aestheticized woman is transformed in *Finnegans Wake* into her opposite, into that which she displaces: the cockle-picking gypsy woman ("you born ijypt" [FW 198.1]) Stephen rele-

gates to the periphery of his vision in "Proteus." The gypsy is herself
a romanticized figure of the homeless, nomadic outcast, and as ALP
shares features of the cocklepicker, she emerges as an impoverished
old woman scavenging rubbish for her livelihood, a precursor of
Beckett's metaphysical female tramps, and of the contemporary
"bag ladies" ("all spoiled goods go into her nabsack" [FW 11.18]) of
our own urban American landscape. ALP is many things in *Finne-*
gans Wake, but chiefly she is a little clown of a crone, insignificant,
mute, repulsive, funny, pathetic, whose stories the washerwomen
tell not to degrade her, but to give her silent social degradation
voice. Anna Livia Plurabelle and HCE are far less Molly and Leopold
Bloom as the washerwomen tell their story, than Josie Powell running after the demented Denis Breen ("that bloody old pantaloon
Denis Breen in his bathslippers . . . and the wife hotfoot after him,
unfortunate wretched woman, trotting like a poodle" [U 12:253])
and failing to save him from losing his precarious hold on the margins of social integration and respectability. Like the derision Denis
Breen's decaying appearance earns him, ALP's strange get-up makes
her a social joke, "O gig goggle of gigguels. I can't tell you how! It's
too screaming to rizo, rabbit it all! Minneha, minnehi, minaaehe,
minneho!" (FW 206.14), a fashion unintelligibility, a sartorial mu-
tation in huge "ploughboy's nailstudded clogs," a pointed "sugarloaf
hat" with streamers, weird round spectacles that like "owlglassy bi-
cycles boggled her eyes," a "fishnetzeveil" over her face, potato-rings
for earrings, spotted and speckled stockings, "bloodorange" knick-
erbockers perhaps of the kind worn by the feminist McCann in *Ste-*
phen Hero, and many other items of castoff clothes of all descriptions, like a walking sartorial garbage heap.[1] Stephen's poverty, cultural dispossession, and feelings of alienation take on the cast
of romantic solipsism against their sharply reduced social radical in the figure of ALP as mute, homeless, wandering crone with
her worldly goods slung on her back. The washerwomen's gossip
functions as a discursive social work, a deinstitutionalized counterpart of philanthropic efforts to save endangered human creatures
from social disintegration, by committing their history to the narrative remembrance that assures salvage of their human significance and worth. Instead of making the modern world possible
for art, the washerwomen's gossip makes art responsible for correct-
ing its own occlusive practices and discharging neglected social responsibilities in the modern world. They do this by making their
discourse represent in its form (their own manual and discursive
labor) and its content (the description and story of ALP) that which
is non-art.

1. Samuel Butler and the Desublimation of Myth

In a strategy explicitly contradicting T. S. Eliot's notion of Joyce's "mythical method," Joyce desublimates myth to restore it to historical realism, turning pearls back into dead men's eyes, as it were, or the Nibelungs' Rhinegold (O loreley! [FW 201.35]) back into the quotidian rhinestones of pebbles and rocks in the river where washerwomen wash their clothes, "a jetty amulet for necklace of clicking cobbles and pattering pebbles and rumbledown rubble, richmond and rehr, of Irish rhunerhinerstones and shellmarble bangles" (FW 207.5). Joyce differs from Eliot in his use of myth precisely because he degrades myth from instrument of desire—desire for order, for form, for significance—into an instrument of self-critique, a means of uncovering the repressed truths of the social real, of history, buried under mythic desire for heroism, fidelity, idealism. Joyce's inspiration for this practice was, I will follow Hugh Kenner in arguing, Samuel Butler—the nineteenth-century utopianist, novelist, and classicist, whose *The Authoress of the Odyssey* used gender reversal to make woman the radical other of Western culture with the same gesture that restored the Odyssean myth to history. In arguing for a female Homer, Butler doubles the archeological analogue Sarah Kofman borrows from Freud to open her own exploration of the female's otherness:

> Freud compares this revolutionary discovery of the *entirely other* to finding the Mycenean civilization behind that of the Greeks: 'Our insight into this early, pre-Oedipus, phase in girls comes to us as a surprise, like the discovery, in another field, of the Minoan-Mycenean civilization behind the civilization of Greece." (33)

Had it been taken seriously, Butler's argument, that a woman was Homer's historical and literary other—that is, that Homer was authoress, not author, of the *Odyssey*—might have disrupted received notions about Western classical culture with the force of a metaphysical turn. Hugh Kenner, who began arguing in 1969 that Joyce made significant use of Butler's *The Authoress of the Odyssey*, concedes that the nearly total rejection of Butler's thesis cannot be justified by a failure of scholarship, and is attributable to no intrinsic weakness in his logic—"Had it not obtruded that unacceptable female Homer, Butler's book might have been taken rather seriously. . . . Instead he chose to be the man with the silly bee in his bonnet about a poetess, and his most serious reader, it may be, was James Joyce" ("Homer's Sticks and Stones" 294). As a classicist

Butler worked in the nineteenth-century empirical and scientific tradition, a practice reflected also in his vigorous, lifelong debate with and over Darwinian evolutionary theory, and his enlightened attacks against religion, which earned him George Bernard Shaw's praise. Settling himself in the map room of the British Museum, studying Italian Ordnance maps and Admiralty charts, aided by an assortment of scholars, travellers, archeologists, and friends, and eventually checking his theories with field trips to Sicily, Butler transformed myth into history, and gave the *Odyssey* the novelistic translation and interpretation that Kenner, seconded by Michael Seidel in *Epic Geography*, treats as an important precursive discovery for Joyce's writing of *Ulysses*: "Butler's was simply the first creative mind—Joyce's was the second—to take the archaeologist's Homer seriously: to consider what it might mean to believe that the *Odyssey* was composed by a real person in touch with the living details of real cities, real harbors, real bowls and cups and pins and spoons, real kings, real warriors, real houses. His book is the first about the *Odyssey* to be illustrated with photographs: of the actual Trojan walls, or of an actual cave that might have been the Cyclops' " (293). Butler's argument relies both on historical evidence for a thriving female literary tradition,[2] and on inferences about female gender reference drawn from the material and social realism of the story's details.

Whether or not Butler's argument is sustainable on archeological or historical grounds, it should pose a formidable imaginative challenge to what we would now call the phallologocentrism of the Western Classical heritage. Had Butler been taken seriously without androcentric resistance, literary history should have been rewritten, the principles of canonicity should have been reconsidered, a plethora of theoretical centrisms should have been dislodged. Instead, Butler's gender reversal argument has been trivialized (even Kenner and Seidel do not elaborate it) except in the rare instance, such as Vicki Mahaffey's book, where she argues, "Samuel Butler also draws attention to the unusual parity between men and women in *The Odyssey*, but he does so by exaggerating, in a way that is both comic and startlingly credible, the importance of women in the poem" (203). But in general, Butler's gender theory has been reduced to a minor point, as impetus for Joyce's satirical treatment of "Nausicaa"'s ludicrous female prose.

But I wish to argue that Butler's thesis, whether historically or merely imaginatively, transformed the *Odyssey* into a double or intersected text, a text cut through by gender difference that bears the double configuration of many of Joyce's own fictions. The Butler

Odyssey becomes a text riven by the intersection of desire and truth, by male need to sustain idealism with fantasies of heroism and by female experience with the daily labor required to sustain life. It becomes a subverted legitimation myth. The Butler *Odyssey* is metaphysically intersected by male Mastery and by female Bondage, by an anthropogenetic mythology that undercuts the Hegelian originary fight, the founding of idealism in man's willingness to risk life in battle, with the Kojèvian exploration of the Slave's subordination to the Master who risks life. Alexandre Kojève argues, in his reading of Hegel, that the Slave, though oppressed and forced to transform nature for the Master in order to supply him with the necessities for life, achieves his [sic] own metaphysical mastery through the self-transformation of labor and suffering (22–27). In Butler's *Odyssey*, then, a female writer has men risk life and shed blood, but spares Eumaeus as a final victim because "possibly the writer felt that she should be shorthanded with the cleaning up of the blood and the removal of the dead bodies" (156). Considerations of housework alter the dimensions of massacre in this version of the classic text.[3]

Butler identifies his female author as a Sicilian gentlewoman living in Trapani on the western coast of Sicily, who inscribes herself into the *Odyssey* as Nausicaa, the Phaeacian maiden who mounts a massive laundry expedition at the oneiric urging of Minerva. Butler has that colossal wash day, which required the loan of "a good big waggon" and mules to transport the laundry, firmly in mind when trying to identify Scheria on the island of Alcinous: "There must be no river running into either harbour or Nausicaa would not have had to go so far to wash her clothes. The river when reached might be nothing but a lagoon with a spring or two of fresh water running into it, for the clothes were not, so it would seem, washed in a river; they were washed in public washing cisterns ('Od.'vi.40, 86, 92) which a small spring would keep full enough of water 'to wash clothes even though they were very dirty'" (159). Butler gives the mythical events a thoroughly naturalistic plausibility, and his discovery of the clever installation of the cistern, through which running clear water flows for a continual rinse, allows him to further describe the actual laundering technique: "They took the clothes out of the wagon, put them in the water and vied with one another in treading them in the pits to get the dirt out" (72). Although Joyce does not transpose Butler's mythical wash day into "Nausicaa," it reinforces his interest in laundries that began in "Clay," although there, as I have argued, it is repressed on the grounds of the narration's class and social prejudice. The narrator in "Nausicaa" does the same, and although there is much coy talk of the undies that are Gerty's chief care, the washerwomen who launder them are not foregrounded, narratively, socially, discursively, or subjectively, until "Anna Livia Plurabelle."

Joyce's treatment of washerwomen in his fiction reflects the critical lesson of Butler's *Odyssey* as a fable of an originary gender doubling and repression, the Greek classic as genesis not only of Western literary history, but of literary history as founded on acts of patriarchal repression and suppression. Butler's *Odyssey* retroactively demonstrates the silencing of the female voice at the origins of Western art, the obscuring of its social realism with translations of florid and heroic prose, and the trivialization of its foregrounding of the prosaic labor, the housework, without which warriors could not proceed to their heroic deeds. (As Jean Gardiner writes in a different vocabulary, "domestic labor is a necessary component of the labor required to maintain and reproduce labor power" [175]). That textual self-contradictoriness that forms the ground of interpretation, and that post-structuralism treats as an inherent constitution or nature of textuality, Joyce saw, I believe, as the product of both history and the oppressive social function of art and texts. But as I have been arguing in my previous chapters, his response to this insight was not polemic but dramatization and reenactment. The classic as gender masquerade, as cross-dressed pantomime in which the historical readership does not want to see the girl behind the principal boy, serves as analogue for Joyce's own fictional masquerades, the genteel voice that lies to us about Maria and Gerty, the myth that conceals a contradictory myth, as I will show, in "Nausicaa," the patriarchal narration of "The Dead," that promotes the male artist *manquée* at the expense of women's lives. The textual concealment of its own otherness is revealed as politically pernicious in the Joycean text, and becomes the object of its own self-critique.

2. The Social Politics of Washerwomen in History

Joyce's art, I have tried to demonstrate, is essentially an art of gesture, less in the rhythmic sense Stephen promotes in *Stephen Hero*, than in the dramatic sense of an acting out of unconscious behavior, that Joyce would have learned from Ibsen and Hauptmann. His narrations make perceptual gestures that are motivated politically, and we can construct quite precisely both how and why this is done. Joyce chooses for the setting of "Clay" a laundry fraught with oppressive political implications that far exceed any usefulness to provide local color. "The meaning of *Dublin by Lamplight Laundry?*"

Joyce wrote to Stanislaus in November 1906, "That is the name of
the laundry at Ballsbridge, of which the story treats. It is run by a
society of Protestant spinsters, widows, and childless women—I expect—as a Magdalen's home. The phrase *Dublin by Lamplight*
means that Dublin by lamplight is a wicked place full of wicked and
lost women whom a kindly committee gathers together for the good
work of washing my dirty shirts. I like the phrase because 'it is a
gentle way of putting it'" (*Letters* II, 192). Joyce's own concluding
gesture is here double: the "gentle way of putting it" is an ambiguous motive, possibly aestheticist and poetic, an enamorment with a
turn of phrase, but also potentially politically critical, turning our attention to the way the bourgeois discourse mimicked in "Clay" will
occlude and marginalize every politically significant aspect of the
washerwomen's situation. The washerwoman is a doubly degraded
colonial victim: first forced by need and male betrayal ("I suppose
that's your doing" [D 53] Lenehan says of the woman Corley drove
onto the turf) to a life of handling the sexual bodies of strangers, and
then, when she is too old, forced by Protestant philanthropists to a
life of handling the sexual linens of strangers. By making himself
rhetorically the beneficiary of their penance through "the good work
of washing my dirty shirts," Joyce articulates, too, his own male
implication in their oppression, the sexual difference that demeans
only the women, but not the men who enjoy them, for their whor-
ing. Yet Joyce's significant gesture is that having clearly created a
politically complex and significant situation for his story, he
chooses not to have the story elaborate and analyze it, but instead
to have the story repress and occlude it, until all that remains of his
analysis is a residue of narrative gaps and incongruities, as I have
tried to show. Joyce clearly deems it more important to write the
story as a dramatization of the way bourgeois consciousness will-
fully denies social reality, than as a polemical critique of Dublin
institutions. In enacting these repulsed denials and finicky repressions of its social reality, the story enacts, and self-critiques, a submerged aspect of its own modernism.

It is in his treatment of class, and specifically of women of the
lower class, that Joyce sets himself apart, artistically and politically,
from T. S. Eliot. "Anna Livia Plurabelle" will function as anti-
modernism, and specifially as an anti-"Waste Land," for it presents
a flooded, fertile post-diluvial terrain that has washed ashore an impotent fisher king, whose Parsifal is a little scavenger woman shor-
ing up junk and refuse against her ruins, her futility narrated not in
the poetry of Tiresias, but in the idiomatic low brogue of humble
washerwomen. Joyce's insertion into the historical Irish discourses

on population control, as Mary Lowe-Evans terms his immersion in the various forms of public address to the population's survival, may account for his different poetic response to modern mass culture. Eliot's poem fears the disintegration of personality and culture threatened by waste and filth, as Maud Ellmann explains—"However, it is difficult to draw taxonomies of waste, because the text conflates the city with the body and, by analogy, the social with the personal. Abortions, broken fingernails, carious teeth, and 'female smells' signify the culture's decadence, as well as bodily decrepitude. The self is implicated in the degradation of the race, because the filth without insinuates defilement within" (93). But the *Wake* text does more than will to become a refuse dump of textual detritus and abject language. It repeatedly dramatizes the tension between the bourgeois artistic desire for order, control, and cleanliness in art, language, and society, and the double-edged suppression that this desire aims against the very lower classes whom it designates to carry the slops and scour the copper pots and launder the filth of the world. Joyce's own *déclassée* condition, a heritage of bourgeois ambitions and prejudices obliged to come to terms with the reality of plebeian deprivations and humiliations, allowed him to embody and enact, but also critique his own class denials and repressions.

His comportment toward the "Anna Livia Plurabelle" chapter plays out this class conflict, for Joyce created a series of pretty fictions about the chapter's origins that repress both its point of departure in "Clay," and in other analogues in both his life and fiction. Joyce made Livia Schmitz, the wife of Italo Svevo, the model of ALP's beautiful name and hair, "They say I have immortalized Svevo, but I've also immortalized the tresses of Signora Svevo. These were long and reddish-blond. My sister who used to see them let down told me about them. The river at Dublin passes dye-houses and so has reddish water. So I have playfully compared these two things in the book I'm writing. A lady in it will have the tresses which are really Signora Svevo's" (JJ 561). The dye-works, the Dublin industries staffed by living workers who put the color in the cloth that his washerwomen will eventually wash in the river, are marginalized as an insignificant detail to account for the river's ruddy color. But Joyce suppresses a great deal more with this misleading anecdote. What was Joyce's sister doing in Livia Schmitz's household that would allow her to see her with her hair down, and what sort of familiarity was there between the Svevos and the Joyces? To Ellmann's account of Svevo's generous friendship to Joyce, Brenda Maddox gives a devastating modification:

Joyce did enter fine houses, such as the elegant Villa Veneziani
with its tiled floors and walls hung with portraits, but only as a
teacher. It was the home of Ettore Schmitz and his proud and
beautiful wife, Livia. The Schmitzes never received Joyce socially. Livia Schmitz employed Nora to do her ironing (which
Nora did at her own home and returned when it was finished).
The Schmitz family thought Eileen more refined than Nora and,
in order to help Joyce financially, employed Eileen as a governess
for their daughter. But the sense of social distance was very great.
Joyce, who regarded Signora Schmitz as a model of the beautiful
gentlewoman, never forgot that he never crossed the threshold
except as an employee and that Livia Schmitz snubbed Nora
when she saw her in the street (111).

During those lean years in Trieste, Nora was forced to return to the
work that the 1901 Galway census lists as her occupation. "That
she did washing and ironing for a living, as the census report says, is
probable," (20) Maddox speculates, and reports that Joyce confided
Nora's forced return to taking in laundry to Byrne in 1909, who later
passed on the information in a letter to Ellmann, "that same Nora
being the young woman who, as Jim himself told me, took in washing during Joyce's illness in Trieste to help make money for herself
and her family" (*Nora* 94). The anecdote about the inspiration of
Livia Schmitz' flowing red-gold hair thus becomes fraught with humiliating social implications, as the haughty gentlewoman is admired by the domestics she patronizes and snubs in the street, these
domestics being Joyce's wife and sister. ALP's double identity as Si-
ren and ugly little crone gives Joyce's compliment to Livia Schmitz
a potentially malicious edge,[4] and the text makes it even crueler as
the washerwomen speculate about the authenticity of ALP's wave
and hair, "was she marcellewaved or was it weirdly a wig she wore"
204.23). Joyce's Anna Livia Plurabelle may have acted out his own
social *ressentiment* on behalf of his family's women. Joyce's second
fiction of the source of the washerwomen is consequently also
double and devious. He told Stanislaus that the idea for the chapter
was inspired on a trip to Chartres, by seeing women washing clothes
on both banks of the river Eure. But behind this picturesque pasto-
ralism lies Joyce's immediate, if second-hand, experience with the
drudgery, the hardship, the humiliation of this hard labor. Its social
humiliation can best be measured by the class prejudice Joyce put
into the mouth of a babe: little Stephen, wanting to punish Father
Dolan for the cruel, unjust pandy-batting, invests him with this so-

cial identity as his most stinging insult—"Dolan: it was like the name of a woman that washed clothes" (P 55).

Joyce's clue about Livia Schmitz' presence in the ALP chapter pointed his readers of "Work in Progress" back to the Trieste years, which were for him the "moment of modernism," as William Johnsen puts it, "when Joyce modernised himself" (6). But his retrieval, many years later, in *Finnegans Wake*, of the complex social hierarchies experienced by his household of women and their world, suggests that the moment of modernism, when Joyce should have been steeped in the poetic solipsism, the ontological isolationism, the totalitarian aesthetic of form, rigor, totalization, and mastery that has become defined as the ideology of modernism, may have been for Joyce rather a moment of significant social awareness and shrewd analysis. Instead of the artist's isolationism ostensibly celebrated in *Portrait*, he may have been keenly aware that while he and Svevo conversed as aspiring artist to neglected artist, Joyce's wife and sister were acting as servants to Svevo's wife and daughter. Behind the solipsistic artist about to fly by his aesthetic wings, there is a mother putting his second-hand clothes in order. While Joyce has Telemachus brooding on his dispossession in the metaphorical language of service, "A servant too. A server of a servant" (U 1:312) and "I am a servant of two masters" (U 1:639), he has, I believe, a very literal sense of hierarchies of literal servants, of the spiral of degradation and labor that organizes the female community of "Clay" into matrons and board ladies and washerwomen and slaveys, with a mute or mentally retarded dummy at the bottom, whose silenced subjectivity could produce its own further turns. Woman as *other* is not an ontological monolith in Joyce's fiction, and it is in his ability to translate the historical and political particularity of woman's situation into fictional emplotments in which her experience is marked by varying degrees of occlusion and attention, by denials and falsifications of her status, by repressions and enablings of her speech, that the class-coded *other* of the female *other* is restored to literary history and to modern poetic representation.

Joyce's strategies in "Anna Livia Plurabelle" form an ideological gesture that contradicts Georg Lukács' characterization of modernism's existential solipsism. Lukács' sense that "Man, for these writers, is by nature solitary, asocial, unable to enter into relationships with other human beings" (20) is countered in the Joycean text, and in the ALP chapter especially, with the form of discursive connectedness that we call "gossip," and whose function in the process of "dereification" Fredric Jameson discusses in his essay on "'Ulysses'

in History" (135). But Joyce's attempt to invert poetic solipsism has
been difficult to discern through the filter of social and cultural criticism that marginalizes female interests and domestic labor[5] that
were a central feature of the Irish colonial experience. Franco Moretti renders the relevance of Irish colonialism to *Ulysses* virtually
nugatory: "The hypothesis of this study, then, is that a 'structural
homology' exists between the specific social nature of the British
crisis and the specific literary structure of *Ulysses*: if they appear as
mutually integrative of each other, the question of Ireland is no
longer pertinent" (*Signs Taken for Wonder* 190). But for my purposes in exploring "Anna Livia Plurabelle" as a song of labor, it is
important to make a distinction between industrialized England, the
heavily industrialized north of Ireland, and the rest of the country of
which Mary E. Daly writes, "The only area of increased employment
for women during the nineteenth century was domestic service, so
that by 1911 one working woman in three was a servant, while another large group was employed in agriculture" (71). Washerwomen,
whose unskilled labor might seem politically insignificant in English labor history, were numerous and oppressed enough in Ireland
to have been organized by the Irish Women Workers Union as early
as 1911—that is, at a time when only 19.5 percent of Irish women
were employed at all (MacCurtain 48). "One of the union's greatest
achievements was the organisation of laundry workers, a group of
women engaged in unpleasant, poorly-skilled labour. By 1932 a total
of thirteen hundred workers had joined the Union and won a guaranteed forty-seven–hour week, fixed overtime rates, one week's
holidays with pay and a minimum wage of thirty/-" (Daly 72–73).

Joyce may not make his washerwomen conscious of the causes of
their oppression, but he certainly imprints on their thoughts and
words their awareness of its effects. They are not petty bourgeois in
the way "Clay"'s narrator is bent on social denials, and if they are
comical in their complaints, their curiosities, and their frankness,
neither are they treated as emblems of spiritual sewage and aridity,
like Eliot's lower class women in "The Waste Land." Joyce's washerwomen may be gently patronized—Joyce's wheedling imitation of
their speech in his 1929 reading for the Ogden recording does not
preclude this—but they are spared the misogynistic judgment implicit in Eliot's twice-told tale of his Lillith of a Lil, and her sordid
female sociology of conjugal coercion, multiparity, abortion, cal-
cium deficiency, toothlessness, premature aging, and adultery. Joyce,
like Eliot, implicates the feminine in his writing, but, I will argue,
in fructification rather than in decadence. "If writing is in league
with death, however, it is also in cahoots with femininity," Maud

Ellmann writes of Eliot. "In *The Waste Land*, the 'hearty female stench' converges with the odour of mortality—and both exude from *writing*, from the violated and putrescent corpse of speech. To use the text's sexology, writing and the stink of femininity have overpowered the priapic realm of voice" (106). In "Anna Livia Plurabelle," Joyce reintegrates the feminine, voice, poetry, and labor into an avant-garde textual performance of art's staging of non-art as art. In speech marked with their labor—"Wring out the clothes! Wring in the dew! . . . Will we spread them here now? Ay, we will. Flip! Spread on your bank and I'll spread mine on mine. Flep! It's what I'm doing. Spread! It's churning chill. Der went is rising. I'll lay a few stones on the hostel sheets. A man and his bride embraced between them. Else I'd have sprinkled and folded them only. And I'll tie my butcher's apron here. It's suety yet" (FW 213.19)—the washerwomen enact their social relations to each other and their community, even including in their poetic worktalk the greasy non-aesthetic object of the butcher boy's apron. In "Anna Livia Plurabelle," Joyce comes closest, I believe, to fulfilling the artistic socialist prophecy extruded, like Stephen's butcher boy, from the end of *Portrait*: "To those multitudes not as yet in the wombs of humanity but surely engenderable there, he would give the word" (P 265).

3. Washerwomen's Working Talk

Joyce's political gesture is not so much representational as performative of representational occlusions and incompletions. His procedures are intertextual and intratextual, as I have tried to show—sometimes using external texts as references to show gaps or deceptions in his own, sometimes having his own texts trip themselves and expose their ruptures, seams, and blind spots, and sometimes turning one of his texts against another of his own texts to turn it inside out, or to supplement it, thereby exposing its lacks and absences. Having argued that "Clay" exposes itself as a "blind" text, a text that can't see itself and therefore doesn't know what motivates its own narration, I would now argue that the "Anna Livia Plurabelle" chapter of *Finnegans Wake* (I.8) retrieves some of what is elided in "Clay" and therefore supplements some of its gaps—while, of course, opening others. "Clay" occludes the labor of the washerwomen and suppresses their speech ("Then Ginger Mooney lifted up her mug of tea and proposed Maria's health . . . and said she was sorry she hadn't a sup of porter to drink it in" [D 101]) with ashamed apology, "she knew that Mooney meant well though, of course, she had the notions of a common woman." The ALP chapter

restores both the washerwomen's labor and their speech, rolling
back the narrative sequence of "Clay" that introduces the washerwomen at the end of their labor, as they roll down their sleeves and
come in to tea, "In a few minutes the women began to come in by
twos and threes, wiping their steaming hands in their petticoats and
pulling down the sleeves of their blouses over their red steaming
arms" (D 100). "Clay" leaves us only the synecdochic trace of the
steam on their reddened arms to indicate the effaced labor of the
women's laundering; *Finnegans Wake*, like a film played in reverse, begins with the washerwomen rolling up their sleeves in
order to begin washing and talking, "Tuck up your sleeves and
loosen your talktapes" (FW 196.8). Joyce's political message lies in
the difference between these two texts, these two narrations and
their discursive modes: a difference of repression, of not wanting to
know those who do the dirty labor of the world—who pick up the
tab of civilization, as Adorno put it—and not wanting to recognize
them as speaking and thinking and feeling subjects. The repression
practiced by "Clay"'s narration constitutes a social oppression and
political reification that does not become visible until it is reversed
in *Finnegans Wake*.

Georg Lukács, who opens his attack on the ideology of modernism with an attack on Joyce's use of the interior monologue in *Ulysses* (17), would find his objections rebutted by the dialogical performance of the washerwomen in the text of the ALP chapter. The text
performs dialogue and constitutes social exchange, and its dialogue,
furthermore, is imprinted with the material and social reality of the
outer world. The washerwomen's discourse is created by their labor:
they speak because their hands are occupied but their mouths and
minds are free while they work; at the same time their gossip is
frequently interrupted by the contingencies of their work: the need
to pass laundry supplies back and forth, to attend to the condition
of the clothes in their hands, to supervise and criticize each other's
work. The fabled lyricism of their musical discourse is impregnated
with the realism of social reference to their class, their gender, their
religion, their nationality. Richard Wall tracks Anglo-Irish pronun-
ciation throughout the washerwomen's speech in this chapter, and
its political significance as Joyce's true vernacular, in opposition to
the literate Anglo-Saxon English that we assume as his normative
narrative speech, must be understood as a choice Joyce makes in
favor of the urban working class and against the Gaelic League's efforts to artificially revive Gaelic from remote western rural com-
munities such as those of the Aran Isles. "We can imagine Synge's
excitement as the music of the islanders' speech began to catch his

ear," Ulick O'Connor wrote. "He must have known that if he could set it down in some form and transfer its melody to English, he would have brought a new sound to literature" (192). I would argue that Joyce, hearing similar music in working women's Irish brogue, set it down in "Anna Livia Plurabelle" and so too brought a new sound to literature. But the music of their lyricism does not drown out its performance as labor.

"What am I rancing now and I'll thank you? Is it a pinny or is it a surplice? Arran, where's your nose? And where's the starch?" (FW 204.30) signifies their occupation and social relation as laundresses ("Where's the starch?") working for families with babies in diapers as well as for Catholic priests in surplices. Their labor and their speech are therefore sometimes congruent, when they must speak to facilitate their work ("Throw us your hudson soap for the honour of Clane! . . . Ay, and don't forget the reckitts I lohaned you" [FW 212.24]), and the rest of the time analogous, when the social function of their discursive gossip serves to flush the moral dirt out of reputations while they wash the personal filth out of the community's linen. Their physical ablutions double their discursive absolutions of the community's involuntary confession to them, and through them.

In "Anna Livia Plurabelle" Joyce has art produce a representation of the otherness of art, of that which art precludes and on whose negation it is founded as a surplus: manual labor. If an ontological homology could be established between labor as not-art, and woman as not-man, then the laboring woman, the washerwoman, becomes the otherness of woman as aesthetic object, she becomes woman-as-not-art. Insofar as manual labor is the other of bourgeois consciousness, what bourgeois consciousness represses in its human ontology, the washerwomen's discourse works or labors: it does not merely describe or narrate their work, it facilitates and participates in their work, and it acts on their work. The rhetorical structures of their dialogue, obscured by "the rhythms of the poetry" as labor is obscured by art, must therefore be retrieved for their social and working *activity*, as a contending force against their own lyricism.[6] In the washerwomen's dialogue the laundering tasks become discursive activity, and every step and operation in the manual laundering of clothes is therefore acted out, in a roughly coherent sequence, by the sequence of their conversation. First they *soak* the dirtiest clothes, like HCE's filthy shirt ("Look at the shirt of him! Look at the dirt of it! He has all my water black on me. And it steeping and stuping since this time last wik" [FW 196.11]). Then they *sort* cleaner and dirtier clothes, separating diapers from priestly vestments by their smell ("What am I rancing now and I'll thank you? Is it a pinny or is it a surplice? Arran, where's your nose?". Then they *starch* the finer linens, "And where's the starch? That's not the vesdre benediction smell" [FW 204.30]). They use *ashes as an abrasive* for tough spots ("Lynd us your blessed ashes here till I scrub the canon's underpants" [FW 206.26]) and *pass the soap* to each other as they commence with the scrubbing ("Throw us your hudson soap for the honour of Clane!" [FW 212.24]). When they are done washing, they *wring* the wet laundry ("Wring out the clothes!" [FW 213.19]) and *spread* it out to dry ("Throw the cobwebs from your eyes, woman, and spread your washing proper! It's well I know your sort of slop" [FW 214.16]), first *anchoring* large items like sheets so the rising wind, "Der went is rising" [FW 213.23] won't blow them away ("I'll lay a few stones on the hostel sheets" [FW 213.24]). They *sprinkle* the linens for ease of ironing ("Else I'd have sprinkled and folded them only" [FW 213.25]), having earlier heated the iron ("Hustle along, why can't you? Spitz on the iern while it's hot" [FW 207.21]). One of their last jobs is to *tally* the diverse pieces of laundry to account for all the articles they've washed ("Six shifts, ten kerchiefs . . . the convent napkins, twelve, one baby's shawl" [FW 213.27]). The washerwomen's conversation works to *perform*, not merely *represent*, their labor. Their discursive exchanges act out the commands, requests, borrowings, decisions, reproaches, criticisms, and so on, necessary to get the job done.

What a bourgeois consciousness like that of the narrative voice of "Clay" elides is not just the fact of manual labor, that it is being *done*, but also its subjective aspect. Since physical labor is done by the body it produces effects on the body, it is felt, and if it is sufficiently heavy and strenuous, it is felt as strain, pain, and injury to the body.[7] Special attention should therefore be paid to the rhetoric of *complaint* that shapes the washerwomen's conversation, for while this is too easily dismissed as a comic effect, their complaint articulates their awareness of labor's effect on their bodies, and their own understanding of their own social reasons for performing it. In the residue of their accents lurks a latent political understanding that connects the burdensome bagfuls of dirty laundry to colonialism and its exaction of tithes from the Irish poor—"My colonial, wardha bagful! A bakereen's dusind with tithe tillies to boot" [FW 212.20]. The strenuous mechanical motions of the scrubbing make the women feel like rusting machines in the pervasive damp, "Wallop it well with your battle and clean it. My wrists are wrusty rubbing the mouldaw stains" [FW 196.16]. Besides the unwholesome dampness, the washerwomen are subjected to extremes of temperature, water too hot or too cold, either scalding or freezing their hands, "My hands are blawcauld between isker and suda like that piece of pattern chayney there" (FW 213.4) and coarsening them with soda and abrasives. Bending over the brook (German *Bach*) makes their backs hurt, "O, my back, my back, my bach!" (FW 213.17). Besides the physical effects, the drudging labor produces a coarsening of their social relations as well, and the women's exchanges are often marked by the aggression of reproach ("And you ought to have aird them. They've moist come off her" [FW 204.34]), interdiction ("Will you hold your peace and listen well to what I am going to say now" [FW 207.30]), accusation and self-defense ("You've all the swirls your side of the current. Well, am I to blame for that if I have? Who said you're to blame for that if you have? You're a bit on the sharp side. I'm on the wide" [FW 212.27]). We're reminded of the climate of threatened violence in the laundry in "Clay"—"And Ginger Mooney was always saying what she wouldn't do to the dummy who had charge of the irons if it wasn't for Maria" (D 99). The *Wake*'s washerwomen offer Maria a worker's prayer, "Lord help you, Maria, full of grease, the load is with me!" (FW 214.18).

The *Wake*'s washerwomen display consciousness not only of the harsh effects of their work on their bodies and their lives, but also that its reasons are the necessities of physical and social survival. They drudge to keep their families from starving and to give their children a chance to enter the middle class, mindful that they are paying the price for the benefit of those who enjoy social progress. The women may not be political analysts or activists, but neither are they oblivious to their social and economic oppression. "Scorching my hand and starving my famine to make his private linen public" (FW 196.15) says one of them, complaining, in effect, that her pain and incommensurate wages barely manage to feed her own family while they allow someone better off than herself to enjoy social presentability in clean clothes. Anna Livia Plurabelle's poem or song reiterates this same crude analysis: she wants a job doing laundry for a lord of the manor or a knight when her barely edible food, her "horsebrose and milk" ("horsemeat" in the first fair copy holograph [JA 47474–110]; or "horsebrose" as an oat mash used as horse feed—McHugh describes "brose" as "made by pouring boiling water on oatmeal" in his *Annotations* 201.16) runs out:

Is there irwell a lord of the manor or a knight of the shire at strike, I wonder, that'd dip me a dace or two in cash for washing and darning his worshipful socks for him now we're run out of horsebrose and milk? (FW 201.13)

The washerwomen's narrative will trace the complex etiology that brings ALP to the point of wanting to join them, and that makes her their proleptic double: a downward spiral in her husband's fortune (*"my frugal key of our larder"*) that begins in poverty without wedding ring or proper home, "Not a grasshoop to ring her, not an antsgrain of ore" (FW 197.27)—rather like Nora Barnacle upon her elopement—and that in spite of the man's efforts ("He erned his lille Bunbath hard, our staly bred, the trader . . . In this wet of his prow" [FW 198.5], ends in his "hungerstriking" (FW 199.4]).

Like Charlie Chaplin left to eat a shoe in *The Gold Rush*, the Dedalus girls in *Ulysses* are left to boil clothes alongside their charity peasoup in their kitchen, "a greyish mass beneath bubbling suds" (U 10:261), and we fear for a moment they will have boiled clothes instead of soup to eat:

> —What's in the pot? she asked.
> —Shirts, Maggy said.
> Boody cried angrily:
> —Crickey, is there nothing for us to eat?
> (U 10:271).

Like ALP's prayer, the Dedalus girls too use a profane Our Father, "—Our father who art not in heaven"—to pray for a daily bread he will not or cannot provide. Little Stephen's social snobbishness toward women who wash clothes receives its comeuppance as his own starving sisters serve as their own washerwomen. The economic condition of Irish women, then—like that of all housewives—is hopelessly tied to the working condition of their men, and when the men don't work, the women starve. Furthermore, as Jean Gardiner points out, "In a time of crisis . . . housewives bear the major burden of working-class loss of real income and are forced to work harder in the home to stretch the reduced wages coming in" (178). Joyce represents this in his earliest fictions when he reports that "Mrs Daedalus had to set her wits to work to provide even one substantial meal every day" (SH 151), and we can see in "Anna Livia Plurabelle" a revisitation of that conversation between Stephen and Cranly at the end of *Portrait*, when the issue of orthodoxy and Stephen's Easter duty occludes the issue Cranly is trying to probe, of the conditions of the mother's life ("I don't want to pry into your family affairs. But was your father what is called well-to-do? . . . Are you in good circumstances at present?—Do I look it? Stephen asked bluntly. . . .—Your mother must have gone through a good deal of suffering, he said then" [P 241]).

In the most extensive complaint by one of the washerwomen, what appear to be almost comical exaggerations of working-class calamity actually produce an effective analysis of the interrelations of the injurious conditions of poverty: "Amn't I up since the damp dawn, marthared mary allacook, with Corrigan's pulse and varicoarse veins, my pramaxle smashed, Alice Jane in decline and my oneeyed mongrel twice run over, soaking and bleaching boiler rags, and sweating cold, a widow like me, for to deck my tennis champion son, the laundryman with the lavandier flannels?" (FW 214.22). This song of the martyred widow[8] creates a small naturalistic novel of a mutilated life, broken prams, injured dogs, unwholesome work, miserable conditions of damp and cold, ruined health, too many children, a consumptive daughter, a parasitic son, and so on and so forth. Furthermore, she is one of "those who pick up the tab for the progress of civilization," and Joyce emphasizes just that "tab." The washerwoman with the tennis-champion son in lavender flannels echoes the imperialism theme implicit in the *Ulysses* joke of Bella Cohen supporting a son at Oxford with her whorehouse in Nighttown. While Joyce may be merely venting Irish plebeian *ressentiment* by making whoresons of his privileged Sassenach peers, he also reiterates a point already elaborated in "Telemachus" when he has Haines's money derive from Britain's African imperialism, "selling jalap to Zulus or some bloody swindle or other" (U 1:156). The budget for supporting the bearers of culture, the public-school tennis champions and Oxford men, is balanced, Joyce seems to suggest, on the backs of blacks, washerwomen, and prostitutes at the turn of the century.

4. Ablution and Absolution

By giving his washerwomen the self-awareness to recognize their social situation, its causes and its effects upon them, by making them socially self-conscious, Joyce is able to demonstrate the transformational power of labor that Kojève finds in exploring the metaphysics of bondage. Labor is metaphysically empowering because it endows the Slave with the experience of overcoming material nature, and with the experience of confronting mortality and death. In "Anna Livia Plurabelle," these intellectual and psychological products of labor are dramatized also as empowering the washerwomen in relation to their community. By making their situation primitive rather than industrialized, their washing not yet mechanized, their clientele a village or neighborhood rather than a city, Joyce lets their labor retain a human and humanizing dimension with which they resist its oppressions. The washerwomen do not wash anonymous and depersonalized cloth; they recognize in the laundry the clothing of individuals in the community, and they therefore wash, in effect, metonymic extensions of their bodies. Their work becomes for them a source of intellectual and narrative stimulation, as they act on the laundry intellectually, "reading" and interpreting their clients' lives from their linens, and connecting themselves, in an intimate way, to the community by their knowledge. What the washerwomen learn about people from their wash is an empowering knowledge beyond the power of blackmail, the power to betray the intimate, personal, sexual secrets that soiled laundry discloses. What they learn, ontologically, is something of the universal materiality of the human body, its exudation of living matter, its corporeal and sexual functioning, that is, its mortality. That is why, I believe, the washer-women become connected for Joyce to the function of the banshees, the women who wail and keen before a death occurs, and who there-fore prophesy death. For the *Wake's* washerwomen, this foreknowl-edge takes a self-reflexive, but purely idiomatic form, as a dead metaphor for the coterminality of death and narration—"Tell me all. Tell me now. You'll die when you hear" (FW 196.5) or "I'm dying down off my iodine feet until I lerryn Anna Livia's cushingloo" (FW 200.35). They will die when they stop talking and when they stop working; conversely they will not be able to stop working and talking until they die. But besides learning from laundry and wash-ing the universal mortality of the body, they also learn its demo-cratic universality. The "worshipful socks" ALP wants to wash for a lord of the manor or a knight of the shire will collect filth and smell like any other socks. In their washtubs, the priest's vestments and his underpants, the baby's diapers, the convent napkins, the poet's combinations or underwear—"Tell me the trent of it while I'm lath-ering hail out of Denis Florence MacCarthy's combies" (FW 200.33)—all have the same status and get the same treatment from them. Washerwomen stand at the point of social leveling (unlike Eliot's Tiresias disconcerted by the squalor of the typist's "drying combi-nations" perilously spread from her window) and have no illusions about the arbitrary and culturally created nature of social hierarchy. Their labor transforms them into social naturalists.

It is this "intellectual" aspect of their labor, the way the laundry imprinted with the human body's matter and effluvia involuntarily confesses to the washerwomen the community's transgressions, animality, and mortality, that mandates the suppression of their dangerous knowledge and their speech. "Baptiste me, father, for she has sinned!" (FW 204.36), Mrs. Magrath's drawers confess to the washerwomen. The washerwomen's work, like that of servants, is considered degraded because it requires the handling of personal wastes and excretions; it is the noisome job of "throwing out the dirt" (U 18:72), presumably emptying slops, that makes Molly hesitate to do without a servant. Yet what is protected by suppressing the washerwomen, by silencing them as subjects, is their knowledge of the producers of personal dirt, "I know by heart the places he likes to saale, duddurty devil!" (FW 196.14). The cruel and hypocritical irony of the washerwomen's oppression is that they are degraded not only for what they do, for being, ostensibly, grossly physical workers with no minds, but precisely for their opposite quality, for possessing sharpness of wit, for their powers of observation and inference, for their ability to read, decipher, and interpret, for their function as semioticians and critics. Fashion, the style of people's clothing, we know from Roland Barthes, constitutes a language system, a way for people to create social identities for themselves (Mahaffey 161–171). But when fashion is reduced back to laundry, the secret writing of its materiality can be read. The text projects the washerwomen as producers of a Lacanian critical "gaze," the enemy of desire, that sees a community as it does not want to be seen. Their narration, then, becomes a synecdoche of the social function of the Joycean *oeuvre*, the Joycean text censored and censured because it, too, saw the community as it did not want to be seen. "Anna Livia Plurabelle" thus fuses the social paranoia produced by critical art with the power of the reconstituted proletarian subject. That is Joyce's avant-garde gesture: to make art self-critical by transforming it into the eye of not-art. The *Wake's* washerwomen represent the reconstituted elision of "Clay" in order to explain why in "Clay" they were silenced. The ALP chapter specifies that the bourgeois text of art suppresses washerwomen because the community does not want its own loss of social identity, its degradation as animal, mortal, and sexual mirrored back to it in their servants' knowledge. Their proletarian "eye" takes on the metaphysical function of penetrating the truth. The washerwomen thus become social analogues to the priest, the psychoanalyst, and the doctor, but because the community bestows its confidence on them involuntarily, they remain beyond institutional social control. This is what makes them dangerous and requires their suppression: first as whores, then as laundryworkers, "Clay"'s washerwomen are capable of disseminating the community's truth in ways beyond its control, and oblige the bourgeoisie to see itself socially, culturally, and aesthetically stripped.

A small digression in the chapter illustrates the process: the washerwomen virtually deduce a miniature novel about Mrs. Magrath

from her underwear.[9] After identifying her drawers by their smell—
"I can tell from here by their *eau de Colo* and the scent of her oder
they're Mrs Magrath's" (FW 204.33)—they proceed to draw their,
and our, imaginations into indecent intimacy to Mrs. Magrath's private parts, "And you ought to have aird them. They've moist come
off her." They then draw inferences about the wealth and social status of their wearer from the material of the lingerie fabric, "Creases
in silk they are, not crampton lawn," and decide that their cultural
embellishments, the cologne that scents them and the frills that
decorate them ("The only parr with frills in old the plain. So they
are, I declare!" [FW 205.2]), suggest that Mrs. Magrath may be extra-
maritally sexually active. The drawers' construction, to facilitate
ease in taking them off, reinforces this inference, and gives new
meaning to the "hip" in the cheer "hip hip hurrah!": "Through her
catchment ring she freed them easy, with her hips' hurrahs for her
knees'dontelleries" (FW 205.1). We are reminded with what complex sexual significance Joyce freighted the construction of drawers
in *Ulysses*. Molly's excitation upon her first flirtation with Boylan
at the DBC takes form as need to go to the bathroom. But she has
trouble extricating herself from a particularly complicated pair of
underpants Bloom makes her wear, "the black closed breeches he
made me buy takes you half an hour to let them down wetting all myself always with some brandnew fad every other week" (U 18:251).
It is almost as though Bloom, fearing that Molly plans to stray, makes
her wear breeches that confine her like a chastity belt. The ease
with which Mrs. Magrath's are designed to come off leads the washerwomen to speculate that she plans to exhibit them to old men
(Old Parr, English centenarian accused of incontinence [McHugh
205.2]) as well as young men (parr = young salmon, "the only parr")
like young Belvedere students working on exhibitions and in rowing
clubs, "Welland well! If tomorrow keeps fine who'll come tripping
to sightsee? . . . The Belvedarean exhibitioners. In their cruisery caps
and oarsclub colours" (FW 205.3), but that she perhaps plans to
charge money as well, "O, may the diabolo twisk your seifety pin!
You child of Mammon, Kinsella's Lillith!" (FW 205.10). Eventually
they detect the initials of her maiden name, L. K., on the drawers
("And here is her nubilee letters too. Ellis on quay in scarlet thread"
(FW 205.7) and the garment now becomes a text bearing scarlet letters as her heraldic insignia, "Linked for the world on a flushcal-
oured field." As good readers, the washerwomen recognize the function of *difference* in signification: "Annan exe after to show they're
not Laura Keown's" (FW 205.9), an X distinguishes the initials for
Lillith Kinsella from those of Laura Keown. Mrs. Magrath's under-

wear tells a story, or so the washerwomen seem to infer, that generically belongs to scandal magazines, something about a young, recently married wife (who still has panties from her maiden days) showing off her frilly drawers to well-heeled young boys. But unlike writers of trash journalism or fiction, the washerwomen's gossip is uncommodifiable. It is a power without social utility except to dereify social relations, as Jameson suggests of gossip. The washerwomen's gossip is devalued by gender as what Joyce elsewhere in the *Wake* calls "Woman. Squash" (FW 390.32), that is, "woman's *Quatsch*" or woman's prattle.[10]

The washerwomen's dialogue allows them to recognize that a part of themselves returns to the bodies and lives of their clients, and that they have imprinted themselves, by a curiously reverse writing that is actually an erasure, an erasure of dirt, on the community's textile texts. They attach to their labor an awareness of what they have done, that disperses their laboring subjectivity, themselves as laboring subjects, into every linen press and onto every body their cleaned clothes will ultimately inhabit. The invisible writing of their labor will be repressed, ignored, and misunderstood, but it will be there, like the ironmould mark Mrs. Fleming burnt onto Molly Bloom's drawers, and that Molly fears the artist, Stephen, might misread as a personal stain rather than as the mark of labor. As not-artists producing not-art, the washerwomen replace woman as aesthetic and erotic object with woman as the producer of the sign of her labor.

CHAPTER EIGHT

Modernism, Myth, and Desire in "Nausicaa"

FROM THE PERSPECTIVE OF both its content and its form, Joyce's "Nausicaa," his pulp fiction narrative of erotic titillation between strangers, could emblematize the most characteristic moral and poetic features of the modernist nightmare. The sterility of its meretricious sexuality could be inserted into Eliot's "Waste Land" and the cheapness of its meretricious art into Pound's "Hugh Selwyn Mauberley," to serve as the double exemplar of a modern age of debased passion and debased form—a parable in which the Fisher King has become lost in the Five and Dime. "Nausicaa" therefore has a special relevance for determining Joyce's relationship to the way high modernism institutionalized a particularly elevated and disciplined form of aesthetics as the moral project of the early twentieth century. If "Nausicaa"'s grace, its redemptive maneuver, is what Eliot in his essay "Ulysses, Order, and Myth" called "the mythical method," then this *Ulysses* chapter would indeed function as an exemplary high modernist text. "Instead of narrative method, we may now use the mythical method," Eliot writes. "It is, I seriously believe, a step toward making the modern world possible for art" (178). "Nausicaa" would then function as aesthetic analogue to "The Waste Land," and share with that poem Eliot's ideological assumptions underlying the transcendentalizing potential of myth. Myth for Eliot appears highly overdetermined, but functionally unified—serving as a template of ordered form that brings timeless aesthetic tradition to modernity's artistic proliferations, as a moral norm to bring timeless values to modernity's spiritual disintegrations, and as a critical norm to stabilize modernity's uncontrollable perspectivism. The extent to which Eliot inscribes the foreseen failure of these aims into his poem ("Poetry separates itself from life by feigning wholeness, by declaring itself a *sign* of wholeness. It is nostalgic for the old order" [Riddel 267]) determines his implication in postmodernism.

But the failures to recenter and restabilize itself that modernist poetry may figure as its nascent postmodernity, I will ascribe in Joyce's text to an avant-garde gesture of a historically self-conscious, and a socially self-critical, kind. To Joyce's "mythical method," especially, I will impute a particularly devious procedure: a Penelopean gesture of weaving one myth into the text only to unravel it with another, in order that the logic of the mythic effect in modernism's aesthetic ideology may be interrogated. Specifically, Joyce uses the Homeric narrative of Nausicaa to enact the repression of one of its own causal myths: the "Trial of Paris," the beauty contest whose outcome leads to the Trojan War. The story of frustrated romance between Nausicaa and Odysseus is thus disrupted as a formal template in Joyce's text by the countermythology of an allegory of aesthetic response that implicates artistic genres and their various social functions in a political problematic relevant to questions of modern aesthetic desire. If this formulation resonates to Stephen's aesthetic theory in *Portrait*, with its focus on genre and aesthetic response (static, kinetic, etc.), then it may be precisely because "Nausicaa" offers a dramatic or gestural countertext, a pantomime from the popular arts, to just that problematized set of issues. Although I will limit my parameter to the *Ulysses* chapter, the spectacle of mythic displacement that I find in Joyce's "Nausicaa," the unraveling of one myth with another, could be widened into larger questions of modern mythopoeia and their negotiations between the empirical historicizing impulse of such nineteenth century figures as Samuel Butler and David Strauss, on the one hand, and the political refunctioning of mythology in radically different ways in the works of Richard Wagner and Friedrich Nietzsche, on the other. Joyce's project in "Nausicaa," I will contend, glosses modernism's own privileging of classicism not only as a consolidation of its aestheticism for metaphysical ends (Eliot) or their deconstruction (see Riddel's discussion of William Carlos Williams' use of the Cloisters tapestries in *Paterson* [274–288]), but also as an extension (if against the grain of Eliot's criticism of Arnold) of liberalism's use of classicism as a cultural commodity used to defend against mass education and mass culture.

In Eliot, especially, a double and paradoxical gesture toward liberalism is enacted, which gives it metaphysical resistance at the same time that it appeals to its project of cultural retrieval. In spite of his refusal, in "What is a Classic?," to situate himself in the classicism-romanticism controversy, his position in his later attacks on Arnold makes clear his protest against the forms of supplementarity to which a range of cultural secularisms (including T. E. Hulme's figu-

ration of romanticism) were prone. "Eliot denounces Bergson and
Matthew Arnold with equal vehemence for instigating modern
heresy," Maud Ellmann writes. "Both supplanted true religion with
a glittering sham, and the substitutes have pullulated ever since"
(48). Against this protest, classicism becomes itself a form of supplementarity—a nostalgia for the metaphysical presence that once was
God. The transcendental aura of Eliot's modernism is thus produced
by the hidden metaphysics of its desire—"Eliot's interpretation,
that is, reconstructs the 'structure' of an historical *episteme* in
terms of an aesthetic, of an Image that is, in his term, autotelic, but
which by its very formal wholeness acknowledges itself as art, or
ritual. This 'form' is the symbol of an otherwise imperfectly known
perfection, and thus a shadow representation of desire" (Riddel 267).

But if the modernist project in the 1910's and 1920's takes form as
abstract or pure desire to preserve *value-as-such*, the formal and the-
matic enactment of that desire in the poetry nonetheless betrays an
instrumentality or use. Aimed against the tide of modern insignificance that threatens to level the entire social and cultural order,
religious hierarchy and aesthetic judgment, political stability and
economic control, intellectual precision and emotional discrimination, the classic as code of pure desire becomes inserted into Arnoldian distinctions between "high" and "low" art that reinstate classicism in aesthetic discourse as a cultural commodity. Eliot may
decry the degradation of Philomel's tragedy as ornamental home
decor in "The Waste-Land"—"Above the antique mantel was dis-
played . . . The change of Philomel"—but the allusion itself contributes to the therapeutic recuperation of formal virtuosity and classical erudition needed to expunge the vulgarity. A poetry like Pound's
"Mauberley" laments the usurpation of the classical lyre by the
pianola in a language of poetic virtuosity that reinstates the lyre.
But Joyce's parodic form in "Nausicaa" problematizes the mythical
method and its classical instrumentality at the outset. To be sure,
the parodic form appears to denigrate popular culture's colonization
of the female mind with vulgar desire. But the narration's simulta-
neous impregnation with a failed classical erudition could, as surely,
parody the text's self-consciousness of its own modernistic colonization. In its reflexive complexity, the play of desire in "Nausicaa"
seems to rebuke Arnoldian liberalism's snobbishness by reproducing in its Philistinism desires identical to those that animate high
art. The critique produced by "Nausicaa"'s ironic doubling of desires deflates its metaphysical pretensions at the same time that it
exposes modernism's scholarly exhibitionism.

Under the influence of the structuralist anthropology that was just becoming available to the American academy in the early seventies, I tried to argue, in *The Decentered Universe*, that the function of myth in *Finnegans Wake* was meta-mythopoetic—Joyce's effort to have the text raise questions about the nature, structure, and function of myth, mythology, and mythic language. The aim of this interrogation, I argued, was to destabilize the transcendentalizing effect of myth by decentering its structure in a Lévi-Straussian assortment of deprivileged variants and versions, and decentering its meaning by shifting it from the transparencies of a Jungian collective unconscious or a Campbellian monomyth, to the problematized structural encodings that made Lévi-Straussian mythology homologous to the rebus of the Freudian dream-text. But the meta-mythopoeia of "Nausicaa" strikes me as addressing a different set of issues arising from the problem of how society historically refunctions the role of mythology in its culture. "Nausicaa" explores the way myth's service as an instrument of desire in the symbolic order assimilates to the power of institutions, and becomes, in effect, a condition of institutional formation. "Nausicaa" interrogates the function of mythology in the institutionalization of art, both "high" and "low." More specifically, the myths of "Nausicaa" explore mythological allegories that wed sexuality to aesthetics ("The Trial of Paris," for example) that naturalize an intrinsic connection between conventionalized notions of "beauty" and sexual desire into gender and class ideologies shaping social institutions (courtship, romance, marriage, prostitution) as well as artistic institutions (literary and popular genres and entertainments, standards of erudition and taste, etc.). Myth in "Nausicaa" demythifies itself as a social construct capable of being unmasked by the particularities of history.

Modernism's special contribution to refunctioning mythology in the early twentieth century was to make it the guarantor of cultural value, and the connector to cultural tradition. "Nausicaa"'s demystification of this conservative function takes the form of exposing the way this abstract valorization conceals its class reference by appealing to forms of erudition and taste that are ultimately determined by class, and that therefore depend on specific class exclusions and disqualifications. This process of problematizing the relation of myth and class becomes apparent even in the question of how to assess the function of the mythic structure, the Homeric narrative, giving shape to the narrative of the chapter. The function of the classical myth in "Nausicaa" is paradoxical, because by the same gesture with which it performs its implicit transcendentalizing function, to inflate and enhance Joyce's text, making the chapter seem larger and more significant in its assimilation to an ancient classical tradition, it also makes the constrictions and barrenness of the chapter's language and values painfully palpable. This results in a strange dissonance of both generic and aesthetic register. Without the Homeric parallel, *Ulysses* becomes merely "Mr. Bloom's Day in Dublin," and "Nausicaa" becomes merely "Miss MacDowell's Evening on the Beach," fictions stripped of their classical aura at the same time that they are seemingly stripped of their self-critical apparatus. The status and function of this mythic doubling has been the source of some of the critical controversy surrounding the chapter, which might be formulated as the difference implicit in two questions: Is "Nausicaa" pulp fiction tricked out as a classic, or is "Nausicaa" a classic tricked out as pulp fiction? My own mediation of this controversy is to argue that "Nausicaa" is the spectacle of pulp fiction wanting to be a classic, because "high" art sets standards and aspirations that are internalized by "low art," and that condemn its consumers to a perpetual cultural frustration. The Gerty MacDowells and Leopold Blooms of the world have the same cultural and spiritual aspirations that are set forth by high art, and their constraints in pursuing and achieving them are produced not by innate limitations (stupidity or indifference) but by historical constraints. Gerty's narrator tells us "Had kind fate but willed her to be born a gentlewoman of high degree in her own right and had she only received the benefit of a good education Gerty MacDowell might easily have held her own beside any lady in the land and have seen herself exquisitely gowned with jewels on her brow" (U 13:99). Such sentences work perversely, creating in their fatuity effects opposite from those intended—suggesting that Gerty is a hopeless scrub, whom no amount of money or education could have improved. But the sentence performs its own truth of a sentiment lacking the poetic tradition and expressive means (breeding and erudition) to achieve the elevation it desires. Like Gerty, the language suffers the pathos of thwarted poetic desire—too low bred and poorly educated to escape the deformations of archaism and artificiality produced by its lack of taste, discipline, and experience.

Joyce implements his indictment of the social effects of the idealizations at the heart of learning and taste with a strategy that is the obverse of the high modernist display of classical and international erudition. Joyce conspicuously displays in "Nausicaa" a deprivation (not an absence) of education and culture, a lack of taste and erudition that is not simple dullness or ignorance but an ardent, yet doomed desire, for high culture. The narration's faulty learning is not stupidity, but the thwarted, yet eager, desire for learnedness. Joyce marks in the poetic desire of the language a crucial difference between two kinds of cultural lack—a Philistinism that is contemptuous of culture versus a Philistinism that is enslaved by desire for a culture from which it is debarred—in order to rediagnose the cultural malaise of modernity not as spiritual bankruptcy, but as social disqualification. The spiritual condition of Joyce's Philistines is like that of heathens in Catholic theology who would believe in God if someone taught and enlightened them, but who cannot invent their own conversion. They are held to experience what the Catholic Church calls "a baptism of desire."

Furthermore, Joyce puts the failed erudition of "Nausicaa" in the service of thwarted romantic desire, for reasons that the chapter's mythological undertow, the competing currents of the tales of Nausicaa and the Trial of Paris, eventually bring to the surface. Gerty MacDowell appears, like Nausicaa, a winner in the arena of regal beauty, only to have her victory retracted by a logic that eventually questions the role of myth, art, and culture, in the consolidation of an ego whose friability they simultaneously insure. The display of Gerty's beauty produced by the inflated and pretentious narrative rhetoric is a dramatization not of vanity, but of vanity masking profound sexual insecurity. Gerty's narration is not a paean to her beauty but the fantasy of how such a paean might sound, could someone be found to utter it. The nexus of beauty and sexual desirability, narrativized in the Trial of Paris, is shown in the "Nausicaa" chapter to depend for its vehicle on modes of expression whose model is found in art and poetry. The problem of finding articulation for the erotic power of her beauty is therefore critical to Gerty's social ontology—whose cruel truth is that there is no plausible speaker in her real world who could or would offer an adequate or convincing testimonial to her beauty, virtue, and desirability. The voice that speaks of Gerty in "Nausicaa" therefore makes best sense as a phantom narrator constructed by Gerty's imagination to produce the language of her desire, that is, to produce the hypothetical praises that she fears no one will ever offer, and that she equates with art. Her narration therefore represents Gerty not as she is, nor even as she is not, but as she would like to be, as she would like people to think about her, and indeed, to write about her, given the conspicuous and emphatic literariness of her narration. Art's mission in the chapter's tacit philosophy is to create models of idealization into which the modern self may pitch its desires, and hope for validation of their possible realization.

Gerty's narrative voice inscribes a grasp of erudition's force in producing the cultural prestige of "high" art, and therefore endows Gerty's hypothetical praise, her language of desire, with what it imagines to be erudition. But merely imagined erudition is doomed to produce merely "highfalutin'" prose that condemns "Nausicaa"'s narration to self-betraying excesses, slips, and solecisms. As a result the chapter's prose is riven by a yawning gap between its poetic reach and its poetic grasp—a cultural failure whose abuse of the classics may especially be laid at modernism's door. The myth of Nausicaa promotes its desires throughout Gerty's narration. She would like to be a princess, or at least to be thought as beautiful as a princess, but in giving her a metaphorical aristocracy, her narration merely succeeds in making her an aristocrat manquée, less queen than "queenly" (U 13:97). The narration's metaphorical exigencies doom Gerty to occupy the lack inherent in adverbial displacements, and in classicisms that are not quite classical allusions but tags that sound vaguely classical. In the discrepancy between Homeric poetic diction and the narration's allusive adverbial forms, its ignorance of Homer is inscribed. The sentence "her rosebud mouth was a genuine Cupid's bow, Greekly perfect" (U 13:88) pretends to know something of classical perfection, but Greek harmony of proportions and relations is to be found, probably neither in the shape of Gerty's mouth, nor, certainly, in the shape of the phrase "Greekly perfect."

The classic, ancient and modern, expressed in its twin form by Ezra Pound's wonderful double metaphor, "His true Penelope was Flaubert," haunts "Nausicaa" as an impossible model of desire. It is as though "Nausicaa," both text and woman, are haunted by a cultural ideal they do not know, but whose prestige they covet. It is as though the language of the text—limited, as Hugh Kenner claims Joyce himself was, to translations and popularizations—knows there are great classics out there in the culture somewhere, but deprived, like Gerty herself, of "the benefit of a good education," has access to them only in mediated, secondary, and often corrupted form. Even the scholarly or quasi-scholarly studies Joyce consulted, like Victor Bérard's *Les Phéniciens et l'Odyssée*, and Samuel Butler's *The Authoress of the Odyssey*, argue for the classical text's primordial reversions, displacements, and dislocations. Similarly, it is as though Gerty, knowing there is a French romance tradition in the culture, aspires to be not the Flaubertian heroine who is destroyed by that tradition (and who, in turn, destroys it) but a bizarre elevation of the very role Emma Bovary found unbearable and humiliating, the role as Charles' *petit-bourgeois* "dear little wifey" (Lawrence 121). In Gerty's world, aristocracy has been reduced to a code of hyperbolic prestige, like her father's linoleum ad, "Catesby's cork lino, artistic, standard designs, fit for a palace" (U 13:323). The French romance

tradition survives merely as a verbal residue of desire, as franco-
phonic affectation, "a languid queenly *hauteur*," or "patrician suitors at her feet vying with one another to pay their devoirs to her"
(U 13:97–104). In the narration of "Nausicaa," the Greek classic
and French romance traditions announce their modern functions as
instruments of pretension, as vehicles of a mimic erudition that can
reap merely specious prestige.

But the object of Joyce's critique in this representation, is less, I
believe, the abuse of the classic than it is the consequence of its
internalization by figures whose desires are simultaneously inspired
and frustrated by it, and who are barred from recognizing little more
in the classic beyond its cachet. Joyce, whose Penelope was not only
Flaubert but Ibsen as well, learned from his modern masters to recognize ordinary behavior as a *mise en scène* with a logocentric script.
It makes a significant difference whether Joyce deploys his figures as
mere puppets blindly enacting self-indicting Homeric gestures, or
whether he constructs them as actively desirous and idealizing figures who acquire their amorous and aesthetic models from a classical culture that has passed through extensive linguistic and generic
deformations. Joyce deplores, I believe, not the disregard of high art
by ordinary people, but rather the way their desire for it, and for the
prestige they hope to achieve from it, is doomed to frustration by
their inescapable detours through popular culture. Joyce has, I believe, more pity and liking for Bloom's attempts to spruce up his
home's decor with pictures of a nymph from the slick magazine
Photo Bits or a plaster statue of Narcissus, than Eliot does for mythological scenes on the walls of the boudoir, or Pound for his "two gross
of broken statues" and "a few thousand battered books." Joyce recognizes that ordinary Dubliners were bound to acquire their myths,
legends, and folklore mainly through the Pantomime, in forms that
often give their fantasies and dreams the exotic shapes of a strange
orientalism. But I believe he also recognized that the Dubliners' access to Homer in the deformed and truncated fragments that man-
aged to survive as tropes in their language and as plots in their entertainment was different in degree, rather than in kind, from his
own displaced acquisition of the *Odyssey* in Butcher and Lang's
translation or Charles Lamb's tales. What Joyce makes of these debased internalizations of the classics is a psychological anatomy of
desire for high culture that, in turn, critiques the modernist temper.

The Trial of Paris serves a useful function as a counter-myth to
"Nausicaa" because it harbors beneath its romantic surface, the
judgment of the fairest goddess and the winning of Helen, the parable of an unscrupulous critical act that compromises both beauty's

formalistic integrity and criticism's power to pledge it a disinterested evaluation. The Trial of Paris thus challenges Stephen's aesthetic theory. The myth begins with the exclusion of Eris, the goddess of Discord, from the marriage feast of Peleus and Thetis. In revenge, Eris throws a golden apple labeled "For the Fairest" among the wedding guests, and three goddesses, Athena, Hera, and Aphrodite, fight for its possession. They submit their dispute to Paris of Troy for judgment, and each goddess offers a bribe to win his favor. Paris awards the golden apple, and his judgment of superior beauty, to Aphrodite, who promised him in return the most beautiful woman in the world, Helen, wife of Menelaus. The Trial of Paris problematizes both the notion of Platonic or intrinsic beauty and the possibility of its independent and objective judgment by inserting desire and relativity (the "fairest" as always a possible another) into its determination. By subordinating beauty to the mediations and manipulations of desire, The Trial of Paris dramatizes the irony of modernism's adulation of the classical myth for exemplary parables of truth and beauty. As classical philologist, Joyce is a disciple of Nietzsche rather than T. E. Hulme.

Gerty MacDowell's narrator alludes to the Trial of Paris by referring to the disputed sand castle of the twins as "the apple of discord." "But just then there was a slight altercation between Master Tommy and Master Jacky. Boys will be boys and our two twins were no exception to this golden rule. The apple of discord was a certain castle of sand which Master Jacky had built . . . " (U 13:40). This allusion raises once again the question of the status of narrative knowledge and narrative erudition. Does the narrator of "Nausicaa" know the Trial of Paris and understand its applicability to the events about to be narrated, the flirtation on Sandymount strand between the three girls and Leopold Bloom? Or is the narrative voice ignorant of Euripides' plays, ignorant of mythology, retaining the metaphor of "the apple of discord" only as a proverbial saying, its mythical origins forgotten or repressed, in order to inflate the infantile quarrel over a sand castle to mock-epic proportions, and thereby display its own rhetorical powers to produce an inflated discourse?

Joyce introduces the Trial of Paris into an earlier fiction with just this motive, albeit by an educated and knowledgeable speaker. Gabriel Conroy in "The Dead," uses the myth in his after-dinner speech, "He ran over the headings of his speech: Irish hospitality, sad memories, the Three Graces, Paris, the quotation from Browning" (D 192). Gabriel intends to flatter his spinster relatives with a hyperbolic and inappropriate analogy, whose insincerity he patently admits to himself ("What did he care that his aunts were only two ignorant old women?" [D 192]) and whose function is clearly to parade his erudition:

> —I will not attempt to play to-night the part that Paris played
> on another occasion. I will not attempt to choose between them.
> The task would be an invidious one and one beyond my poor
> powers. (D 204)

The classical allusion merely abets pretension, and its victims in the story "The Dead," as in "Nausicaa," are the three spinsters who are never serious contenders for the prize, but are offered vain and empty homage in order that their judge may flatter himself as a producer of honeyed prose inflected by classical erudition. Paris really chooses Helen, Gabriel really chooses Gretta, and Bloom really chooses Molly—"That's where Molly can knock spots off them" (U 13:968) is his true judgment.

The layering of myth in "Nausicaa" takes the form of rhetorically foregrounding the Homeric myth of the Phaeacian maiden, Nausicaa, while relegating the Trial of Paris to reduced and miniaturized allusions on the periphery of the narrative. This produces the effect of repression, and, indeed, the narrator who works hard to award the palm of beauty to Gerty MacDowell, pronouncing her at the very outset "as fair a specimen of winsome Irish girlhood as one could wish to see" (U 13:80) and claiming that "of a surety God's fair land of Ireland did not hold her equal" (U 13:121), has good reason to suppress the spectacle of Gerty's vigorous and indecent competition for the prize. To this effect, the Trial of Paris is presented in infantile miniature in the interrogation of four-year-old Tommy Caffrey:

> —Tell us who is your sweetheart, spoke Edy Boardman. Is Cissy
> your sweetheart?
> —Nao, tearful Tommy said.
> —Is Edy Boardman your sweetheart? Cissy queried.
> —Nao, Tommy said.
> —I know, Edy Boardman said none too amiably with an arch
> glance from her shortsighted eyes. I know who is Tommy's
> sweetheart. Gerty is Tommy's sweetheart. (U 13:66)

The "apple of discord," identified ostensibly as the disputed sand castle, is more pointedly the baby's rubber ball, whose trajectory between the girls and Bloom outlines the choreography of a perfect ballet of desire. The ball, like the sand castle, is disputed by the twins and is intercepted by Bloom. Bloom, confronted by identical twins, must choose where to throw it. When Cissy asks Bloom to throw the ball to her, she shifts the semiotic power of his gesture onto the women, thereby establishing him as Paris, who will award his attentions and his favor along with the ball. Bloom's decision is a curve ball as symbolically devious as it is literally crooked: Bloom tosses the ball to Cissy, but it veers, rolls down the strand, and comes to rest at Gerty MacDowell's feet. Bloom's action is as ambiguous to himself as to the reader, as he cannot really say whether it resulted from athletic ineptitude ("Course I never could throw anything straight at school. Crooked as a ram's horn" [U 13:951]) or from the workings of romantic fate ("But the ball rolled down to her as if it understood. Every bullet has its billet" [U 13:950]).

Why does Bloom award "the apple of discord" to the passive and silent Gerty rather than to the vividly capering Cissy? Why is Edy Boardman, the only person who never touches the ball, so thoroughly extruded from the competition? In their competition to win the attention of the exotic stranger on the beach, Cissy, I would argue, takes the part of Hera, Gerty, the part of Aphrodite, and Edy Boardman, the girl with the glasses and the probing questions, the critical gaze that sees through the whole game, plays the part of Athena. The contest on Sandymount strand is fought, like the mythical contest, not on its merits but with bribes that in "Nausicaa" take the form of artistic presentations or performances. The outcome will be paradoxical and, in its own way, perverse. Bloom will choose Gerty's failed attempts to trick herself out in the forms of high art over Cissy's burlesque-like minstrel show performance, but he makes this choice for essentially pornographic reasons. Bloom is the most literal of art lovers, exhibiting in his approach to classical figures the kinetic approach that Stephen Dedalus denounces as improper in his aesthetic theory. Bloom is much like Stephen's friend Lynch, who writes his name on the backside of the Venus of Praxiteles, or Molly Bloom who falls in love with a plaster statue of Narcissus—"that lovely little statue . . . theres real beauty and poetry for you I often felt I wanted to kiss him all over also his lovely young cock" (U 18:1349). Bloom has already played Paris earlier in the day when he examined the statues of goddesses in the museum for rectal orifices. Like Lynch, he too is a graffiti artist, privileging the erogenous zones of art. "Unseen, one summer eve, you kissed me in four places," the nymph in the picture from *Photo Bits* accuses him in "Circe," "And with loving pencil you shaded my eyes, my bosom and my shame" (U 15:3264). Bloom, as Paris, will choose Gerty because she impersonates classical statuary but offers him, unlike the unyielding museum goddesses, a peek at her bottom. But as a figure of "high art" she remains for him a masturbatory fetish, an object of libidinal rather than metaphysical desire. Bloom, who happily sees modern nakedness in classical nudity, and who, Judge Woolsey notwithstanding, enjoys art as an aphrodisiac, is, at any rate, not a modernist.

Cissy Caffrey's strategy for winning Bloom's attention is pure theater, drawn from the popular and low comedic forms of her day, the Pantomime and the minstrel show. Her namesake may be a Pantomime character from the production of *Babes in the Woods*, a giant baby girl named Cissy, usually played by a man in baby clothes. Cissy is implicated in various displacements of age, race, and gender, of the sort that constitute the fracture of personality at the heart of this particular genre of comedy. In her physical appearance, with her "golliwog curls" that Gerty claims won't grow longer, she physically resembles her four-year-old twin brothers, and she does not hesitate to use them and the baby as props ("Cissy took off the twins' caps and tidied their hair to make herself attractive of course" [U 13 : 571])—a stratagem penetrated not only by Gerty, but by Bloom himself, "Caressing the little boy too. Onlookers see most of the game" (U 13 : 902). The infantile is a major trope of the Pantomime whose intertexts are drawn from fairy tales and nursery rhymes, like the famous *Mother Goose* production, and whose baby talk, games, and play— "O my! Puddeny pie!" (U 13:613) or "What's your name? Butter and cream?" (U 13:65)—Cissy produces to amuse the baby. Her discourse on the strand ultimately consists entirely of this play language, and we learn from the narrator that Cissy has habitually formalized her lovability into a series of comic turns that have earned her a reputation as an entertainer. The narrator's precious rhetoric gives us both an inventory and a favorable review of Cissy's repertoire:

Madcap Ciss with her golliwog curls. You had to laugh at her sometimes. For instance when she asked you would you have some more Chinese tea and jaspberry ram and when she drew the jugs too and the men's faces on her nails with red ink make you split your sides or when she wanted to go where you know she said she wanted to run and pay a visit to the Miss White. That was just like Cissycums. O, and will you ever forget her the evening she dressed up in her father's suit and hat and the burned cork moustache and walked down Tritonville road, smoking a cigarette? (U 13.270)

Cissy's performances owe their conventions to the popular comic theatrical forms of her day, the cross-dressing like that of the "principal boy" of the Panto, her miniaturizing and multiplying herself in her finger play like the clown turns of the circus, and her jokes echoing those of interlocutors and endmen in the minstrel show—"Edy asked her the time and Miss Cissy, as glib as you like, said it was half past kissing time, time to kiss again" (U 13:531). But these displacements of age, dress, scale, and race are dangerous strategies with respect to the kind of attention or estimation they provoke, earning laughter at the price of derision. These comic incongruities and discordances, being at the same time artificially male and female, young and old, black and white, too large and too small, act like a fragmentation or mutilation of personality, a castration of the ego, as it were, that snuffs the very desire it is intended to provoke and thereby creates the doomed pathos of the clown. The popular theatrical forms of the turn of the century, Pantomimes, minstrel shows, variety acts, tended to force to the cultural surface—though generally without address—the problematic of social divisions, differences, marginalizations, and exclusions in art and representation that high culture, too, embodied and repressed (Herr, Kershner).

Cissy's third displacement of race, her transition in the chapter's discourses from romantic gypsy to buffoonish "black-face," becomes one of the critical implements that turns the Trial of Paris in this chapter inside out and lets us judge the judge. Bloom transforms, in his imagination, many of the cute narrative descriptions of Cissy by Gerty's narrator into crude racial stereotypes. Her "golliwog curls" become a "mop head" in his language, and he changes her "cherryripe red lips" into "fat lips" and "nigger mouth" (U 13:897). Bloom will see in the performances of the girls on the strand versions of several current Dublin plays, and in Cissy's performance he sees Eugene Stratton's minstrel show. In spite of the sexual glamour their racial exoticism gives the Blooms, the Semitic foreignness that makes him so attractive to the girls on the strand, and the Moorish voluptuousness he himself finds so exciting in Molly ("That's where Molly can knock spots off them. It's the blood of the south. Moorish" [U 13:968])—Bloom is quite capable of treating race as a sexual freak. "Curiosity like a nun or a negress or a girl with glasses" (U 13:776) he thinks, reflecting on the erotic value of Gerty's lameness. Bloom's embedding of race in this series of three (nun, negress, and girl with glasses) identifies, however unconsciously, all three spinsters on the beach as marred or disfigured: lame, celibate Gerty, dark, negroid Cissy, and lilliputian, bespectacled Edy), like "The Three Spinners" (*Die drei Spinnerinnen*) in Grimms' fairy tales, who are uglified by an exaggerated feature: a huge foot, lip, or thumb. Bloom's titillation by such special markings in women is, alas, not liberalism, but its perverse double: a difference desired perversely for its undesirability. He expresses this sentiment in his "Circe" fantasy of Molly's slumming:

> She often said she'd like to visit. Slumming. The exotic, you see.
> Negro servants in livery too if she had money. Othello black
> brute. Eugene Stratton. Even the bones and cornerman at the
> Livermore christies. Bohee brothers. Sweep for that matter.
> (U 15:408)

By treating race not as real but as an imago, blackness as a marking or code that can be painted on or detached, like the black of a chimney sweep, Bloom makes it clear that the desire for the black signals not the courage to flout or defy prejudice, but its intensified reenactment. "Slumming" becomes the censoring of the desire for the undesirable. Bloom's titillation by the putative sexual mark makes his desire not a compliment but an insult, and thereby subverts the highly conventional aesthetic ideology that governs the rules of The Trial of Paris. "Nausicaa" thus re-addresses in a more culturally and historically specific form the problematic Stephen raises, and neutralizes, when he gives himself only two alternatives—biologism or formalism—for explaining the conundrum of aesthetic relativism, "The Greek, the Turk, the Chinese, the Copt, the Hottentot, said Stephen, all admire a different type of female beauty" (P 208). "Nausicaa" goes much farther in exploring the role of ethnocentrism, social construction, and gender politics in shaping aesthetic ideology.

Gerty fares better than Cissy in claiming Bloom's attention, for she imitates high art rather than low art, gives a static rather than a kinetic performance, and portrays an idealized and romanticized figure rather than, like Cissy, a fragmented and multiplicitous human type. She thereby exploits and creates the illusion that beauty is ideal, singular, and timeless, rather than socially constructed, historically conventionalized, and consequently culturally relative and multiple. Gerty chooses a static performance not only to conceal her lameness, but also to defeat her great enemy, time—"the years were slipping by for her, one by one" (U 13:649). Gerty's preoccupation with the passing of time, youth, and opportunity is betrayed by the inadvertent, but persistent, reference to time in all her scant speech, "I was only wondering was it late" (U 13:527), or "I can throw my cap at who I like because it's leap year" (U 13:590), or her unspoken and startling cry, "she was just going to tell her to catch it while it was flying" (U 13:617) in reference to the clot of milk Baby Boardman spits up. Like Cissy Caffrey, who hopes to reverse time by becoming a little girl or a tomboy again, and who regresses to infantile language and infantile art, Gerty MacDowell too tries to catch time while it is flying by regressing. But she retreats culturally and historically to the venerable art of the past, to classical or neo-classical forms, the marble statue, the icon of the Madonna, the aristocratic arts of the eighteenth century. In composing herself into a classical pose, Gerty tries to assimilate to herself the excess significance that accrues to representation, and to multiply her injured personal worth by making herself abstracted and representative, an idealized type, "a specimen of winsome Irish girlhood." She overdetermines her roles by playing, albeit in reverse, the parts of both Pygmalion and Galatea, transforming her living desiring self into a beautiful frozen sculpture, the "waxen pallor of her face" (U 13:87), her "hands . . . of finely veined alabaster" (U 13:89), "her throat, so slim, so flawless, so beautifully moulded it seemed one an artist might have dreamed of" (U 13:582).

But Gerty's aim is undermined because her access to concepts of classical form are already mediated by popular, ephemeral art that will lend her beauty neither the permanence of marble or oil, nor its prestige. She cannot imitate classical statuary except by way of another reversion, by imitating the imitation of the classical figure in the *tableau vivant*, the transient representation of mythological, classical, or Biblical subjects by living figures, who enacted them as a sort of parlor entertainment in the aristocratic homes of the eighteenth century. But the *tableau vivant*, when not itself embedded in a classic like Goethe's *Elective Affinities*, is vulnerable to ridicule as pretentious kitsch. Even so, the *tableau vivant* retains some cultural distinction precisely because it is both expensive and ephemeral, and the spectacle of living figures dressed and posed to represent a classic work of art cannot be mass produced. But Gerty's cultural model for the picture of romance she wants to compose, of herself with Reggy Wylie, or Leopold Bloom, or any man who who can be enlisted as a prop in an adoring attitude ("drinking in her every contour, literally worshipping at her shrine" [U 13:564]), *is* a mass produced picture presumably called "Halcyon Days," whose archaism so eludes Gerty that she has to look up "halcyon" in Walker's pronouncing dictionary. The picture is a temporal anachronism, with its aristocratic subject, a "ladylove" in "studied attitude" receiving flowers and homage from a young man in a tricornered hat, attached to an almanac that is already out of date, and that represents a bogus past, a golden age existing only in the insipid conventions of calendar art (U 13.334–344). And Gerty has hung this picture of "Halcyon Days" in her privy, where it functions much as her narration does in "Nausicaa"—to mask and neutralize the squalor of her life, like the chlorate of lime she remembers to apply every fortnight. Gerty's notions on how to idealize or aestheticize her life appear to be either ephemeral, like trying to fix in her imagination a scene of Dublin at twilight in pastels, "like the paintings that man used to do on the pavement with all the coloured chalks and such a pity too leaving them there to be all blotted out" (U 13:406), or vulnerable to disruption by time and mortality. Even the photograph, that seemingly permanent mode of fixing the self aesthetically, can be preempted by death. The happy family portrait the MacDowells and the Dignams were to have made ("they were to have had a group taken. No-one would have thought the end was so near" [U 13:318]) is overtaken by Dignam's alcoholic death. Its idealization would have been fraudulent in any case, eliding drunkenness, penury, and domestic violence.

Joyce writes "Nausicaa" with the technique of Penelope, weaving texts only to unravel them again, reversing genres into their opposites, and shifting perspectives and values until his text, like Bloom's women, have "Eyes all over them" (U 13:912). Gerty's "namby-pamby- jammy marmalady drawersy" style (*Letters* I, 135) is only a failed imitation of ambitious and thwarted writing that aspires to be significant and admired, to be treated as high art. In its failure other failures are inscribed, and we may read between the lines and in the evasions and circumlocutions of the prose, a naturalistic version of Gerty's life in which she is not the Princess Nausicaa, but a poor crippled spinster whose mother suffers migraines and takes snuff and whose father probably beats both women when he is drunk. But this melodramatic naturalism itself offers only a half-truth, unless it is linked to the strivings of Gerty's desire, and to our recognition that because of this squalor, not in spite of it, Gerty dreams the dream of art as steadfastly as any modernist. Joyce argues in "Nausicaa," I believe, that modern squalor produces not the Philistine, the ignorant lout contemptuous of culture, but the crippled connoisseur and the castrated idealist, men and women who long for beauty and significance forever outside their ken. For Gerty MacDowell classical art may be only the hearsay of her culture, yet she is determined to imitate that which she cannot know and to body it forth.

Joyce embeds the tragedy of Gerty's desire in a subversive reading of his own mythical method. He appears to offer us the classics and myth in order to gratify our own aspirations to high art but gives us instead mainly the inscription of their absence. He elicits our homage to the Homeric superstructure of this episode while entertaining and titillating us with the stunts and antics of figures whose taste we are allowed to ridicule and whose sexual desires we are permitted to censure. At the same time, Joyce undermines his own mythical intertext with a hidden mythical countertext, Homer's "Nausicaa" reinterpreted by the Trial of Paris. In the end, Joyce's "Nausicaa" itself serves as a modern countertext to this mythical countertext, prompting us to reexamine the great mythic beauty contest that is the prototype for some of the most resistant sexist rituals in our own contemporary society. The point is not that modern culture has lost its aesthetic compass. The invocation of the repressed Trial of Paris rather dramatizes that the internalization of the myth's desires by modern women and the men who install themselves as judges of their desirability is tragically ironic because it is served by a primordially corrupt model of the judgment of beauty. Joyce indicts the psychological power of myth rather more than he indicts its absence in the modern consciousness. And by earning from his contemporaries praise for his use of myth, Joyce further dramatizes modernism's blind eye to the cruelties of its own elitism, the libidinal impulses behind its attack on what is poor, mean, squalid, and cheap in the culture, and the dishonesties of its own pretensions. In the spectacle of the multiple criticisms and censures that we ourselves bring from modernism to "Nausicaa" is reflected the spectacle of modernism's denial of its slumming.

PART III
The Children

CHAPTER NINE

The Politics of Childhood in "The Mime of Mick, Nick, and the Maggies"

"THE MIME OF MICK, NICK, AND THE MAGGIES," Book II, Chapter 1 of *Finnegans Wake*, stages an infantile failure of knowledge, the inability to guess a children's riddle, that disrupts the progress of *Bildung* and makes itself, in its regressive generic forms, an *anti-Bildungsroman*. The concept of *Bildung* coincided with the Enlightenment, which made the child as educable creature the focus of pedagogy and socialization (Pelzer-Knoll 45). But the "Mime"'s extensive children's play of magic, superstition, and animism, resists the disenchantment that the Enlightenment hoped would free humankind from irrational enslavement to nature, and thereby disrupts *Portrait*'s collusion with its project. To argue that the "Mime" functions as an anti-*Portrait* is, of course, to reduce that work's own self-ironizations and internal subversions to an ideological simplicity it does not possess.[1] But as I have noted earlier, I see in *Portrait*'s critical tradition a privileging of artistic individualism that seems to me to have survived as a putative liberalism even in contemporary Althusserian readings of the novel. Indeed, the heroicizing of the artist that is the donnée of the *Kuenstlerroman* can be found in a naturalized form even in fine Marxist readings like Trevor Williams' analysis of Stephen's social construction. The critical tradition has resisted the destabilizing effects of an ironized Stephen, and as a result an Enlightenment narrative has been produced as the fiction of the Joycean fiction, that celebrates the apotheosis of the artist—the individual's rational self-liberation from the mythologizings of religion, state, and home.

But I hope to show that in another children's fiction in *Finnegans Wake*, in "The Mime of Mick, Nick, and the Maggies," the Enlightenment ideal in which childhood, education, and maturation is implicated, is subjected to an artistic self-critique. The "Mime" follows *Ulysses* in revisiting and re-exploring some of the more glaring opening gaps and dissonances in *Portrait* with the result that it criticizes artistic separatism and exile to argue instead that the developing artist fails his community on precisely the ground it fails him: the ground of class (Naremore). In the plot of the rejected and repulsed child, the fear of the loss of class standing that historically afflicted the Joyces is dramatized: the *Deklassierungsangst* peculiar to an Ireland that in modernity experienced a far weaker version of the *embourgeoisement* that Herbert Marcuse found emerging throughout the modern West. In *Portrait* Stephen tenaciously clings to his bourgeois identification as long as he can ("He had tried to build a breakwater of order and elegance against the sordid tide of life" [P 98]), but fails because his declassed condition gives him the purpose of neither the bourgeois child, who, Walter Benjamin argues, is trained as heir to its class privileges, nor the proletarian child, trained to be avenger and liberator of its dispossessed community. Instead, he trains to become a pioneer of adversary culture by becoming emplotted in the modern *Bildungsroman*, subjected to development into non-conformity rather than conformity in accordance with the liberal legitimation narrative of the artist. Emigration, the fate of his class, is romantically translated into exile, and with his *Non Serviam*, the figure of the artist itself becomes epiphanized and transcendentalized in order to legitimate the isolation of art from the sphere of ordinary social life. S. L. Goldberg writes, "In the long run, Stephen extends the exile of the artist to the exile of art" (64). Art and the artist ostensibly achieve class transcendence as they are fetishized in the tropes of religion, occultism, and mythology: Lucifer, Icarus, "a priest of eternal imagination, transmuting the daily bread of experience into the radiant body of everliving life" (P 221). *Portrait's* progress inscribes the dialectic of the Enlightenment's sublimated failure: the return, in secularized and aesthetic form, of the spiritualized mystifications it sought to dispel. "Just as the myths already realize enlightenment, so enlightenment with every step becomes more deeply engulfed in mythology" (Horkheimer, Adorno 11). Even with its abrupt demystification by the diary entries at the end, and by *Ulysses'* exposure of the failure of exile and artistic isolation, the legitimation narrative of *Portrait* has become assimilated as a key figure in the mythology of Modernism.

"The Mime of Mick, Nick, and the Maggies" would seem to represent the infantile version of the artistic autonomy that *Portrait* legitimates in the apotheosis of the bird-girl in the stream: the purely aesthetic and decorative play of a children's game, "Angels and Devils or Colours," the unencumbered aestheticism of flower girls and rainbow colors, the rhythms of nursery rhymes and the lilt of children's laughter. Childhood, like woman in *Portrait*, seems to have been extricated from the troubled social matrix of *Dubliners*—"I think the piece I sent you is the gayest and lightest thing I have done in spite of the circumstances" (SL 355) Joyce wrote Harriet Shaw Weaver on 22 November 1930. But the qualification—"in spite of the circumstances"—argues for a separation of the sunny text from the material and social life of the artist that, on closer inspection, turns out to be specious. The depressing circumstances of Joyce's life out of which the "Mime" is born can be recognized in transcribed form in the children's chapter: Joyce's worsening eye problems become Glugg's inability to see and determine colors; the unintelligibility of Lucia's worsening madness becomes the enigma of female nature and desire encoded in the heliotrope riddle; Joyce's dental pain becomes little Glugg's toothache ("His mouthfull of ecstasy . . . shot pinging up through the errorooth of his wisdom" (FW 231.9); and the colitis symptomatic of the ulcer that would kill him a decade later appears as Glugg's tummy ache, "Lookery looks, how he's knots in his entrails! Mookery mooks, it's a grippe of his gripes" (FW 231.34). That these problems became legendary within the Joyce family is suggested in a 1980 memoir by Joyce's niece, Bozena Delimata, when she asks "With his painful eyes, his stomach trouble, and his bad teeth, how did he manage?" (59).

Joyce's comment to Miss Weaver about the "Mime"'s effacement of the difficult circumstances of its genesis betrays the dialectical structure of this chapter. "The Mime of Mick, Nick, and the Maggies" purports to offer a Pantomime, a carefree children's entertainment, that on closer inspection suppresses and displaces the material and social reality of children's lives. The "Mime"'s text is like the evening newspaper in *Portrait* with the picture of the beautiful Mabel Hunter—"—What is she in, mud?—In the pantomime, love"—whose edges the boy mauls "with his reddened and blackened hands" after dropping the heavy load he has carried in, "stamping crookedly under his stone of coal" (P 67). The text dialectically represents the displacement by a "symbolical" childhood of a "real" childhood that it fails to erase or efface, unlike the *Bildungsroman* that, Franco Moretti argues, eliminates many of the features of the life of youth: "Modern youth, to be sure, is many other things as well . . . Yet the *Bildungsroman* discards them as irrelevant, abstracting from 'real' youth a 'symbolic' one, epitomized . . . in mobility and interiority" (4–5). The "symbolical" childhood with which adult bourgeois society replaces the social reality of children, and with which it denies, particularly, the effects of class upon their lives, represents a lie society tells itself about its own condition. Max Horkheimer describes the function of "the child ideal" as using an idealized notion of the child and childhood to preserve a faith in utopianism no longer sustained by the experience of social reality: "Children symbolized the Golden Age as well as the promising future. The rationalistic society gave children legends and fairy tales so that they might mirror hope back to their disillusioned elders" (41). In "The Mime of Mick, Nick, and the Maggies" Joyce gives us both the lie and its demystification.

Children's culture with its nursery rhymes, theatricals, stories, and games, is then especially implicated in the creation of utopian visions of home, family, and domesticity. William York Tindall stressed the way "Polly Put the Kettle On," with its closing tea party refrain, "and they all drank tea," becomes a major motif of peace, happiness, and unity after conflict in *Finnegans Wake*. Indeed, using "The Mime of Mick, Nick, and the Maggies" for his example, Tindall argued that "tea" in its tea-party connotations gives unified closure to the text of the *Wake* as a whole, "Take tea, another recurring theme. Appearing several times in this chapter . . . tea carries its usual meanings of home, marriage ("Tea for Two"), urine, and peace after conflict to support these matters here and, by recurrence, to weave the book together" (155). Tindall's optimistic reading of the chapter reflects the philosophical sanction of the philosopher who is given a prominent place in *Finnegans Wake* in general, and in this flower chapter in particular: Edgar Quinet. Joyce sent the sentence from Quinet's essay on Herder and Vico,[2] to Harriet Shaw Weaver with the explanation: "E. Q. says that the wild flowers on the ruins of Carthage Numancia etc. have survived the political rises and downfall of Empires. In this case the wild flowers are the lilts of children" (SL 355). But I will argue that this Herderesque vision of perpetually self-regenerative nature should be placed in dialectical relation to another set of texts by Edgar Quinet implied, if not named, in this chapter: his work on the Wandering Jew, which supplies an antithetical vision of perpetual vagrancy, homelessness, and alienation as a poignant counterpoint to the optimistic concept of eternal survival. Joyce uses Quinet to universalize the extremes of infantile fate these allegories evoke in the chapter, in order to have "The Mime of Mick, Nick, and the Maggies" suggest that if children will always laugh and play, they also will always fear and suffer.

Against Quinet's cosmic metaphors of fate, Joyce gives children in the "Mime" an allegorical function as colonized subjects, to stand for the social reality of Ireland itself in relation to its symbolization at the hands of its artists. Ireland's idealization by the Celtic twilight and the Irish revival, that in its folk retrievals and occultism recreates the kind of magical, animistic children's culture Benjamin sees as an antidote to the Enlightenment's hypocritical promises of social and scientific progress, is frequently invested in the trope of the child at the expense of its social reality. The symbolically idyllic Yeatsian child—

> Dance there upon the shore;
> What need have you to care
> For wind or water's roar?

is precisely the child exempt from concern with social reality—

> Being young you have not known
> The fool's triumph, nor yet
> Love lost as soon as won,
> Nor the best labourer dead
> And all the sheaves to bind.
> ("To a Child Dancing in the Wind")

Joyce gives this Irish troping of the child as figure of romantic nostalgia a negative revision in his satiric portrait of Irish poetic desire, when he makes the infant the enemy of poetry in "A Little Cloud." Chandler's child vociferously avenges his race, as it were—the race of Irish children that the story's narrator encodes in a symbol that Freud believed stood universally for children in the adult mind (*Interpretation of Dreams* 392) but that bears overtones of the specifically British racist animus against the populous Irish: "A horde of grimy children populated the street. They stood or ran in the roadway or crawled up the steps before the gaping doors or squatted like mice upon the thresholds. Little Chandler gave them no thought. He picked his way deftly through all that minute vermin-like life" (D 71). Joyce, unlike Chandler, gives careful thought to the way in which adults give real children, especially grimy and ragged children, no thought except as a mass. This is true even of *Portrait*, which leaves the names and numbers of Stephen's numerous siblings largely indeterminate precisely in order to let both Stephen and the narrative disavow them. "How many children had she?" Cranly asks about Mrs. Dedalus. "Nine or ten. Stephen answered. Some died." (P 241). Stanislaus wrote in his diary, "Many fathers I know do not know the names of their children" (Healey 118). The "Mime" offers a critique and a discursive reparation of this disavowal—not by treating the children now as significant individuals, but rather by treating them with some seriousness as a class rather than as a mass. The text gives thought both to their culture and to what their culture teaches them, and goes on to explore the extent to which children can recognize and resist the ideological freight they thus inherit. The "Mime" further obliges the reader to retrieve the child's material and social reality from the play and games in which it is enacted and reenacted, and thus to reverse the earlier disavowals. Joyce, whose relation to his siblings has been biographically mythologized chiefly for his parasitism, should surely be recognized for at least attempting to reverse their abandonment. "We do weeks on one chance insufficient meal" (Healey 77), Stanislaus wrote in his diary in 1904, and although Eileen later told her daughter "their poverty was often exaggerated in books" (Delimata 53), the family mythology seems to have confirmed Stanislaus' feeling of destitution. Joyce used Stanislaus' perception of the lean 1904 period to limn the plight of the Dedalus children in *Ulysses,* and Ellmann reports that James was disturbed by the family condition on his visit to Dublin in 1909, "Still with John Joyce were the five sisters, May, Eileen, Eva, Florence, and Mabel. Joyce felt a burst of pity for them and resolved to do something" (JJ 285). He eventually brought three of his siblings, Stanislaus, Eileen, and Eva, to live with him, Nora, and their children in Trieste.

Joyce cast his dialectical exploration of children's symbolical and social lives into the form of the Pantomime (Atherton, Weir), "The Mime of Mick, Nick, and the Maggies" performed in the free theater of Phoenix Park, the "Feenichts Playhouse" during "childream's hours, expercatered" (FW 219.2). As a highly heterogeneous medium, the Pantomime and its various ingestions of high and low genres, serves a double function in Joyce's political agenda with respect to the child. On the one hand, the pantomime and its attendant popular forms explain how even very young children acquire cultural messages (Herr) along with their first sexual knowledge and experience;[3] on the other, they offer the child media for extricating itself from adult typologies of childhood, and for reinventing itself. Popular, folk, and children's culture play in the "Mime" the role of *geheime Miterzieher,* secret coeducators of children—to borrow a term Heinz-Elmar Tenorth retrieves from the work of early twentieth-century reform pedagogy. The historical consequences Tenorth attributes to this new modern concern with children's culture are reflected in Joyce's texts. On the one hand, the censure of the injurious effects of *Schmutz und Schund,* filth and trash, on children's minds is indignantly voiced by Father Butler in "An Encounter" (Kershner 31–46); on the other, the politically progressive appropriation of new media explored by Bertolt Brecht, and by Walter Benjamin in his children's radio broadcasts (Buck-Morss, Schiller-Lerg,

Mueller), is reflected in the children's resistance to what Benjamin calls the *Kolonialpaedagogik* of children's education. For the Irish child, the imperialistic imprint on the curriculum takes literal form in the classroom that spills over into their leisure play (Naremore): Clongowes boys compete as York and Lancaster at sums; they play cricket, the British public school game; Stephen plays Napoleon with his Dublin friends; the Caffrey twins build Martello towers like their colonial masters. But they also practice, like the Pantomime genre they enact, the kind of *bricolage* Benjamin finds in children's play, that lets them create out of the leftover scraps of culture a little world of their own, that is both reflective and oppositional to the big world they inhabit. Transgressive and creative—*smugging* and *miching* are among its paedocentric names—the play of truant children in Joyce's fictions renders adult power more brutally transparent, and invents new forms and new identities ("let you be Murphy and I'll be Smith" [D 26], "Let Pauline be Irene. Let you be Beeton. And let me be Los Angeles" [FW 154.23]) for children to resist its force. The richly evocative form of "The Mime of Mick, Nick, and the Maggies" is such a product of paedocentric *bricolage:* a juvenile transformation in its own image and interests of a great, heterogeneous, overdetermined mass of cultural, and specifically Joycean, textual material. The "Mime" is a child's rewriting of those aspects of the Joycean *oeuvre* that deal with childhood and adolescence.

"The Mime of Mick, Nick, and the Maggies" could be inserted into various moments in Joyce's earlier fictions that allude to children's play—usually in nostalgic and sentimental reminiscence that occludes the interior experience and social significance of children's unsupervised activities. "The cold air stung us and we played till our bodies glowed" (D 30), "Araby" 's narrator warmly remembers of childhood winter evenings, and Eveline, recalling fondly that "One time there used to be a field there in which they used to play every evening with other people's children," notes without rancor that this playground was usurped by an Ulster developer, "Then a man from Belfast bought the field and built houses in it—not like their little brown houses but bright brick houses with shining roofs" (D 36). "The Mime of Mick, Nick, and the Maggies" recapitulates such childhood evening play but offers its content: a riddle game with many versions, in which the little boy must guess a color to win a little girl, and fails. Joyce described it as "Angels and Devils or colours. The Angels, girls, are grouped behind the Angel, Shawn, and the Devil has to come over three times and ask for a colour, if the colour he asks for has been chosen by any girl she has to run and he tries to catch her. As far as I have written he has come twice and been twice baffled" (SL 355). This game, with its romantic donnée of yearning desire, sexual bafflement, frustration, and ostracism could serve as figure for the occluded interior drama of several little boys' romances in *Dubliners* and *Ulysses*,[4] and for Stephen's bafflement by girls and women throughout *Stephen Hero* and *Portrait*—from infantile oedipal desire ("Was it right to kiss his mother or wrong to kiss his mother?" [P 14]) to adult lovelessness ("How to win a woman's love. For me this. Say the following talisman three times with hands folded:—*Se el yilo nebrakada femininum!*" [U 10.847]).

The "Mime," then, represents the possible paedocentric rewriting of many Joycean plots. But it is especially consequential to explore its revision of *Portrait*, because its dialectical movement in simultaneously demystifying the artistic legitimation myth and restoring infantile social reality to a plane of serious consideration can be foregrounded with this maneuver. In the "Mime" plot of a little devil unable to guess the little girls' riddle, rebuffed and ostracized from the game, going off to write literature, and returning to a miserable home, Stephen's Icarean odyssey and vocation is rescribed. Reread through this infantile narrative, *Portrait* becomes the tale of a sensitive boy whose poverty eventually made him an unfit suitor for a bourgeois girl. He emigrates for the same reason so many other Irishmen, politically activist or not, were forced to leave their native land: because he has no material or social prospects there. He transforms emigration into exile, and cloaks his *Deklassierung*, his loss of class, in the bohemian imperatives of heresy, freethinking, and art. After an exile more squalid than romantic, plagued by hunger and the specter of depravity, he returns ignominiously to further derision, neglect, and need in *Ulysses*. But if the "Mime" demystifies *Portrait*, the narrative residues of *Portrait* also retrieve the "Mime" with its infantile play from the trivialization its miniaturization and desacralization invites. The great Miltonian theme of *Paradise Lost* that shadows Stephen's Luciferian gestures in *Portrait* is reduced and hollowed in "Angels and Devils or colours"—"Chuffy was a nangel then and his soard fleshed light like likening" (FW 222.22)—by transforming the sacred symbolic figures into decorative cherubs and imps. We are invited to read children's play with the fatuous optimism of "Nausicaa"'s narrative ("building castles as children do, or playing with their big coloured ball, happy as the day was long" [U 13:19]), dismissing children's distress as ephemeral and minor ("smoothing over life's tiny troubles" [U 13:57]), and treating even their violence as a joke, like Father Conmee and Father Dolan having a famous laugh together over Stephen's pandy-batting. But by challenging the heroic myth of Stephen, the "Mime" simultaneously challenges the trivialization of childhood. By making the social reality of the artist homologous with the social reality of the child, both are restored to validity and significance.

In exploring the politics of childhood in "The Mime of Mick, Nick, and the Maggies," then, I will focus on three moments—the tea party, exile, and home—that this chapter relates narratively in a way none of Joyce's individual works do. This is the "Mime"'s *bricolage*, assembling from the submerged Joycean pretexts that we have received only accidentally—the epiphanies, Stanislaus' diary, *Stephen Hero*—the larger social plot that rewrites the Irish artist's plight as a historical and class issue. These topoi—tea party, exile, and home—imbricate each other in complex ways. The "Mime" conflates nursery and parlor, infantile games and adolescent courtship rituals, to show that older children enact social values already imbibed in nursery rhymes and fairy tales, and that their success or failure is already predicated on class determinants. The "Mime" allows us to reconsider as primordially exiled the child whose class dislocations cause it to be marginalized and ostracized—the child relegated to a collective narrative otherness in Joyce's earlier fiction as member of a savage race, "the rough tribes from the cottages" ("Araby" [D 30]) or "the ragged troop screaming after us '*Swaddlers! Swaddlers!*' thinking that we were Protestants because Mahony, who was dark-complexioned, wore the silver badge of a cricket club in his cap" ("An Encounter" [D 22]). The "Mime"'s retrospective arrangement allows the complex effects of class on children's assumptions of identity and power to emerge into the foreground of our reading. Artistic exile, in turn, is deromanticized and likewise restored to its class implications: that the disenfranchisement and poverty of home are exported to new worlds to merely double the feeling of dispossession and alienation. Finally, the return home in the "Mime" becomes, paradoxically, a return to the homelessness that is the permanent condition of all colonial subjects who do not possess their native land.

1. Tea Parties

John Gordon, in his plot summary of II.1, not only speculates that "there is a tea party going on downstairs in the kitchen, complete with pot and kettle, cups and saucers" (170), but argues that Shem is the tea kettle, Shaun the phallic teapot, and the seven rainbow girls "the seven cups of a tea-set," as well as tea leaves. Read a little less literally, as children playing at tea party by transforming themselves into the implements of the tea table (as in the song "I'm a little teapot" or Bloom's "teapot" game with Josie Breen, "I'm teapot with curiosity to find out whether some person's something is a little teapot at present" [U 15:457]) Gordon's quirky picture allows us to recognize a nursery creation by children into an animistic children's world peopled by animate things. The teapot world of the "Mime" may first have been conjured by the Joyce children and chronicled in Stanislaus' diary. After a visit from Thomas Kettle, who reminded the children to tell their father he had called—"You won't forget now—Mr. Kettle—what you boil water in"—Joyce's sister Eva remarked, "Unfortunately he didn't know that it's Mr. Teapot we boil the water in" (Healey 24). Stanislaus' explanation— "We have no kettle"—transforms Eva's little joke into a child's comment on the poverty of the Joyce household after the death of their mother. Joyce fictionally confirms this in the triste children's tea party Stephen finds in *Portrait* when he returns home after rejecting a religious vocation, a tea party where besides having no kettle, the children have no cups: "Tea was nearly over and only the last of the second watered tea remained in the bottoms of the small glassjars and jampots which did service for teacups" (P 163). Joyce here uses the trope of the children's tea party to critique the way a "symbolical" childhood—children's carefree, playful, mimicry of bourgeois adult social rituals—is substituted for the grim reality of many children's social lives. In the *Wake* we find a glorious Mr. Kettle restored as a theater patron, "Galorius Kettle" (FW 219.12) and "Jampots, rinsed porters, taken in token" (FW 219.6)—as poor children bring their recycled teacups to gain admission to the children's theater in which they will mime their fears of poverty and their dreams of wealth.

Gordon's further elaboration of the tea pouring in the "Mime" as sexual (the "girls, as the seven cups of a tea-set, may have exalted aspirations to . . . Shaun's spout") and as social ("Issy is also a tea-party hostess frustrated by Shem's perverse unwillingness to understand the social rituals" [174–175]) widens the tea party into the bourgeois theater of courtship in which the class transactions of the marriage market occur. One of the salient differences between *Portrait* and *Stephen Hero* is that *Portrait* suppresses the social context, the "at homes" in the Daniel household that provide the background for the courtship of Emma Clery and Stephen, and whose function as a marriage fair for the many Daniel daughters the earlier work makes perfectly explicit: "There were several marriageable daughters in the family and whenever any promise [was] on the part of a young student was signalled he was sure to receive an invitation to this house" (SH 42). The Blooms court in the context of a similar, if more opulent, social setting, the parties hosted by Mat Dillon for his bevy of six daughters in Roundtown. Its complex romantic and sexual play notwithstanding, the Bloom marriage—aided by some manipulation of their social tokens and tenders (the concealment of Molly's illegitimacy; the inflation of Bloom's political promise— "all the Doyles said he was going to stand for a member of Parliament" [U 18:1186])—is a remarkably well-calibrated social match. The Dillon girls, with their father's wealth behind them, have higher aspirations, and even though Atty is jilted by a "fellow that was something in the four courts" (U 18:741), Floey Dillon ends up "married to a very rich architect if Im to believe all I hear with a villa and eight rooms" (U 18:720).

The bevy of flower girls in the "Mime," then, represents not only the erotic and aesthetic bounty of massed femaleness—an effect socially localized in the girls' school, the convent, the brothel—but they also symptomatize the social crisis resulting from the Famine that, according to Florence Walzl, gave turn-of-the-century Ireland not only the lowest marriage and birth rates among civilized nations, but also "the highest rate of unmarried men and women in the world" (33). The pretty flower bunches of girls in Joyce's texts—"Mat Dillon and his bevy of daughers: Tiny, Atty, Floey, Maimy, Louey, Hetty. Molly too" (U 13:1106) or, in the "Mime," "Winnie, Olive and Beatrice, Nelly and Ida, Amy and Rue. Here they come back, all the gay pack, for they are the florals, from foncey and pansey to papavere's blush, forsake-me-nought, while there's leaf there's hope, with primtim's ruse and marry-may's blossom, all the flowers of the ancelles' garden" (FW 227.14) may be bouquets of flowers in the *Kindergarten*, but they are also implicated, precisely in the field of romance, in the social danger of class loss. This becomes more readily apparent when we consider that the Wakean flower girls, especially, might also represent the social opposite of the Dillon girls: the motherless, starving Dedalus girls—Katey, Boody, Maggy, Dilly—or, for that matter, the six Joyce sisters—Poppie, Eileen, May, Eva, Florrie, and Baby—two of whom, Poppie ("papavere's blush") and Mary or May ("marry-may's blossom") are named in the "Mime." Their fates, taken as a group, were possibly typical of Irish women of their day: Poppie, the surrogate mother of the group, became a nun in New Zealand; Eva and Florrie remained unmarried and worked in separate law offices until Eva's death; May and Eileen married, had children, and were widowed, and Baby died in 1911 of typhoid fever, a fatality of the poor, caused by drinking contaminated milk or water. Fortunately, none committed suicide (though Eileen's husband

did, in the face of bankruptcy) and Stephen's fear for his sister Dilly
("She is drowning. . . . She will drown me with her, eyes and hair.
Lank coils of seaweed hair around me, my heart, my soul" (FW
10.875) is displaced onto the flower girls of the "Mime" in what
Vincent Cheng describes as "a dense cluster of allusions to Ophelia"
(68). He points out that the Floras variously appear to be depressed,
wilting and dying—"The flossies all and mossies all they drooped
upon her draped brimfall. The bowknots, the showlots, they wilted
into woeblots" (FW 225.35)—like Dilly Dedalus grieving the loss of
Dan Kelly, I would argue, "Late lieabed under a quilt of old overcoats, fingering a pinchbeck bracelet, Dan Kelly's token" (U 10:860).

In following a version of the traditional romance plot of the Pantomime—the successful suit of a charming poor boy against a
swank and foppish rival for the hand of a greedy man's daughter (Wilson 27)—the children in "The Mime of Mick, Nick, and the Maggies" also embrace the dream of class mobility and ascendance while
at the same time resisting it with two very different strategies.
While their seemingly "innocent" courtship, marriage, and kissing
games teach them the commodification of sex they will later encounter in both the marriage market and the brothel—"Quanty
purty bellas, here, Madama Lifay! And what are you going to charm
them to, Madama, do say?" (FW 224.28)—the children cling to
magic, superstition, divination, and necromancy in an implicit hope
that love and marriage are mystical and spiritually ordained rather
than the product of commercial transaction. The "Mime" practices—like the children's divination game in "Clay" ("He halth kel-
chy chosen a clayblade and makes prayses to his three of clubs"
[FW 222.28]), Gerty's superstitions about her underwear ribbons, and
Molly's casting cards in the morning—various kinds of denial of the
hidden social and class laws that dictate that a midget-like Maria
will never marry, that lame, lower-class Gerty is ineligible for marriage into the well-to-do, Trinity-educated, Protestant, Wylie family,
and that a Polly Mooney can wed a respectable clerk only at the
point of a rhetorical shotgun. Matthew Hodgart finds all twenty-two
Major Trumps of the tarot in this chapter (86), as well as much
other magic, religion, and superstition. But I would argue that the
chapter's magic and necromancy is here, as elsewhere in the Joycean
corpus, tied to resistance and denial of social reality. Kate, the char-
woman in the Wake, who assumes the guise of "Miss Rachel Lea
Varian, she tells forkings for baschfellors, under purdah of card
palmer teaput tosspot Madam d'Elta" (FW 221.12), is cook and
dishdrudge ("kook-and-dishdrudge") when not reading palms or tea
leaves. In a gloss on "Clay," the tea party as gypsy divination rite

both colludes with dreams and fantasies of socially redemptive romance and resists the truth of the class and social determinants of love and marriage.

But the children learn the truths of social reality from contradictions among their own games and entertainments. If the Pantomime and fairy tales encourage them to fantasize plots of morganatic marriage into gentry and aristocracy—"Cinderynelly angled her slipper; it was cho chiny yet braught her a groom" (FW 224.30)—their play teaches them to recognize their own social disqualifications by presenting them with conventions and conducts they will never master. Cinderella able to escape her cinders as bride (German: *Braut*) promises the child little more than the sort of game Stephen plays in Paris "But you were delighted when Esther Osvalt's shoe went on you: girl I knew in Paris. *Tiens, quel petit pied!*" (U 3:449) that makes him fearful of his own effeminacy. Stephen traveling abroad will never be a male Cinderella, and the crass Ignatius Gallaher, who sails forth in the "Mime" like one of Columbus' ships searching for treasure, "three shirts and a wind . . . the bruce, the coriolano and the ignacio" (FW 228.9), is exposed for the marital adventurer he is. Having told Little Chandler "I mean to marry money. She'll have a good fat account at the bank or she won't do for me" (D 81) his type proceeds in the "Mime" to seduce Gloria Vanderbilt, "to melt Mrs Gloria of the Bunkers' Trust, recorporated" (FW 228.19). Little Glugg in the "Mime" suffers such an embarrassment of feminine riches that he has to use counting rhymes on the order of "Eeny, meeny, miney, moe" ("Tireton, cacheton, tireton, ba!" [FW 224.27]) to choose, and yet he will fail to get the girl. The reason may well be that he is plebeian and of humble and dubious origin, "weed-hearted boy of potter and mudder" (FW 240.22), pitied in the gossiping low brogue of his class, "This poor Glugg! It was so said of him about of his old fontmouther. Truly deplurabel! A dire! O dire! And all the freightfullness whom he inhebited after his colline born janitor. Sometime towerable" (FW 224.9). The morganatic marriage plot evoked in the reference to *The Colleen Bawn* serves as further caution against class transgression, as do references to Bulwer-Lytton's *The Lady of Lyons*, "malady of milady made melodi of malodi, she, the lalage of lyonesses, and him, her knave arrant" (FW 229.9). This is one of the plays Stephen takes his family to see with his exhibition money, during his last stand against the family's social decline, and it is the figure of its hero, Claude Melnotte, the gardener's son in love with a woman above his station, who is revived in Glugg, twice referred to as "their commoner guardian" (FW 224.24, 32) to the haughty flower girls. Glugg eventually will write lies about his

parents now socially elevated to "the sabbatarian" and "her Letty-
shape" (FW 229.19), much as Stephen did at Clongowes, "You told
the Clongowes gentry you had an uncle a judge and an uncle a general in the army" (U 3 : 105). Glugg is baffled by the feudal courtship
rituals imprinted on the children's games, a troubador ("trapadour")
who fails to guess the colors his ladies wear ("fand for himself by
gazework what their colours wear" [FW 224.26]). But the chivalric
code of the games becomes an aristocratic figure of romantic conduct that survives infantile discourse. "Was that boyish love? Was
that chivalry? Was that poetry?" (P 115)—is the language in which
Stephen riddles and castigates himself after the gothic retreat sermon in *Portrait*. Max Horkheimer writes that "Poise, rank, pro-
priety, gallantry, still are what pragmatism mistakes them to be, ha-
bitual forms of the individual's adjustment to the social situation.
In the distant past all who behaved at variance with these norms
were threatened with loss of class standing" (32). Rather than "prepare children for associating with adults of many social levels, especially the royalty and other national figures" (91), as Grace Eckley
conjectures, I would argue that the kissing, courtship, and marriage
games they play imbue children with an ideology of class distinction, desire, and transgression. Aristocracy remains for most Irish
children and adults either the mysterious presence hidden in the
carriages of cavalcades or figures of fantasy and desire.

The "Mime" more specifically dramatizes social desire and rejection in a children's game that has two ideologically divergent versions: a utopian, that promises marriage, babies, kissing, and happiness, and a dystopian, that brings rejection and humiliation. The
game is "Lady on a Mountain," and its donnée is the crossing of
social distance by marriage:

> There stands a lady on the mountain,
> who she is I do not know.
> All she wants is gold and silver;
> all she wants is a nice young man.
> (Rose, O'Hanlon, 129); rhyme structure mine)

In Alice Gomme's versions the game ends happily, in choice
("Choose one, choose two, choose the fairest of the few"), marriage
and children ("Now she's married I wish her joy, / First a girl and then
a boy") and kissing ("Kiss her once, kiss her twice, / Kiss her three
times three" [321]). But Rose and O'Hanlon report a different version in which the little boy's proposal is rebuffed ("He then asks the
lady: 'Madam, will you marry me?' and she replies *No!*" [129]) and is

followed by a dystopian tea party in which the oral play of the children is changed from kissing to eating—or worse, I will argue, to not eating. Joyce's own changes in the game shift the emphasis from romance to food:

> As Rigagnolina to Mountagnone,
> what she meaned he could not can.
> All she meaned was golten sylvup,
> all she meaned was some Knight's ploung jamn.
> (FW225.15; rhyme structure added)

In Joyce's early draft of the "Mime," the line "All she meaned was multimoney" (JA 47477–10) still preserves the allusion to the gold and silver in the wedding vows current at the time of *Ulysses:* "Though the Irish Catholic service at this point has since been modified, in Gerty's day the groom said, 'With this ring I thee wed: this gold and silver I thee give: and with all my worldly goods I thee endow" (Thornton 362). But by changing "multimoney" to "golten sylvup," Joyce adds to the echo of gold and silver an allusion to little Tommy Caffrey in "Nausicaa": "Cissy Caffrey . . . was awfully fond of children, so patient with little sufferers and Tommy Caffrey could never be got to take his castor oil unless it was Cissy Caffrey that held his nose and promised him the scatty heel of the loaf or brown bread with golden syrup on" (U 13:30). The cloying language of "Nausicaa" does rhetorically what the golden syrup does medically: it tries to artificially disguise, with concentrated sweetness, the grimmer truth about infantile life and to deny the colics and gripes that plagued malnourished children, making them literal rather than idiomatic "little sufferers," who were dosed with the hateful castor oil.

In Rose and O'Hanlon's dystopian version of "Lady on a Mountain," the menu of the tea party that is part of the riddle (Roland McHugh gives the question as "What's for tea, love? What's for tea, love?" [*Annotations* 225.15]) degenerates from "Bread & butter, water-cress" (*Annotations* 225.15) to "Squashed flies and black-beetles" (Rose, O'Hanlon 129). In the "Mime" the effect of this riddling tea is a fiendish stomach pain—

> So olff for his topheetuck the ruck made raid, aslick aslegs would run; and he ankered on his hunkers with the belly belly prest. Asking: What's my muffinstuffinaches for these times? To weat: Breath and bother and whatarcurss. Then breath more bother and

more whatarcurss. Then no breath no bother but worrawarra-
wurms. (FW 225.9)

Did Glugg stuff too many muffins, or did he get nothing to eat? Perhaps his colic is the product, as Bloom predicts, of trying to eat air
or "breath," what oriental mythology calls Barmecide food, like
Baby Boardman, "Oughtn't to have given that child an empty teat to
suck. Fill it up with wind" (U 13:958). Is Joyce playing here with
the traditional way children play "tea party"—that is by sitting at a
table and pantomiming the drinking of tea and eating of food in the
air—by shifting from the figurative to the literal, from the ludic to
the real, that is, by alluding to children for whom this play is a reality because they have nothing to eat?

Is the dietary sequence suggested here—breath and bother and
more breath and bother followed by no breath no bother but only
worms—even grimmer and more macabre than it seems, suggesting
that being alive but having no food ("breath and bother") will eventually lead to being no longer alive, and becoming food for worms
instead? Although Atherton records no references in the *Wake* (114–
123) to Swift's *A Modest Proposal* ("... *for preventing the Children
of poor People in Ireland, from becoming a Burden to their Parents
or Country; and for making them beneficial to the Publick*" [1729]),
could this passage echo a veiled allusion to the fear in Swift's satire,
of hungry Irish children themselves becoming unpalatable food? Or,
less melodramatically, did Glugg get worms (a taste for heresy, a
Diet of Worms?) from eating pieces of dried cowdung, like Lynch in
his Carmelite school, "please remember, though I did eat a cake of
cowdung once, that I admire only beauty" (P 206), or like Issy protesting that she is not a whore, "Though I did ate tough turf I'm not
the bogdoxy" (FW 225.20). The allusion to Lynch's words in this line
is interesting, because the discussion of aesthetic theory between
Stephen and Lynch is contextualized by physical hunger, as the two
boys smoke, eat air or breath, while they walk and talk. When
Donovan, who is a member of a field club, departs for his supper of
pancakes ("that yellow pancakeeating excrement" Lynch calls him,
[P 211]), Stephen twice asks him "Bring us a few turnips and onions
the next time you go out . . . to make a stew" and "Don't forget the
turnips for me and my mate" (P 211). His request, no doubt joking,
nonetheless resonates to the Irish peasants' attempts to supplement
their diet of "potatoes and water" with forage from the fields both
before and during the famine years. In their topographical survey
of the Irish diet in 1836, Clarkson and Crawford write, "The same
line of reasoning suggests that berries, wild fruit, nettles, rabbits,

hedgehogs and game were eaten more often than the Inquiry suggests" (173).

The utopian vision of childhood represented in the game of "tea party" is repeatedly revised through the Joycean tea party. Even at Clongowes with its gentrified clientele, the boys are fed damp bread they cannot eat and weak tea—while the richer boys are sent hampers and tins of cocoa from home, and the Jesuits, according to Mr. Dedalus, live in Dickensian hypocrisy, "You saw their table at Clongowes. Fed up, by God, like gamecocks." (P 71). The children in "The Mime of Mick, Nick, and the Maggies" play at bourgeois marriage games from which class has already disqualified them, and at tea parties for which there is inadequate food. Indeed, the utopian tea party in the "Mime" is the British tea party rather than the Irish proletarian tea, the utopian tea of "Polly Put the Kettle On" translated into the imperialist idiom of "tiffin"—"So they fished in the kettle and fought free and if she bit his tailibout all hat tiffin for the thea" (FW 229.24). Or, to put the proper British accent on the children's mimed utopian tea party, it is a "Teapotty. Teapotty" (FW 247.15). But the "real" Irish children's tea party is the one described by the narrator of *Portrait*—"Discarded crusts and lumps of sugared bread, turned brown by the tea which had been poured over them, lay scattered on the table. Little wells of tea lay here and there on the board and a knife with a broken ivory handle was stuck through the pith of a ravaged turnover" (P 163). This scene is not fantasy, according to Stanislaus' diary, which argues that the specter of famine, which had cast its apocalyptic shadow over modern Irish history, haunted in its depoliticized form the everyday lives of the Joyce children. "*December 1904.* It is now December and for this year we have lived in this house on practically starvation rations. There has been a very small breakfast, perhaps, no dinner, and no tea, and at about seven o'clock I find the house intolerable and go down town" (Healey 138).

2. Exile

Stanislaus, unable to bear the family hunger and squalor, goes downtown; James goes abroad to France, leaving his sisters behind in poverty in Ireland. "But if he'll go to be a son to France's, she'll stay daughter of Clare," the "Mime" tells us (FW 226.9), and the Dedalus girls, begging for charity soup from the nuns, do indeed enact the mendicancy of the order of the Poor Clares. "I told her of Paris," Stephen muses about Dilly, but exactly what did Stephen tell her? Did he tell her of the squalor, poverty, and hunger, and his own ascetic Franciscan life there, or did he fill her head with romance and sugarplums—"Late lieabed under a quilt of old overcoats, fingering a pinchbeck bracelet, Dan Kelly's token" (U 10:860). Did Stephen go off to Paris to study, like Laertes, and leave Dilly behind to be jilted, like Ophelia? After what he told her about Paris, Dilly squanders the precious coppers she badgered from her abusive father ("An insolent pack of little bitches since your poor mother died. . . . I'm going to get rid of you" [U 10:682]) in order to buy Chardenal's French primer. (McMichael 113). "What did you buy that for? he asked. To learn French?" (U 10:867). Dilly will starve to learn French in order to go to Paris like her brother. Does she dream, lying under her quilt of old overcoats, of a "Fashionable Intelligence" of French aristocrats and sweet food, like Issy in the "Mime"—"And the Prince Le Monade has been graciously pleased. His six chocolate pages will run bugling before him and Cococream toddle after" (FW 236.2)? Does she dream of Prince Le Monade, or lemonade, because Stephen told her his own impression of Paris as a city that is—like Glugg's second riddle in the "Mime"—"a symphony in yellow," to borrow William York Tindall's phrase (160): "The sun is there, the slender trees, the lemon houses. Paris rawly waking, crude sunlight on her lemon streets" (U 3:207). Or did he confess to Dilly that he was constantly hungry in Paris, that the yellow light glinted off the gold teeth and yellow custards in people's hungry mouths, "In Rodot's Yvonne and Madeleine newmake their tumbled beauties, shattering with gold teeth *chaussons* of pastry, their mouths yellowed with the *pus* of *flan breton*" (U 3:212) and that he suffered "Hunger toothache" (U 3:186) like little Glugg in the "Mime"— "shot pinging up through the errorooth of his wisdom" (FW 231.10). "—Haps thee jaoneofergs?" (FW 233.21) Glugg asks in the second riddle, perhaps fearing, like Stephen, that France, the country that burned Joan of Arc, may not prove hospitable to a heretic like himself. But in an early draft of the "Mime" the line read "Haps thee ore candy?" [JA 47477–10]—that is, 'Do you have rock candy, or candy, gold candy, lemon platt?' The "Mime" is full of hungry children dreaming of candy, like the urchins of *Ulysses'* Dublin, "Two barefoot urchins, sucking long liquorice laces, halted near him, gaping at his stump with their yellowslobbered mouths" (U 10:244).

The "Mime" continues the demystification of exile begun in "Proteus" by confounding the specious distinction between the different kinds of emigration that Robert Hand makes in *Exiles:* "In exile, we have said, but here we must distinguish. There is an economic and there is a spiritual exile. There are those who left her to seek the bread by which men live and there are other, nay, her most favoured children, who left her to seek in other lands that food of the spirit by which a nation of human beings is sustained in life" (E 99). Hand's distinction—promoted in Stephen's interest in *Portrait*—is made implicitly along the lines of class, and proleptically incorporates Trilling's later assertions that the adversary culture of modern artists constitutes a transcendent class. But for Ascendancy literati like Lady Gregory and Yeats, extended stays in England or on the Continent constituted neither emigration nor exile precisely because class and poverty played no role in their departures. The "Mime" reinterprets the flight of little Glugg, expelled after having failed to guess the riddle, "atvoiced ringsoundinly . . . to go to troy and harff a freak at himself by all that story to the ulstramarines" (FW 225.2), to encompass a wide range of emigration motives and activities: the patriotic flight of the wild geese ("Hark to his wily geeses goosling by" [FW 233.11]); clerical expulsion ("they provencials drollo eggspilled him" [FW 230.4]); criminal transportation ("carberry banishment care of Pencylmania, Bretish Armerica . . . and fire off, gheol ghiornal" [FW 228.18–33]); adulterous elopement ("Fuisfinister, fuyerescaper!" [FW 228.28]); and, like Joyce himself, search for a sanctuary with a pension so that he can write poetry, "He would si through severalls of sanctuaries . . . on a demi panssion for his whole lofetime . . . while he, being brung up on soul butter, have recourse of course to poetry" (FW 230.17–240).

For one of these—cultural missionary to expatriate Irishmen ("Mischnary for the minestrary to all the sems of Aram" [FW 228.14])—Stephen sarcastically excoriates himself in "Proteus": "You were going to do wonders, what? Missionary to Europe after fiery Columbanus" (FW 3 : 192). Joyce gives to Glugg, as to Stephen in his Paris memories of "Proteus," the fear that turns saint into martyr. The courage of the heretic, of his bold *Non Serviam*, is chastened by his confrontation with its possible violent consequences: that his bold provocation—"If you were a genuine Roman Catholic, mother, you would burn me as well as the books" (SH 135)—might come true. In the second riddle, Glugg "asks not have you seen a match being struck nor is this powder mine" (FW 233.18), like Kevin Egan lighting a dynamite fuse ("The blue fuse burns deadly between hands and burns clear" [U 3:239]) or one of his "gunpowder cigarettes . . . Loose tobaccoshreds catch fire" (U 3 : 116, 239), or setting fire to Joan of Arc, "—Haps thee jaoneofergs?" (FW 233.21). In Paris, Stephen's moral courage turns into paranoia and cowardice— "Yes, used to carry punched tickets to prove an alibi if they arrested you for murder somewhere" (U 3 : 179). He desperately tries to dissociate himself from the wild geese, "To yoke me as his yokefellow, our crimes our common cause" (U 3:228), and he strips the Irish revolutionary Kevin Egan of all glamour and political relevance: "In gay Paree he hides, Egan of Paris, unsought by any save by me. Making his day's stations, the dingy printingcase, his three taverns, the Montmartre lair he sleeps short night in, *rue de la Goutte-d'Or*, damascened with flyblown faces of the gone. Loveless, landless, wifeless" (U 3:249).

Artistic exile in "The Mime of Mick, Nick, and the Maggies" takes on the features of criminal transportation rather than Icarean flight. Among the insights Glugg's hunger toothache gives him—"pinging up through the errorooth of his wisdom" (FW 231.11)—is his historical recontextualization among a quartet of minor nineteenth-century Irish writers[5] with bad teeth and no bite who merely flap their gums. They are "gumboil owrithy prods wretched some horsery megee plods coffin acid odarkery pluds dense floppens mugurdy" (FW 231.13), that is, John Boyle O'Reilly (transported to an Australian convict settlement in 1869 for being an Irish Republican Brotherhood agent) plus Thomas d'Arcy McGee (a member of the Young Irelanders, "yank islanders" [FW 228.7], who emigrated to the U.S. and Canada, and was shot in Montreal in 1868) plus Kevin Izod O'Doherty (also transported, according to McHugh, [*Annotations* 232]) plus Denis Florence MacCarthy. There are earlier references as well to another Young Irelander, the author of *Knocknagow*, Charles Joseph Kickham, who eventually served four years of penal servitude for Fenian activities, and, to John Mitchell's "gheol ghiornal" (FW 228.33) or *Jail Journal, or Five Years in British Prisons*, who was transported to Van Diemen's Land ("Or Van Diemen's coral pearl?" [FW 225.26]) for treasonous articles in 1848. The reference, of course, also encompasses Oscar Wilde's *The Ballad of Reading Gaol* and the letters he wrote from abroad as Sebastian Melmoth, "gheol ghiornal, foull subustioned mullmud" (FW 228.33).

Behind the romantic exile of Irish writers there are more tales of banishment, incarceration, isolation, futility, and failure than there are tales of triumph like Joyce's own. Indeed, it is the distortions that Joyce's own success will work upon Stephen's cautionary tale of Irish artistic emigration, that may have prompted Joyce's ironical references to his own odyssey, his own flight to Paris by way of detours over twenty or thirty ("getrennty") years to Trieste and Zurich in German-speaking railroads, "catch the Paname-Turricum and regain that absendee tarry easty, his città immediata, by an alley and detour with farecard awailable getrennty years" (FW 228.22). He mentions his support by the "satiety of arthurs" (FW 229.7), and attributes the success of *Ulysses* ("Ukalepe. Loathers' leave. Had Days.

Nemo in Patria. The Luncher Out. Skilly and Carubdish. A Wondering Wreck. From the Mermaids' Tavern. Bullyfamous. Naughtsycalves. Mother of Misery. Walpurgas Nackt" [FW 229.13]) to the titillation and notoriety it provided to the British public, "the old sniggering publicking press and its nation of sheepcopers" (FW 229.8). He then shoots this narration of literary exile and putative success through with more than a dozen references to lines from James Macpherson's bogus translation of the Gaelic epic of Ossian, to signal, I believe, that this Irish epic, too, is romanticized fiction, and that the romantic artistic flight of Joyce from Ireland, in the form of an elopement, has acquired an epic romantic mythology that he wants to dispel. He therefore reinterprets Glugg's rejection by Issy and return to Iseult of Ireland not as the operatic epic romance *Tristan and Isolde*, but as the tawdry, commonplace, adulterous affair between Richard Wagner and a putatively promiscuous Mathilde Wesendonk, "a hadtobe heldin, thoroughly enjoyed by so many so meny on block at Boyrut season and for their account ottorly admired by her husband in sole intimacy" (FW 229.33), her husband having been Otto Wesendonk. The analogy of Glugg's aspirations to Wagner's are deromanticized in spite of the Parisian setting and the allusion to *Tristan*, "he would accoster her coume il fou in teto-dous as a wagoner would his mudheeldy wheesindonk at their trist in Parisise" (FW 230.11). Vicki Mahaffey writes of Joyce's attitude toward Wagner, "Joyce, like Emerson, came to believe that 'The secret of Genius is to suffer no fiction to exist for us,' and he consequently rejected Wagner's operas as enticing and seductive lies celebrating a tragic heroism that was all posturing" ("Wagner, Joyce and Revolution" 239).

By overdetermining the causes of Glugg's emigration or exile in the "Mime," the text reopens the question of its interpretation and posture for the artist that Cranly raises to Stephen—"you need not look upon yourself as driven away if you do not wish to go or as a heretic or an outlaw" (P 245). By linking exile or emigration to rejection in love or failure in rivalry, the "Mime" particularly points us back to the troublesome disjunctions and contradictions that mark Stephen's motives for flight at the end of *Portrait*. "Yes; he would go. He could not strive against another. He knew his part" (P 245) the text tells us, although a moment later, Stephen confidently asserts to Cranly "I do not fear to be alone or to be spurned for another" (P 247). The fitful re-emergence and reconvergence of Emma Clery and Cranly in Stephen's diary entries—espied, indeed, having a tea party together: "Saw her drinking tea and eating cakes . . . He tells me Cranly was invited there by brother" (P 250)—suggests that Stephen's rejection by Emma and the successful rivalry of his best friend (at least as Stephen imagines it) play a large, but suppressed, part in Stephen's Icarean gesture of flight and exile. Love, sexual desire, and exile—concepts powerfully idealized and socially decontextualized in *Portrait*—have, on the contrary, definite social determinants. *Stephen Hero* limns these more clearly, while *Portrait*, true to its legitimation ideology, suppresses them and admits them only as gaps.

> "A louse crawled over the nape of his neck and, putting his
> thumb and forefinger deftly beneath his loose collar, he caught
> it. . . . The life of his body, illclad, illfed, louseeaten, made him
> close his eyelids in a sudden spasm of despair. . . . Well then, let
> her go and be damned to her. She could love some clean athlete
> who washed himself every morning to the waist and had black
> hair on his chest. Let her." (P 233–233)

Clearly the narrative of *Portrait* fails to report a missing scene, an incident we are asked to infer from the ruptured logic of Stephen's musing, in which Emma, or someone in Emma's household, says or does something to make Stephen ashamed and defensive about the "life of his body, illclad, illfed, louseeaten," that marks his expulsion from the bourgeois marriage mart. The Shem chapter more explicitly celebrates this elided event, "he had been toed out of all the schicker families" (FW 181.3), and suggests the unwashed artist was ejected by housemaids or servants, "ordered off the gorgeous premises in most cases on account of his smell which all cookmaids eminently objected to" (FW 181.9).

The plot that could be evolved from such an elided expulsion would have the artist, who is thus debarred from bourgeois courtship, deliberately marginalizing himself as a romantic outlaw, a heretic, a traitor, and a libertine. In a scene from *Stephen Hero* that is carefully censored in *Portrait*, Stephen indeed goes on to court Emma "*comme un fou*," like a madman ("To the ordinary intelligence it looks as if you had taken leave of your senses for the time being," Lynch tells him [SH 200])—with an illicit proposal of reckless sex—to which her wounded reply is "You are mad, I think" (SH 199). Stephen's railing at Emma's *petit-bourgeoiserie* is then an inverted self-defense, for it inverts his own exclusions from the social requirements, the cleanliness, hygiene, and physical maintenance, that would qualify him as a proper suitor. Indeed, when the little girls dance in prayerful adoration around the angel, Chuff—like Emma Clery and the other Gaelic League girls milling around Father Moran—it is for his cleanliness they celebrate their "dear sweet Stainusless": "Unclean you are not. Outcaste thou are not . . . Untouchable is not the scarecrown is on you. You are pure. You are pure. You are in your puerity" (FW 237.27). Other analogues to this configuration of the adoration of the priest, saint, or Christ figure by a group of young girls can be found in the Gaelic League's girl students surrounding Father Moran (to Stephen's chagrin) in *Portrait*, and in Père Marcel Jousse's linguistic demonstrations—"Around the lecturer was a group of girls, who addressed him as 'Rabbi Jesus'" (Mary Colum, quoted in Weir [313]). Glugg duly learns his lesson, and when he returns from the dead, or the harrowing of hell, he not only repents his sins and recants his heresies, like Stephen after the retreat sermon ("Examen of conscience scruples now he to the best of his memory schemado" [FW 240.6]), but he also "ast for shave and haircut" (FW 240.34).

In the "Mime," as in *Portrait*, Emma's social rejection of Stephen is repaid with a social revenge. The vulgar *petit-bourgeoiserie* Stephen holds against her in *Stephen Hero* and *Portrait* is magnified and burlesqued in the "Mime" as *nouveau riche* greed and upwardly mobile ambition:

> Should in ofter years it became about you will after desk jobduty becoming a bank midland mansioner we and I shall reside with our obseisant servants among Burke's mobility at La Roseraie, Ailesbury Road. Red bricks are hellishly good values if you trust to the roster of ads. (FW 235.10)

The girls' aspirations to *Burke's Peerage* or *Burke's Landed Gentry* and a superb address on Ailesbury Road in Ballsbridge—still the Embassy Row of Dublin, with its handsome red brick mansions—as well as the desire for a house named as a French rose garden, "La Roseraie," expose the fatuousness of Stephen's adolescent dream of Mercedes, and her figurative transformation into the simplicity of his revised Emma Clery—"And if he had judged her harshly? If her life were a simple rosary of hours" (P 216). The transformations of women in Stephen's adolescent imagination represent not only moral and sexual oscillations, as is often pointed out—their perceptions as virgins or whores—but social extremes as well. When Stephen wants to punish Emma in his imagination, he refigures her as a beggar, a scullery maid, a factory girl:

> Rude brutal anger routed the last lingering instant of ecstasy from his soul. It broke up violently her fair image and flung the fragments on all sides. On all sides distorted reflections of her

image started from his memory: the flowergirl in the ragged
dress with damp coarse hair and a hoyden's face who had called
herself his own girl and begged his handsel, the kitchengirl in the
next house who sang over the clatter of her plates with the drawl
of a country singer the first bars of *By Killarney's Lakes and
Fells* . . . a girl he had glanced at . . . as she passed out of Jacob's
biscuit factory." (P 220)

The kind of magical transformations both Bloom and Stephen practice on women in their imaginations, Joyce uses in the "Mime" to
mark the dialectical relationship between their symbolical and their
socially real versions. The figure of the flower girl as the subject
of social transformation was popularized in 1916 with the London
publication and production of George Bernard Shaw's *Pygmalion*.
Joyce's own complex maneuver socially decontextualizes and recon-
textualizes her in order to make, I believe, a somewhat different
critical point: that flower girls provide art, and particularly the male
aesthetic imagination, with a perennially pleasing symbolical type—
"youngly delightsome frilles-in-pleyurs . . . showen drawen, if bud
one, or, if in florileague" (FW 224.22), or "Just so stylled with the
nattes are their flowerheads now and each of all has a lovestalk onto
herself and the tot of all the tits of their understamens is as open as
he can posably she" (FW 236.33). Yet the de-symbolized source of
these "Happy little girlycums" (FW 234.34), these pretty flower girls
from Klingsor's magic garden in Wagner's *Parsifal*, is the grimy, ill-
spoken near-beggar in *Portrait*. As a social reality, flower girls—
ragged young women on streetcorners obliged to hawk flowers for
pennies—have none of the erotic and aesthetic appeal of symbolical
or mythical flower girls, as Stephen's repulsion makes clear:

> The blue flowers which she lifted towards him and her young
> blue eyes seemed to him at that instant images of guilelessness;
> and he halted till the image had vanished and he saw only her
> ragged dress and damp coarse hair and hoydenish face. (P 183)

Stephen's harsh refusal to buy her flowers—"Did you hear what I
said? asked Stephen, bending towards her. I told you I had no money.
I tell you again now" (P 183)—prefigures Glugg's failure to guess the
riddle of the "blue" or blueish flower—heliotrope—in the "Mime."
Stephen hurrying to escape "that moment of discouraged poverty"
(P 184) that unites him with the ragged hoyden, disavows class identification with her.

We can see the extent to which Stephen's relationship with Emma

Clery is troubled by class, in the abusive metaphors that erupt in his anger at her rejection of him—"He had done well to leave her to flirt with her priest, to toy with a church which was the scullery-maid of christendom" (P 220) and "His anger against her found vent in coarse railing at her paramour, whose name and voice and features offended his baffled pride: a priested peasant, with a brother a policeman in Dublin and a brother a potboy in Moycullen" (P 221). The "Mime," in turn, avenges the young woman for the confusions Stephen's class and sexual *Angsts* visit upon her. In a scene Joyce described to Harriet Shaw Weaver as "the girl angels sing a hymn of liberation around Shawn" (SL 355), they prophesy a better world with no more famine for the Irish poor and their children ("When there shall be foods for vermin as full as feeds for the fett, eat on earth as there's hot in oven") and with merry political, sexual, and religious liberation for the scullerymaids and scullions of Stephen's derision, "When every Klitty of a scolderymeid shall hold every yardscullion's right to stimm her uprecht for whimsoever, whether on privates, whather in publics. And when all us romance catholeens shall have ones for all amanseprated" (FW 239.16). The patriarchal begettings ("bigyttens") of the Bible are invested with infantile *jouissance* in the language of coquettes and cocks and cherries and curly hair ("to tell Cockotte to teach Connie Curley to touch Cattie Hayre and tip Carminia" [FW 239.23])—like the pert riposte to his bold stare with which the young factory lass from Jacob's biscuit factory, a kind of Irish Carminia or Carmen in a Biblical concern, disconcerts Stephen:"—Do you like what you seen of me, straight hair and curly eyebrows?" (P 220). The girls' prayer ends with an inverted *Our Father* to an unlocatable god—"though where the diggings he dwellst amongst us here's nobody knows save Mary" (FW 239.25). This prayer echoes other bitter prayers of Joycean children, like Boody's bad grace over her charity soup in *Ulysses*, addressed to a god and a father who fail to give the girls their daily bread: "Our father who art not in heaven" (U 10:291).

3. Home

The children's games in "The Mime of Mick, Nick, and the Maggies" end, as they must, at dusk, with the onset of darkness, "It darkles, (tinct, tint) all this our funnaminal world" (FW 244.13), at nine o'clock, "whilest nin nin nin nin that Boorman's clock, a winny on the tinny side, ninned nin nin nin nin" (FW 257.8). Their ending is protracted with delays, reprieves, and last rounds of riddling as the children resist the end of play even after the father's thunderous threats, "Housefather calls enthreateningly. From Brandenborgen-thor. . . . In thundercloud periwig. With lightning bug aflash from afinger" (FW 246.6). Eveline and her siblings, too, used to elude the menacing father, "father used often to hunt them in out of the field with his blackthorn stick" (D 36), until Eveline learned, like other Joycean children, that paternal violence can make the home itself unsafe, "When they were growing up he had never gone for her, like he used to go for Harry and Ernest, because she was a girl; but latterly he had begun to threaten her" (D 38). Stanislaus Joyce reported similar fears about his sisters, recording in his diary on 29 March 1904:

> "We—Jim, Charlie, and I—relieve one another in the house like policemen as the girls are not safe in it with Pappie. A few nights ago, not knowing I was in—I do most of the duty—he attempted to strike some of them. He catches at the thing nearest to hand—a poker, plate, cup or pan—to fling at them. This has been the cause of many rows here. If the children see two of us preparing to go out, they run up to the third to ask him to stay in." (Healey 24)

But Joyce, perhaps mindful of the lurid beating by her uncle Tom Healy that drove Nora from Galway to Dublin, adds a particular critique of the pornological hypocrisy of men who beat daughters or nieces for sexual transgressions. The little girls dancing home to rhymes about old men, Edward Lear's "O My Aged Uncle Arley" and the nursery rhyme "Old Daddy Dacon," hear echoed in them par-enthetical sadistic threats that might have been lifted from the por-nographical discourses of "Circe":

> (You'll catch it, don't fret, Mrs Tummy Lupton! Come indoor, Scoffynosey, and shed your swank!) . . . (The nurse'll give it you, stickypots! And you wait, my lasso, fecking the twine!) . . . (You're well held now, Missy Cheekspeer, and your panto's off! Fie, for shame, Ruth Wheatacre, after all the booz said!) . . . (Ah, crabeyes, I have you, showing off to the world with that gape in your stocking!) (FW 257.13–24)

In 1926, when it seems he began thinking about the "Mime," Joyce described his writing to Harriet Shaw Weaver as a game, and re-marked, "Children may just as well play as not. The ogre will come in any case" (*Letters* III, 144).

In "The Mime of Mick, Nick, and the Maggies," Joyce uses the coming of the ogre to carry his dialectical treatment of childhood into the home. The symbolical fiction of home as the locus of infantile security, nurturance, and comfort is critiqued by the social reality of homes in which the child is at greatest risk from parental abuse and violence. "They are subdued, even terrorized at home, and regard it as a great pleasure to be allowed to run about the roads," Stanislaus wrote about his cousins (Healey 37). So it is with the children of the "Mime," who become subdued at nightfall in the home, after their exuberant play abroad. Joyce brings his chapter to the closure of a somber crescendo, by troping the imbricated ironies of the politics of the Irish home in the discourses of religion—the rhythms of Biblical language and the rhetoric of prayers and sacred texts. His philosophical point in this chapter, that faith in benign spiritual agency (magic and superstition as governing love and marriage, prayer and faith as governing life with divine providence) allows people to deny the grimmer social, class, political, and economic determinants of the reality of life, has a Marxist overtone that is underscored by the futility of children's prayers throughout his *oeuvre*. "Loud, graciously hear us!" the children pray in the "Mime," and their prayer seems to be answered by its narrative "Now have thy children entered into their habitations . . . Gov be thanked! Thou hast closed the portals of the habitations of thy children and thou hast set thy guards thereby" (FW 258.27). But its echo of little Stephen's nighttime prayer at Clongowes—"*Visit, we beseech Thee, O Lord, this habitation and drive away from it all the snares of the enemy*" (P 18)—is less reassuring when we remember that his prayer fails to protect Stephen from being beaten by the prefect of studies, any more than a *Hail Mary* saves little Tom Farrington in "Counterparts" from a vicious caning by his father. "Alice told me that on one occasion Bertie, then an infant of six or seven, begged Uncle William not to beat him and promised to say a 'Hail Mary' for him if he didn't" (Healey 37), Stanislaus writes in his diary. He does not report whether Bertie's prayer worked.

Tom Farrington's father—harassed and humiliated all day by a little Ulster martinet—practices on his child the displaced aggression of the colonial subject. The brutal Irish father, we are reminded, is the colonial father caught in the impossible situation of making a home safe when his nation is not safe. Joyce uses the Biblical analogue of the Jews in Egypt throughout the "Mime"'s ending, praying the Passover prayer for the safety of children to keep the firstborns preserved from the avenging angel, "Go to, let us extol Azrael with our harks, by our brews, on our jambses, in his gaits" (FW 258.7), to illuminate the insecurity of the Irish home. The lamplighter is described as lighting Sabbath candles for peasant cottages and gypsy tents, "Bring lolave branches to mud cabins and peace to the tents of Ceder" (FW 244.4) in a reprise of little Stephen's fantasy of the safe comfort of the Irish cottage, "It would be lovely to sleep for one night in that cottage before the fire of smoking turf, in the dark lit by the fire, in the warm dark" (P 18). But the "Mime" already hints the political truth that Stephen learns only much later from the "dull stare of terror" in the eyes of his friend Davin. The mother, like a clucking hen calling her chicks home, is the dreaded curfew—"And, the hag they damename Coverfew hists from her lane. And haste, 'tis time for bairns ta hame. Chickchilds, comeho to roo. Comehome to roo, wee chickchilds doo, when the wildworewolf's abroad. Ah, let's away and let's gay and let's stay chez where the log foyer's burning!" (FW 244.8). But later these shushing admonitions (in German) to the brood of chicks ("Side here roohish, cleany fuglers!" [FW 250.11]) take on foreboding poignancy by alluding to Macduff's lament at losing "all my pretty chickens and their dam/ At one fell swoop" (IV.3) just before a set of Macbeth references—"For a burning would is come to dance inane. Glamours hath moidered's lieb and herefore Coldours must leap no more. Lack breath must leap no more" (FW 250.16). The "Mime"'s children will go to sleep in prayers that they be saved from cold, murder, bedwetting, and madness—("That they take no chill. That they do ming no merder. That they shall not gomeet madhowiatrees" (FW 259.5). In the days of the famine, the curfew made every Irishman abroad after dark a felon, and the smallest glint of light from a cottage could occasion search and seizure. This is the fear Stephen sees in Davin's eye: "the terror of soul of a starving Irish village in which the curfew was still a nightly fear" (P 181).

Rose and O'Hanlon remark of the Biblical prose at the end of the "Mime"—"Joyce seems to equate the wandering of the children in the village streets with the wandering of the Jews in the desert. This last section is full of Hebrew words and allusions" (143). Indeed, the *Wake* father is "in deesperation of deispiration at the diasporation of his diesparation" (FW 257.25)—continuing a family diaspora begun years before Simon Dedalus threatens Dilly: "I'm going to show you a little trick. . . . I'll leave you all where Jesus left the jews" (U 10:697). The children's diaspora was already staged in *Stephen Hero*, when the Daedalus children illegally rescue the family portraits, their *lares* and *penates*, from their evicted lodgings by stealth in the dead of night (SH 159). It was staged again in *Portrait*, at the end of the children's squalid tea, when to Stephen's "Why are we on the move again, if it's a fair question?" the children answer "Becauseboro theboro landboro lordboro willboro putboro usboro outboro"

P 163). The Dedalus children are indeed wandering Jews, and their perpetual evictions, which both Stephen and the reader are allowed to treat with bourgeois condescension as symptoms of the father's fecklessness, have nonetheless powerful political resonances for Ireland with its history of brutal peasant evictions, particularly during the bitterest times. The narrative of *Stephen Hero* treats Simon Daedalus's logic with amused derision—"Mr Daedalus had not an acute sense of the rights of private property: he paid rent very rarely. To demand money for eatables seemed to him just but to expect people to pay for shelter the exorbitant sums which are demanded annually by houseowners in Dublin seemed to him unjust" (P 150). But as political analysis of the situation of the Irish tenantry, having to pay rent for their own appropriated lands, Daedalus's complaint is not without insight.

In using Edgar Quinet's gloss on Herder's vision of nature to figure the lilts of children as never-ending generations of wildflowers, Joyce repeats in the "Mime" the imbricated intertextual gesture of Stephen in *Portrait*, in keeping the melancholy of his siblings' lost childhoods at bay:

> He heard the choir of voices in the kitchen echoed and multiplied through an endless reverberation of the choirs of endless generations of children: and heard in all the echoes an echo also of the recurring note of weariness and pain. All seemed weary of life even before entering upon it. And he remembered that Newman had heard this note also in the broken lines of Virgil *giving utterance, like the voice of Nature herself, to that pain and weariness yet hope of better things which has been the experience of her children in every time.* (P 164)

Stephen suppresses the pain and weariness of the real children by intertextualizing, universalizing, philosophizing, intellectualizing, and aestheticizing it; by invoking a classical illustration from Newman's *An Essay in Aid of Grammar*, in which eternal and ubiquitous children become a trope for humankind itself. Poststructuralist criticism does no less. The "Two Words for Joyce" from *Finnegans Wake* that Jacques Derrida privileges in his *homage* to Joyce's Babelian deconstructions, HE WAR, are embedded in the children's Passover prayer—"Of their fear they broke, they ate wind, they fled; where they ate there they fled; of their fear they fled, they broke away . . . And shall not Babel be with Lebab? And he war" (FW 258.5). In Derrida's essay the children of this chapter too are displaced by the dispersed voice of god, as language becomes the focus of concern at the expense of the children who eat air or breath or wind, and who flee, perhaps from their parents' creditors, like the Dedalus children, or from their parents, like the Farrington boy. But if the dispersed god is the inspiration of prayer in a dispersed language, it is the dispersed children for whose benefit the utterance is made. Joyce counters Quinet's optimistic view of nature, and the culture's ability to imagine a utopian childhood, with an implicit gesture toward Quinet's somber vision of eternal suffering and perpetually deferred redemption, in texts that are silently mimed in the "Mime": his *Tablettes du juif errant* and the prose poem "Ahasvérus," that made Quinet one of the chief nineteenth-century chroniclers of the legend of the Wandering Jew.

"The Mime of Mick, Nick, and the Maggies" revisits some of Joyce's most famous textual terrain: the paedocentric visions of childhood with which he opens *Dubliners* and *Portrait*. But these works establish the legitimation myth of art, the story of the sensitive child apart from its culture, able to transform suffering into infant martyrdom—the tiny Stephen traumatized for ecumenical heresy, the beaten Stephen placing himself in a heroic revolutionary tradition after his pandy-batting—that prefigures the eventual social and class transcendence of the artist into the liberal empyrean of adversary culture. "The Mime of Mick, Nick, and the Maggies" retroactively challenges and critiques this myth of art and the artist by producing an art of childhood that reintegrates the child into its social and political matrix. The "Mime" revisits childhood with a dialectical perspective of its utopian and dystopian versions, its function as the colonized site of adult desires and hopes that suppress and conceal the social and class reality of children's lives. "O Loud, hear the wee beseech of thees of each of these thy unlitten ones!" (FW 259.3) the "Mime"'s children pray—little ones *unlitten*, a German neologism that sounds something like *unsuffered*, or not *suffered*. Unlike the lovely Biblical world of Jesus, where little ones are suffered to come unto him, the "Mime"'s children are often literal "little sufferers," in the parlance of "Nausicaa"'s' narrator—suffering rather than suffered. Joyce's "Mime" gives us their play and their pain:

> Loud, heap miseries upon us yet entwine our arts with
>   laughters low!
> Ha he hi ho hu!
> Mummum. (FW 259.7)

Notes

1. Textual Raveling: A Critical and Theoretical Introduction

1. See Derek Attridge and Daniel Ferrer's eloquent articulation of the theoretical premises of a deconstructive approach to Joyce, and their implications for critical practice, in *Post-structuralist Joyce*, whose "Essays from the French" also contain provocative and relevant essays by Jacques Derrida and Stephen Heath. Writing some years after Ihab Hassan's *The Postmodern Turn*, they exhibit none of his anxiety over an unreadable and unread *Finnegans Wake*. Hassan worried, "Yet, how many ever read *Finnegan's Wake?* Ah, Mr. Wilder, though you say some works permeate the culture unread, the question still nags, and nags" (102). For a comprehensive history of post-structuralist engagement with Joyce's work, see Geert Lernout's *The French Joyce*.

2. Jeffrey Segall, in "Between Marxism and Modernism, or How to Be a Revolutionist and Still Love *Ulysses*," discusses the history of the Marxist political reception of Joyce's work in the thirties and forties, and gives an especially interesting summary of Joyce's defense by the American Trotskyist intellectuals. See also "*Ulysses*, Modernism, and Marxist Criticism" by Jeremy Hawthorn in *James Joyce and Modern Literature* pp. (112–125).

3. See the essays in Derek Attridge, Geoff Bennington, and Robert Young's *Post-structuralism and the Question of History* for discussions of these issues.

4. The strategy of Eugene Jolas in his 1929 essay in *Our Exagmination* ("The Revolution of Language and James Joyce," pp. 77–92) was precisely to assimilate "Work in Progress" to an already institutionalized literary avant-garde (Léon-Paul Fargue, Michel Leiris, André Breton, Gertrude Stein, August Stramm). But Jolas stressed the logopoetic metaphysics of these projects at the expense of their ideological subversiveness.

5. Christine Van Boheemen-Saaf has raised the most sophisticated objections to the performative ontological functions of feminine representation (which is, of course, not the same thing as *écriture féminine*) in the Joycean text. She writes, "Joyce is not the only one to use the image of a woman to legitimize the inscription of the idea of ontological otherness within his

text." But she warns that this practice may "suggest a hypostasis of sexual difference, a new idolatry, a mystique of sexual difference as foundational rhetorical figure" (100).

6. Bonnie Scott in *Joyce and Feminism* points out, for example, that in its earliest published incarnations, *A Portrait of the Artist as a Young Man* shared the pages of *The Egoist* with lively feminist debate. Dora Marsden's attack on Christabel Pankhurst's campaign for abstinence to control venereal disease ("Views and Comments: The Chastity of Women," *The Egoist,* February 2, 1914, pp. 44–46) appeared in the same issue as the first installment of *Portrait* (86).

2. Patronage and Censorship: The Production of Art in the Social Real

1. When constrained to severely limit his focus in his compact essay on Joyce in *Four Dubliners*, R. Ellmann selects precisely an idealistic narrative ("Still, if Joyce mocked such immortal longings, it was because he had immortal longings to mock" [65]; "Joyce was convinced that a great future lay in store for him, and on the promise of it he allowed people to help him secure it" [66]; "As Irish artist, Joyce could be contemptuous toward his literary compatriots, whom he derided as serving lesser gods than his own" [79]; "The function of literature, as Joyce and his hero Stephen Dedalus both define it with unaccustomed fervor, is the eternal affirmation of the spirit of man, suffering and rollicking" [89], etc.).

2. Jacques Aubert's *Introduction à l'Esthétique de James Joyce*, an excellent, major examination of the critical writings, and the philosophical education and assumptions they betray, focuses specifically on the texts dealing with aesthetic matters, including the Paris and Pola notebooks.

3. This is, of course, precisely why Joyce received such early strong support from U.S. liberals, because both in life and art he exemplified what Lionel Trilling in "Beyond Culture" describes as the "adversary intention" of modern art: ". . . a primary function of art and thought is to liberate the individual from the tyranny of his culture in the environmental sense and to permit him to stand beyond it in an autonomy of perception and judgment" (preface n.p.).

4. Joyce's experience of having printers and secretaries refuse to reproduce, and subsequently destroy, his texts should not be confused with the "ideological crisis" Raymond Williams describes when printers are denounced as "a threat to 'freedom of the press' " for "refusing to print what others have written" (58). Joyce's printers and secretary enacted a displaced governmental coercion, a fear of liability and prosecution, rather than a seizure of the production of communication.

5. "Grace"'s narrator never offers an explanation of Tom Kernan's fall—thereby tacitly supporting the official ("They agreed that the gentleman must have missed his footing" [D 152]) and unofficial ("It happened that you were peloothered, Tom" [D 160]) judgments to which Kernan, for his own reasons, accedes ("True bill, said Mr Kernan, equally gravely" [D 160]). The reconstruction of an alternative scenario is left entirely to the reader's infer

ence, which is unaided (and, indeed, misled) by both the narrative voice and the reported discourses of the men's ecclesiastical digressions and Father Purdon's sermon. But tipped off by Kernan's evasion about the incident ("He wished the details of the incident to remain vague. He wished his friends to think there had been some mistake, that Mr Harford and he had missed each other" [D 160]) the reader can use explanatory information supplied by the narrator to speculate that, on this day when Mrs. Kernan reports, "We were waiting for him to come home with the money" (D 155]), Kernan was intercepted for a shake-down by Harford, who is described as an urban version of a gombeen man: "He had begun life as an obscure financier by lending small sums of money to workmen at usurious interest. Later on he had become the partner of a very fat short gentleman, Mr Goldberg, of the Liffey Loan Bank. . . . his fellow-Catholics, whenever they had smarted in person or by proxy under his exactions, spoke of him bitterly as an Irish Jew" (D 159).

6. George O'Brien in his *Economic History of Ireland: From the Union to the Famine* discusses the enormous credit problems of small farmers, cottiers, and sharecroppers, who had no access to the larger banking systems but who occasionally faced situations in which "the alternative to obtaining credit was starvation" (546). Shopkeepers "always charged double the market price when they sold on credit" (547); landlord's agents frequently forced tenants to purchase or borrow only from them at usurious rates; cottiers were obliged to buy potatoes during the winter months only at ruinous prices. "Of course these practices amounted to sheer usury, and would never have been possible if there had been in Ireland any general and proper provision for the advancement of small sums to the poor" (548).

7. In the *Wake* episode of "The Ondt and the Gracehoper," Joyce lampoons, I believe, not his own fecklessness—of the kind satirized as recently as Tom Stoppard's *Travesties*—but the way the artist's putative fecklessness is translated, by a tradition extending back to medieval homilies on the vices and virtues of poverty, into the moral discourses of the Aesopian fable or the Christian parable of the prodigal son:

Now whim the sillybilly of a Gracehoper had jingled through a jungle of love and debts . . . wetting with the bimblebeaks, drikking with nautonects, bilking with durrydunglecks and horing after ladybirdies . . . he fell joust as sieck as a sexton . . . and wheer the midges to wend hemsylph or vosch to sirch for grub for his corapusse or to find a hospes, alick, he wist gnit! (FW 416.8–416.15)

8. Hugh Kenner, in his chapter on "Douglas" in *The Pound Era*, writes: "And books? *Prufrock and Other Observations* was published (though with an anonymous subvention) at the expense of Harriet Weaver. So was *A Portrait of the Artist as a Young Man*, so was *Tarr*, and so was the volume called *Quia Pauper Amavi*, which contained the *Sextus Propertius*. *Ulysses* was serialized at the expense of John Quinn, and finally published at the risk of an American lady who had opened a bookshop in Paris. And year

after year a standing donation from Miss Weaver kept Joyce somewhat extravagantly alive. These are not conditions of freedom" (303).

9. Dominic Manganiello finds in Joyce's letters to Harriet Shaw Weaver his most pronounced anti-fascist sentiments, but does not query the reason: that Weaver's leftist views and commitments would have made her their most appropriate addressee (pp. 227–233).

10. Because the nature of their correspondence was so pointedly addressed to business, Joyce's letters to Sylvia Beach were a litany of incessant wheedling ("Can you please send one thousand francs to Giorgio as early as possible on Monday as he has to pay gas, electricity and the girl" 28 April 1928 [137]; "Can you please let Giorgio have two thousand frs by Thursday?" 2 May 1928 [138]); "And have you a *few* more coppers. Have ninety-five francs left but it won't do the morning" February 1927 [116]), and emotionally manipulative demands for money: "This bombshell fell this morning. I see it has to be paid Monday morning. I have about two thousand francs and will not have more till Thursday 25 next. I am heartily tired of this eternal question. We keep no servant, buy no clothes, rarely go out but Paris has become frightfully dear or something. I paid five thousand taxes last October. It is a hard thing, so I am told, to be a 'genius' but I do not think I have the right to plague and pester you night, noon and morning for money, money, and money. . . . I am almost inclined to let the bailiffs in and watch them walk off with the furniture and animals in the ark" (17 March 1927) [116]. A month later, on April 12 1927, Sylvia Beach wrote Joyce a letter she never sent [xi] in which she vents her resentment by mimicking his own epistolary mode: "I see that I owe the English publishers over two hundred pounds. . . . I have not a sufficient provision in the bank to meet all the bills . . . I never try to borrow from my family. They are too poor. . . . I have already many expenses for you that you do not dream of, and everything I have I give you freely . . . When you are absent, every word I receive from you is an order. The reward for my unceasing labour on your behalf is to see you tie yourself into a bowknot and hear you complain" (209).

11. Colbert Kearney in *Coping with Joyce* (pp. 55–72) discusses the mythic value that "being a gentleman" played in the Joyce family epic.

12. World War I added military censorship of civilian correspondence to civil censorship of literature. "Do you want a job in the censors office?" Pound asked Joyce in a letter of July 1915. The suggestion came from H. G. Wells, who wrote Pound that "Hueffer says he can get Joyce a job at the War Office (Censorship)" (P/J 36–37).

13. The highlights of this familiar story are: Grant Richards' insistent demands for changes in *Dubliners* during the six years he held the contract; Maunsel and Company's contract manipulations and breaches ending in their threat to sue Joyce to recover costs; their Dublin printers burning the proofs of *Dubliners* and smashing its type in 1912; Joyce's serialization of *Ulysses* in the American *Little Review* with the subsequent conviction of Margaret Anderson and Jane Heap for printing obscenities; *Ulysses'* independent publication by Sylvia Beach's bookstore, Shakespeare and Com-

pany, and printing by Maurice Darantière in Dijon; its banning and burning by the U.S. Post Office, followed by the piracy of the edition by Samuel Roth; and, finally, Judge Woolsey's exoneration of *Ulysses* from charges of obscenity in 1933.

14. Besides Dennison's *(Alternative) Literary Publishing*, there are excellent discussions of the private publication enterprises in Hugh Ford's *Published in Paris: A Literary Chronicle of Paris in the 1920's and 1930's.* Especially helpful accounts of the roles women played in modernist publishing may be found in Shari Benstock's *Women of the Left Bank* (Chs. 6 and 10), in Scott's *Joyce and Feminism* (Ch. 5), and in Lidderdale and Nicholson's *Dear Miss Weaver.*

5. "Who Killed Julia Morkan?": The Gender Politics of Art in "The Dead"

1. I will argue in the next chapter that the narrative voice of "Clay" also speaks in what I call "the language of desire," that is, it produces a discourse whose function is to garner respect from the other, and it therefore represses and suppresses disruptive information and unpleasant truths. While my construction of "The Dead"'s narrative builds on Hugh Kenner's "Uncle Charles Principle" (*Joyce's Voices* 15–18), I draw a very different class inference from the stylistic pretensions of the story's opening. The social interests of the opening narrative are not Lily's interests, but rather Morkan and Conroy interests—perhaps even Morkan and Conroy constructions of what they would *like* Lily's views to be, what Lily *ought* to be saying and thinking about herself and them.

2. Joyce represents the vulnerability of servants to suspicions of theft in the rather shameful treatment the Blooms inflict on Mary Driscoll. There is no evidence in the text that Mary Driscoll stole the oysters. The scenario we reconstruct is that Bloom flirted with the uneducated girl by giving her a pair of emerald garters, which she unwisely accepted. One day, while Molly was out, he accosted her, and she defended herself with the scouring brush and by screaming, whereby the alarmed Bloom importuned her to be quiet. Mary Driscoll seems not to have told her mistress about the incident, and Molly, snooping in Mary's room on her day off, confirmed her suspicions that something was going on by finding the garters. She therefore trumped up the charge that Mary Driscoll had been stealing potatoes and oysters, gave her a week's notice, and fired her. Bloom apparently interceded by telling Molly she had no proof of the theft, but he seems not to have confessed that the sexual overtures were all on his side, and that the servant had, in fact, stoutly defended her virtue. In "Telemachus," molestation and theft are again linked in relation to the servant, but in reverse: Ursula is protected from Mulligan's predation by her plainness, and he therefore steals from her, taking the cracked mirror he argues she does not need—"He who stealeth from the poor lendeth to the Lord. Thus spake Zarathustra" (U 1:728).

3. See Adrienne Auslander Munich's carefully researched essay, "'Dear

Dead Women,' or Why Gabriel Conroy Reviews Robert Browning" in *New Alliances* 126–134).

4. I refer chiefly to Lacan's essay, "The Signification of the Phallus," in *Écrits* 281–291.

5. The willingness to risk life, to consider some abstract, nonmaterial value greater than life itself, is the cornerstone of idealism, what makes human beings constitutionally idealistic; idealistic by definition, as it were, in the Hegelian genesis of self-consciousness that—by way of the interpretation of Alexandre Kojève—informs Lacan's concept of desire. Lacan gives desire a sexual etiology, however, by replacing the fear of the loss of life with the fear of castration as a central impulse in social and intersubjective relationships. Joyce neatly distributes these ontological imperatives between Gretta's lovers, making Michael Furey the hero, with his willingness to risk life and die, the more archaic figure of ontological mastery and pure idealism, while making Gabriel, with his ontological fear of castration, a psychologically and socially modern man.

6. Joyce may have included these allusions to female domestic sewing skills because Ibsen reflects upon them in *A Doll's House*. In an argument more politically grievous than anything Gabriel produces, Torvald prescribes embroidery over knitting to Mrs. Linde on purely aesthetic grounds, because the graceful, arced gestures of embroidery (which he imitates for her) are much more pleasing to the male eye than the flapping gestures ("the arms tucked in, the needles going up and down—there's something Chinese about it" [182]) of knitting.

7. As a folk ballad, *The Lass of Aughrim* has many versions, none of which can be definitely privileged as the version in "The Dead." Ruth Bauerle reproduces two different, but thematically congruent versions, in her edition of *The James Joyce Songbook* (pp. 177–178) and in her essay on "Date Rape, Mate Rape" in *New Alliances*. I took this stanza from this latter work (pp. 124–125) in which she uses the version recorded by The New Hutchinson Family Singers on the cassette, "The Joyce of Music" (University of Illinois Press, 1983).

8. At the beginning of Act II, Nora and her nurse, Anne-Marie, now her children's nurse, have a conversation about mothers forced to abandon their children. Nora asks "Wait, tell me, Anne-Marie—I've wondered so often—how could you ever have the heart to give your child over to strangers?" Anne-Marie answers "But I had to, you know, to become little Nora's nurse." Nora says "Yes, but how could you *do* it?" and Anne-Marie responds, "When I could get such a good place? A girl who's poor and who's gotten in trouble is glad enough for that. Because that slippery fish, he didn't do a thing for me, you know" (Ibsen 155).

9. The bridal motif is itself implicated in betrayal and politics in Vincenzo Bellini's *I Puritani*, in which Arthur Talbot steals the bridal veil of his bride Elvira, who naively sings *"Son vergin vezzosa,"* in order to smuggle his condemned queen to safety. His seeming treachery drives Elvira mad. Julia Morkan likewise is abandoned and betrayed by a Church she so faith-

fully served, in the interest of a liturgical reform that consolidated papal authority.

10. The relevant text from Pope Pius X's 1903 *motu proprio* may be found in section V.13: "It follows from the same principle that the singers in church have a real liturgical office, and that women, therefore, being incapable of such an office, cannot be admitted to the choir. If high voices, such as treble and alto, are wanted, these parts must be sung by boys, according to the ancient custom of the Church" (Hayburn 228).

11. Vincent P. Pecora's argument would support my contention of Joyce's criticism of the Church in "The Dead." He argues that Gabriel's "imitation of Christ" is made suspect as a posture of transcendence, and with it a Church that creates the structures for such transcendent desires. "For if we question Gabriel's motives here, far more is at stake than simply the interpretation of a particular character's behavior; the very institutions that produce and maintain the viability of those motives are held up for scrutiny" (243).

12. John Scarry seems to have been one of the earliest scholars to identify the "negro chieftain singing in the second part of the Gaiety pantomime" (D 198) as G. H. Elliott. Basing his judgment on the *Freeman's Journal* review of the pantomime on 14 December 1903, Scarry concludes, "Despite his good critical reception Elliott was not the outstanding member of the company nor can we even be sure that he was a tenor" (183). The 28 December 1903 review of *Babes in the Wood* in the *Irish Times* supports the notion that Elliott was a baritone: "Mr. G. H. Eliott as Pete, the negro servant, got a fair amount of work to do, and his contributions were most meritorious. He possesses a pleasant baritone, and his singing of a number of coon songs evoked cordial plaudits." But Scarry is wrong about Elliott's general status, for G. J. Mellor writes of his success after 1895, "After that he went on the 'halls' as the 'Chocolate Coloured Coon' and was a top-of-the-bill attraction for many years. He made his 'Farewell Tour' of the remaining halls in 1955" (73). Benny Green further confirms Elliott's star status when he refers to "a Tivoli programme over forty years old" in which "out of seventeen turns twelve are stars commanding salaries of from £100 to £250 per week—Will Evans, Happy Fanny Fields, George Robey, Wilkie Bard, G. H. Elliott, Harry Fragson, Little Tich" (181). The more troublesome problem concerns Elliott's race. The photograph G. J. Mellor supplies of G. H. Elliott as the "Chocolate Coloured Coon" in *The Northern Music Hall* shows a light-skinned man both with and without "black-face," and has him hail from Rochdale, presumably the Rochdale in Lancashire, given Elliott's early work in Wales and Scotland. Nor is the probability that Elliott was a white "black-face" performer contested by *The Oxford Companion to the Theatre* billing him as the successor to Eugene Stratton, who was also a white "black-face" performer. Freddy Malins could therefore be wrong either about Elliott's race or about the performance itself. At least two other performers who may have been African-American performed in Dublin during the first week of January, 1904. Billy Farrell, nicknamed "the man who

made the cake walk," performed at the Empire Palace Theatre, and had his act reviewed in the 5 January 1904 *Irish Times*: "Billy Farrell, the Creole comedian, sang several selections, and was repeatedly encored." At the same time, "Jim Hegarty, a catching negro comedian" played at the Tivoli, which a few days earlier, on New Year's Eve, had presented a troupe called the "Black Troubadours." The Kingstown Pavilion was offering ethnic shows with "costume programmes" around this time, and held a "Plantation" night promising "coon costumes" on 6 January 1904. I would argue, therefore, that the "negro chieftain" of Freddy Malins's argument is quite simply historically overdetermined, and his point—that black singers, or "blackface" singers for that matter—are relegated to the less prestigious popular entertainments for racial reasons, is valid with or without reference to a particular case in point.

6. Narration under a Blindfold: Reading the "Patch" of "Clay"

1. Although I first noticed the error in my own reading of Tindall, I later discovered that Warren Beck had mentioned it in his book on *Dubliners* (370).

2. For a detailed study of folkloric motifs in "Clay" see Cóilín Owens' essay in *James Joyce Quarterly* 27(Winter 1990) 337–352. Owens' investment of the story's details with folkloric symbology obliges him to ignore the narrative "problem" with the game, the fact that something disruptive happens that the narration does not explain, and to maintain the tradition of reading the story allegorically—"We may grant that the clay can be considered to symbolize Maria's sharing with us a common substance, or alternatively, to represent her personal malleability, for although the immediate folkloric context presages no more than her imminent, physical death, Joyce allows us to take it also as a symbol of her spiritual barrenness: she is one of Dublin's living dead" (344).

3. The impure pedigree of my theoretical assumptions in this essay is, no doubt, recognizable in the blend of the Girardian politics of desire, which lent me the triangulations, imitation, and master-slave oscillations useful for understanding the social configurations of Maria's desire, and the Lacanian etiology of desire in the castration complex, which illuminates the sexual source of the *méconnaissance* and scotomas that characterize the story's discourse, and that recapitulate the semiological inversions (of *parole vide* and *parole pleine*, for example) of therapeutic language. But the uses to which Joyce puts his psycho-ontological insights into the self-preserving discursive fantasies of the old maid are, I believe, socially critical and generically self-critical, indicting society for its treatment of the poor, the old, the female, the unmarried, the deformed, and indicting narrative art for its ideological collusions with that treatment.

4. Cóilín Owens insists that "clay functions here as a standard element in the game" (344) without accounting for the endless anomalies in the narrative that such a reading creates. The narrator carefully inventories the symbolic objects the children receive, "One got the prayer-book and the

other three got the water; and when one of the next-door girls got the ring Mrs Donnelly shook her finger at the blushing girl" (D 105), in a gesture that makes it clear that during five previous tries no one got the "soft wet substance." Why is the soft wet substance not named by the narrator, and why are we not told, simply, that Maria's hand "descended on the saucer with the clay" rather than that it "descended on one of the saucers. She felt a soft wet substance" (D 105) if the clay is a standard item? What did Mrs. Donnelly mean when she said "that was no play" if the clay was precisely play, as Owens suggests, and if it has been on the table all along? If it has not been on the table all along (Owens suggests that sometimes the clay was suppressed in order not to frighten the children) then who introduced it into the game? Surely not Mrs. Donnelly, who disapproves of its presence. But if the children introduce it for Maria's benefit, their logic ("Let's put dirt in the saucer on the table so Maria will think it is the clay in the game that is normally symbolic of death and be disturbed by it") becomes implausibly hyper-sophisticated, and in any event, fails to support Owens' argument that, "Maria's fate is set by forces in nature and society much larger and more ominous than the mere pique of cheeky adolescents can be interpreted to represent" (344).

5. *The Bohemian Girl* is an opera with music composed by Michael Balfe, and libretto by Alfred Bunn (*Songbook* 161; Benstock "Text, Sub-text, Non-text" 357–358). The missing verse is:

I dreamt that suitors besought my hand
     That knights upon bended knee,
And with vows no maiden heart could withstand,
     That they pledged their faith to me.
And I dreamt that one of this noble host
     Came forth my hand to claim;
Yet I also dreamt, which charmed me most,
     That you loved me still the same.

7. The Work Song at the Washerwomen in "Anna Livia Plurabelle"

1. Joyce made a notebook list for ALP's costume which emphasizes its eccentric details: "clogs/ net/ glasses/ potatorings/ swansruff/ brownfur/ fags/ hayrope/ clothespeg/ sugarloaf/ hazeshimmy" (JA VI.B. 4–272).

2. Butler writes, "When, however, we come to the earliest historic literature we find that famous poetesses abounded. Those who turn to the article 'Sappho' in Smith's *Dictionary of Classical Biography* will find Gorgo and Andromeda mentioned as her rivals. Among her fellows were Anactoria of Miletus, Gongyla of Colophon, Eunica of Salamis, Gyrinna, Atthis, and Mnasidica. . . . Turning to Mueller's work upon the Dorians, I find reference made to the amatory poetesses of Lesbos. He tells us also of Corinna, who is said to have competed successfully with Pindar, and Myrto, who certainly competed with him, but with what success we know not" (pp. 11–12).

3. Butler's wry comment on women's concern with the clean-up of carnage may have reminded Joyce of the Scottish version of the figure of the *banshee,* the figure known as *Bean-Nighe* or "Little-Washer-by-the-Ford": "She is seen by the side of a river, washing the blood from the clothes of those who will die" (*Encyclopedia of Occultism and Parapsychology* 131).

4. Joyce took a somewhat defensive posture when he wrote to Svevo on 20 February 1924 that he was naming ALP for his wife—"A propos of names: I have given the name of Signora Schmitz to the protagonist of the book I am writing. Ask her, however, not to take up arms, either of steel or fire, since the person involved is the Pyrrha of Ireland (or rather of Dublin) whose hair is the river" (*Letters* I, 211). Ellmann narrates, "Signora Schmitz was a little disturbed, notwithstanding; she had to be assured again that he was not denigrating her" (*JJ* 561). Brenda Maddox supplies, I believe, the social sub-text of these tensions and suspicions.

5. Ellen Malos in her introduction to *The Politics of Housework* recapitulates Marx's theoretical views on the nonproductive status of housework and "industrialized housework": "In volume one of *Capital* he did say that the reproduction of labour power was *productive consumption,* but he did not say it was productive *labour.* . . . Having said that the work of a seamstress, carpenter or cook or any servant working for wages for a private master is unproductive because 'the same labour can be productive when I buy it as a capitalist, as a producer, in order to produce more value, and unproductive when I buy it as a consumer, a spender of revenue, in order to consume its use-value', Marx goes on to say that the working class must perform this kind of labour for itself' " (24). Malos goes on to argue that while Marx maintained that nonproductive labour can still be socially and industrially necessary, there has been an unfortunate theoretical devaluation of this type of labour, which is traditionally subject to a sexual division, that has worked especially to the detriment of women.

6. Describing traditional Irish work songs, especially those of women, Nóirín Ní Riain writes, "The second category of work songs are those composed and performed during such activities as spinning, weaving or herding. Spinning and weaving were social functions, and so the construction of these songs caters for group participation. . . . With the exception of one herding song, all occupational songs echo the rhythm of the work in hand" (74).

7. The earliest holograph texts of the "Anna Livia Plurabelle" chapter note many references to the washerwomen's speech with the initial F. Joyce does not appear to have included this F among those symbols he explained, and McHugh does not treat it as a siglum like the others. I am tempted (on no particular evidence) to speculate that it stands for "Fleming": the name of one of the washerwomen in "Clay," Lizzie Fleming, and of Molly's incompetent old servant, Mrs. Fleming. It is Mrs. Fleming who ruins Molly's drawers, "with the ironmould mark the stupid old bundle burned on them" (U 18:1096) and who sounds a hard case, like the washerwomen in the ALP chapter—"and now shes going such as she was on account of her paralysed

husband getting worse theres always something wrong with them disease or they have to go under an operation or if its not that its drink and he beats her" (U 18:1098).

8. Saint Margaret Mary Alacoque inspired the devotion for the Sacred Heart of Jesus, an object of special veneration in Ireland. She becomes, therefore, a figure of female devotion to Christ, or to Christ and brother, like the biblical Martha and Mary, "marthared mary allacook," cooking and ministering to both Jesus and their brother Lazarus. McHugh calls Margaret Mary Alacoque in his gloss, the "visionary who preferred drinking water in which laundry had been washed" (214.23). This conjures up an apotheosized version of the starving Dedalus girls nearly having boiled wash water rather than soup to drink. See Henke (183) for a discussion of the washerwomen's female saints in the ALP chapter.

9. Roland McHugh has an entire section on "The Magrath Mystery" in his book on the *Sigla*. He points to later references to a Magrath who appears cuckolded by his wife, thus closing the washerwomen's narrative with a male counterdiscourse—"I heard the irreverend Mr Magraw . . . kuckkuck kicking the bedding out of the old sexton . . . while I and Flood and the other men . . . was gickling his missus to gackles in the hall" (FW 511.7) They even ask if she was wearing drawers, although they confuse drawers as clothing with drawers in German and French furniture, a *Schublade* or a *tiroir* in a chest or desk—"Was she wearing shubladey's tiroirs in humour of her hubbishobbis, Massa's star stellar?" (FW 511.27).

10. William York Tindall tracks several versions of *Lebens Quatsch* appearing in *Finnegans Wake*, and explains, "296.1–296.2 'Lemmas quatsch,' one of many references to 'Lebens Quatsch,' a waiter's interpretation of Joyce's request in Zurich for lemon squash. *Lebens Quatsch* (*Quatsch* is German, nonsense), said Joyce, is what life is" (*A Reader's Guide to 'Finnegans Wake' 185*).

9. The Politics of Childhood in "The Mime of Mick, Nick, and the Maggies"

1. Breon Mitchell's essay on "*A Portrait* and the *Bildungsroman* Tradition" concedes the novel's implicit critique of the very *genre* it enacts, and ends by noting "Consider that *A Portrait* consists of not one, but two, novels of development—one traditional, and one antitraditional" (73). Homer Obed Brown has made a similar point about *Portrait* ("*Stephen Hero* is replaced by a form which contains those contradictions, reveals them and gives them a different meaning" [103]). Franco Moretti more recently has explored the internalization of contradictions as an inherent function of the *Bildungsroman* in *The Way of the World: The* Bildungsroman *in European Culture.*

2. Atherton's discussion of Quinet (pp. 34–35) and Clive Hart's (pp. 182–200) treatment of the sentence as a leitmotif in the *Wake*, give much valuable information, but even more extensive research is needed. Quinet's

work is not readily available in translation, and although Richard Heath's *Edgar Quinet: His Early Life and Writings* translates portions of *Introduction à la Philosophie de l'Histoire de l'Humanité* and *Ahasvérus*, he unfortunately omits Joyce's favorite sentence about the wildflowers.

3. Daniel Ferrer's essay in the summer 1985 *James Joyce Quarterly* supports with holograph evidence an earlier contention by Alison Armstrong in the August 1973 *Wake Newslitter* ("Shem the Penman as Glugg as the Wolf-Man" [pp. 51–57]) that Joyce alludes to Freud's "From the History of an Infantile Neurosis" in "The Mime of Mick, Nick, and the Maggies." "Scoptophilia" is one of Joyce's notes among the cluster that refer to the case of little Hans. Also Joyce noted "child's world"—a reference, according to Ferrer, to the *Collected Papers* translation of Freud's beginning the narration of the Wolf-Man's story with the words, "I shall begin, then, by giving a picture of the child's world" (373). I would argue that in "The Mime of Mick, Nick, and the Maggies" Joyce also gives such a picture of a child's world. But unlike Freud, who subtracts the social and cultural markings that make the Wolf-Man's gentrified prerevolutionary Russian childhood so historically specific and distinct, Joyce explores the way the acquisitions of sexual, social, and cultural knowledge is interrelated in infantile epistemology.

4. "The Mime of Mick, Nick, and the Maggies" transcribes two important concentric narratives that are inscribed in the background of "Nausicaa." There are several verbal clues in the "Mime" that prod us to reconstruct the romantic dynamics of "Nausicaa" as inscribed in its own configuration. The little twin boys (Tommy and Jacky Caffrey as figures of Shem and Shaun) compete for the attentions of pretty girls that may include their sister. Glugg, like Tommy, is unable to guess the sweetheart riddle whose prototype is found among Joyce's earliest epiphanies: "The Little Male Child—[*at the garden gate*] . . Na . . o. The First Young Lady—[*half kneeling, takes his hand*]—Well, is Mabie your sweetheart? [EP 8]). Tommy Caffrey, like Glugg, has to urinate, and is bested in the end by the heliotropic power of Bloom who has all three girls dance around him and to him to attract his attention. Bloom's own memories, evoked by the girls on the strand and by his own version of the heliotrope riddle ("What is it? Heliotrope? No. Hyacinth? Hm. Roses, I think." [U 13.1008]), take him back to his earliest meeting with Molly at Mat Dillon's garden party in May of 1887, when he was twenty-one, Molly was sixteen, and Stephen, who was there with his mother and who may have been a curious and jealous witness to the Bloom's's first meeting, was only five years old. The foregrounding of Mat Dillon's bevy of daughters, and the strong erotic influence of the spring flowers, make this remembered scene a clear prototype of "The Mime of Mick, Nick, and the Maggies"—with the conflation of flower buds and girls in gossamer dresses providing the trope of the *Kindergarten*, the garden of children or of wildflowers become the lilts of children. It would be possible to fruitfully read the "Mime" against these and other scenarios, as I have done in my address "Joyce's Heliotrope" at the Copenhagen Symposium in

1986, and to reread earlier texts against the "Mime," as I did in my earlier essay on "Nausicaa." See also Patrick McCarthy's Chapter 6 ("Whose Hue: Izod's Heliotrope Riddle" [pp. 136–152]) for other ways to read the chapter. But the retrieval of the social reality of children in this chapter is best achieved by reading it against the biographical, quasi-biographical, and fictional texts of the young Joyce and the young Stephen.

5. I here supplement James Atherton's excellent discussion, in Chapter 3 of *The Books at the Wake*, of Joyce's use of Irish writers in *Finnegans Wake*.

Works Consulted

Works by James Joyce

The Critical Writings of James Joyce. Edited by Ellsworth Mason and Richard Ellmann. Ithaca: Cornell University Press, 1989.
Dubliners. New York: Modern Library, 1969.
Epiphanies. Buffalo: University of Buffalo, 1956.
Exiles. New York: Viking Press, 1966.
Finnegans Wake. New York: Viking Press, 1967.
The James Joyce Archive. Edited by Michael Groden et al. New York: Garland Publishing, 1978–.
Letters of James Joyce. Vol. 1, edited by Stuart Gilbert. New York: Viking Press, 1957; reissued with corrections, 1966. Vols. 2 and 3, edited by Richard Ellmann. New York: Viking Press, 1966.
A Portrait of the Artist as a Young Man: Text, Criticism, and Notes. Edited by Chester G. Anderson. New York: Viking Press, 1972.
Selected Letters of James Joyce. Edited by Richard Ellmann. New York: Viking Press, 1975.
Stephen Hero. Edited by John J. Slocum and Herbert Cahoon. New York: New Directions, 1963.
Ulysses. Edited by Hans Walter Gabler with Wolfhard Steppe and Claus Melchior. New York: Random House, 1986.

Other Works

Adorno, Theodor. *Aesthetic Theory.* Translated by C. Lenhardt. Edited by Gretel Adorno and Rolf Tiedemann. London: Routledge & Kegan Paul, 1986.
Adorno, Theodor W., and Max Horkheimer. *Dialectic of Enlightenment.* Translated by John Cumming. New York: Continuum, 1987.
Armstrong, Alison. "Shem the Penman as Glugg as the Wolf-Man." *Wake Newslitter,* August 1973, pp. 51–57.
Arnold, Matthew. *Culture and Anarchy.* Edited by J. Dover Wilson. New York: Cambridge University Press, 1971.

Atherton, James S. *The Books at the Wake.* Carbondale: Southern Illinois University Press, 1974.

———. "*Finnegans Wake:* 'The Gist of the Pantomime.'" *Accent* 15(1955): 14–26.

Attridge, Derek. "Finnegans Awake: The Dream of Interpretation." *James Joyce Quarterly* 27(Fall 1989):11–29.

Attridge, Derek, Geoff Bennington, and Robert Young, eds. *Post-structuralism and the Question of History.* Cambridge: Cambridge University Press, 1987.

Attridge, Derek, and Daniel Ferrer, eds. *Post-structuralist Joyce.* Cambridge: Cambridge University Press, 1984.

Aubert, Jacques. *Introduction à l'Esthétique de James Joyce.* Paris: Librairie Marcel Didier, 1973.

Baker, Houston A., Jr. *Modernism and the Harlem Renaissance.* Chicago: University of Chicago Press, 1987.

Banta, Melissa, and Oscar A. Silverman. *James Joyce's Letters to Sylvia Beach, 1921–1940.* Bloomington: Indiana University Press, 1987.

Baudrillard, Jean. *Selected Writings.* Edited by Mark Poster. Stanford: Stanford University Press, 1988.

Bauerle, Ruth. "Date Rape, Mate Rape: A Liturgical Interpretation of 'The Dead.'" In *New Alliances in Joyce Studies,* edited by Bonnie Kime Scott, pp. 113–125.

———, ed. *The James Joyce Songbook.* New York: Garland, 1982.

Beck, Warren. *Joyce's 'Dubliners': Substance, Vision, and Art.* Durham, N.C.: Duke University Press, 1969.

Beckett, Samuel, et al. *Our Exagmination Round His Factification for Incamination of 'Work in Progress.'* London: Faber and Faber, 1972.

Begnal, Michael H. *Dreamscheme: Narrative and Voice in 'Finnegans Wake.'* Syracuse: Syracuse University Press, 1989.

Begnal, Michael H., and Fritz Senn, eds. *A Conceptual Guide to 'Finnegans Wake.'* University Park: Pennsylvania State University Press, 1974.

Beja, Morris, and Shari Benstock, eds. *Coping with Joyce: Essays from the Copenhagen Symposium.* Columbus: Ohio State University Press, 1989.

Beja, Morris, Phillip Herring, Maurice Harmon, and David Norris, eds. *James Joyce: The Centennial Symposium.* Urbana: University of Illinois Press, 1986.

Benjamin, Walter. "Berliner Kindheit um Neunzehnhundert." In *Gesammelte Schriften* 4(1). Frankfurt: Suhrkamp Verlag, 1972.

Bennett, Tony. "Texts in History: The Determination of Readings and Their Texts." In *Post-structuralism and the Question of History,* edited by Derek Attridge, Geoff Bennington, and Robert Young, pp. 63–81. Cambridge: Cambridge University Press, 1990.

Benstock, Bernard, ed. *James Joyce: The Augmented Ninth.* Syracuse: Syracuse University Press, 1988.

———. "Text, Sub-text, Non-text: Literary and Narrational In/Validities." In *James Joyce Quarterly* 22(Summer 1985):355–365.

Benstock, Shari. *Women of the Left Bank*. Austin: University of Texas Press, 1986.

Berman, Russell A. *Modern Culture and Critical Theory*. Madison: University of Wisconsin Press, 1989.

Bishop, John. *Joyce's Book of the Dark: Finnegans Wake*. Madison: University of Wisconsin Press, 1986.

Boheemen-Saaf, Christine Van. "Joyce, Derrida, and the Discourse of 'the Other.'" In *James Joyce: The Augmented Ninth*, edited by Bernard Benstock, pp. 88–102. Syracuse: Syracuse University Press, 1988.

Booth, Wayne. *The Rhetoric of Fiction*. Chicago: University of Chicago Press, 1961.

Brown, Homer Obed. *James Joyce's Early Fiction: The Biography of a Form*. Hamden, Conn.: Archon Press, 1975.

Buck-Morss, Susan. "'Verehrte Unsichtbare!' Walter Benjamins Radiovortraege." In *Walter Benjamin und die Kinderliteratur*, edited by Klaus Doderer, pp. 93–101. Munich: Juventa Verlag, 1988.

Buerger, Peter. *Theory of the Avant-Garde*. Translated by Michael Shaw. Minneapolis: University of Minnesota Press, 1984.

Butler, Samuel. *The Authoress of the Odyssey*. Chicago: Chicago University Press, 1967.

———, trans. *The Odyssey of Homer*. Edited by Louise Ropes Loomis. New York: Walter J. Black, 1944.

Carroll, David. *Paraesthetics: Foucault, Lyotard, Derrida*. New York: Methuen, 1987.

Cheng, Vincent John. *Shakespeare and Joyce: A Study of 'Finnegans Wake.'* University Park: Pennsylvania State University Press, 1984.

Cixous, Hélène. *The Exile of James Joyce*. Translated by Sally A. J. Purcell. New York: David Lewis, 1972.

Clarkson, L. A., and E. Margaret Crawford. "Dietary Directions: A Topographical Survey of the Irish Diet, 1836." In *Economy and Society in Scotland and Ireland, 1500–1939*, edited by Rosalind Mitchison and Peter Roebuck, pp. 171–192. Edinburgh: John Donald Publishers Ltd., 1988.

Connolly, Thomas E. *James Joyce's Scribbledehobble: The Ur-Workbook for 'Finnegans Wake.'* Evanston: Northwestern University Press, 1961.

Daly, Mary E. "Women, Work and Trade Unionism." In *Women in Irish Society: The Historical Dimension*, edited by Margaret MacCurtain and Donncha O Corráin. Westport: Greenwood Press, 1979.

Deane, Seamus. "'Masked with Matthew Arnold's Face': Joyce and Liberalism." In *James Joyce: The Centennial Symposium*, edited by Morris Beja, Phillip Herring, Maurice Harmon and David Norris, pp. 9–20.

———. "Joyce and Nationalism." In *James Joyce: New Perspectives*, edited by Colin MacCabe, pp. 168–183. Bloomington: Indiana University Press, 1982.

Delimata, Bozena Berta. "Reminiscences of a Joyce Niece." In *James Joyce Quarterly* 19(Fall 1981):45–62.

Dennison, Sally. *(Alternative) Literary Publishing.* Iowa City: University of Iowa Press, 1984.

Derrida, Jacques. "Two Words for Joyce." In *Post-structuralist Joyce,* edited by Derek Attridge and Daniel Ferrer, pp. 145–159. Cambridge: Cambridge University Press, 1984.

———. *The Post Card.* Translated by Alan Bass. Chicago: University of Chicago Press, 1987.

Devlin, Kimberly J. *Wandering and Return in 'Finnegans Wake': An Integrative Approach to Joyce's Fiction.* Princeton: Princeton University Press, 1991.

Doderer, Klaus, ed. *Walter Benjamin und die Kinderliteratur.* Munich: Juventa Verlag, 1988.

Eagleton, Terry. *Criticism and Ideology.* London: Verso Editions, 1978.

Eckley, Grace. *Children's Lore in 'Finnegans Wake'.* Syracuse: Syracuse University Press, 1984.

Eliot, T. S. "*Ulysses,* Order, and Myth." In *Selected Prose of of T. S. Eliot,* edited by Frank Kermode, pp. 175–178. New York: Harcourt Brace Jovanovich, 1975.

———. "*The Waste Land*" and Other Poems. New York: Harcourt Brace Jovanovich, 1962.

Ellmann, Maud. *The Poetics of Impersonality: T. S. Eliot and Ezra Pound.* Cambridge: Harvard University Press, 1987.

Ellmann, Richard. *The Consciousness of Joyce.* New York: Oxford University Press, 1981.

———. *Four Dubliners: Oscar Wilde, William Butler Yeats, James Joyce, Samuel Beckett.* New York: George Braziller, 1988.

———. *James Joyce.* Oxford: Oxford University Press, 1983.

———. *Oscar Wilde.* New York: Random House, 1988.

Encyclopedia of Occultism and Parapsychology. Vol. 1, edited by Leslie Shepard. Detroit: Gale Research Co., 1984.

Ferrer, Daniel. "The Freudful Couchmare of ∧d: Joyce's Notes on Freud and the Composition of Chapter XVI of *Finnegans Wake.*" In *James Joyce Quarterly* 22(Summer 1985):367–382.

Feshback, Sidney. "Marcel Duchamp or Being Taken for a Ride: Duchamp Was a Cubist, a Mechanomorphist, a Dadaist, a Surrealist, a Conceptualist, a Modernist, a Post-modernist—and None of the Above." In *James Joyce Quarterly* 26(Summer 1989):541–560.

Ford, Hugh. *Published in Paris: A Literary Chronicle of Paris in the 1920's and 1930's.* New York: Macmillan, 1975.

Freud, Sigmund. "Family Romances." In *Collected Papers,* edited by James Strachey. 5 vols. New York: Basic Books, 1959. 5:74–78.

———. "From the History of an Infantile Neurosis." In *Collected Papers,* translated by Alix and James Strachey. 5 vols. New York: Basic Books, 1959. 3:473–605.

———. *The Interpretation of Dreams.* Translated by James Strachey. New York: Basic Books, 1971.

Friedman, Susan Stanford. *Penelope's Web: Gender, Modernity, H. D.'s Fiction.* Cambridge: Cambridge University Press, 1990.

Froula, Christine. *A Guide to Ezra Pound's Selected Poems.* New York: New Directions, 1982.

Gablik, Suzi. *Has Modernism Failed?* New York: Thames and Hudson, 1984.

Gardiner, Jean. "Women's Domestic Labor." In *Capitalist Patriarchy and the Case for Socialist Feminism,* edited by Zillah R. Eisenstein. New York: Monthly Review Press, 1979.

Gifford, Don, with Robert J. Seidman. *'Ulysses' Annotated.* Berkeley: University of California Press, 1988.

Gilbert, Sandra M., and Susan Gubar. *No Man's Land: The Place of the Woman Writer in the Twentieth Century.* Vol. 1: The War of the Words. New Haven: Yale University Press, 1988.

———. "Sexual Linguistics: Gender, Language, Sexuality." In *New Literary History* 16(Spring 1985):515–543.

Gillespie, Michael. *Inverted Volumes Improperly Arranged: James Joyce and His Trieste Library.* Ann Arbor: UMI Research Press, 1983.

Girard, René. *Deceit, Desire, and the Novel.* Translated by Yvonne Freccero. Baltimore: The Johns Hopkins University Press, 1965.

Goldberg, S. L. *The Classical Temper.* London: Chatto and Windus, 1961.

Gomme, Alice Bertha. *Traditional Games of England, Scotland, and Ireland.* Vol. 1. New York: Dover Publications, 1964.

Gordon, John. *'Finnegans Wake': A Plot Summary.* Dublin: Gill and Macmillan, 1986.

———. "Haines and the Black Panther." In *James Joyce Quarterly* 27(Spring 1990):587–594.

Green, Benny. ed. *The Last Empires: A Music Hall Companion.* London: Pavilion Books, 1986.

Hart, Clive. *Structure and Motif in 'Finnegans Wake.'* London: Faber and Faber, 1962.

Hassan Ihab. *The Postmodern Turn.* Columbus: Ohio State University Press, 1987.

Hawthorn, Jeremy. "*Ulysses,* Modernism, and Marxist Criticism." In *James Joyce and Modern Literature,* edited by W. J. McCormack and Alistair Stead, pp. 112–125. London: Routledge and Kegan Paul, 1982.

Hayburn, Robert F. *Papal Legislation on Sacred Music 95 A.D. to 1977 A.D.* Collegeville, Minn.: The Liturgical Press, 1979.

Hayman, David. *The 'Wake' in Transit.* Ithaca: Cornell University Press, 1990.

Healey, George, ed. *The Complete Dublin Diary of Stanislaus Joyce.* Ithaca: Cornell University Press, 1971.

Heath, Richard. *Edgar Quinet: His Early Life and Writings.* London: Truebner & Co., 1881.

Heath, Stephen. "Ambiviolences: Notes for Reading Joyce." In *Post-struc-*

turalist Joyce, edited by Derek Attridge and Daniel Ferrer, pp. 31–68. Cambridge: Cambridge University Press, 1984.

Heilbrun, Carolyn G. "Afterword." In *Women in Joyce,* edited by Suzette Henke and Elaine Unkeless, pp. 215–216. Urbana: University of Illinois Press, 1982.

Henke, Suzette. *James Joyce and the Politics of Desire.* New York: Routledge, 1990.

Henke, Suzette, and Elaine Unkeless. eds. *Women in Joyce.* Urbana: University of Illinois Press, 1982.

Herr, Cheryl. *Joyce's Anatomy of Culture.* Urbana: University of Illinois Press, 1986.

Herring, Phillip F. "James Joyce and Gift Exchange." In *LIT.* 1(1989):85–97.

Hodgart, Matthew. "Music and the Mime of Mick, Nick, and the Maggies." In *A Conceptual Guide to 'Finnegans Wake',* edited by Michael H. Begnal and Fritz Senn, pp. 83–92. University Park: Pennsylvania State University Press, 1974.

Horkheimer, Max. "The End of Reason." In *The Essential Frankfurt Reader,* edited by Andrew Arato and Eike Gebhart. New York: Continuum, 1987.

Hulme, T. E. *Speculations.* Edited by Herbert Read. New York: Harcourt, Brace, and Company, 1924.

Huston, John, dir. *The Dead.* Vestron Pictures, 1987.

Ibsen, Henrik. *The Complete Major Prose Plays.* Translated by Rolf Fjelde. New York: Farrar, Straus, Giroux, 1978.

The James Joyce Archive. Edited by Michael Groden. New York: Garland, 1978.

James Joyce: The Critical Heritage, Vol. 2. Edited by Robert H. Deming. "Karl Radek on Joyce's Realism," pp. 624–626. London: Routledge & Kegan Paul, 1970.

Jameson, Fredric. *The Political Unconscious.* Ithaca: Cornell University Press, 1981.

———. "'Ulysses' in History." In *James Joyce and Modern Literature,* edited by W. J. McCormack and Alistair Stead, pp. 126–141. London: Routledge & Kegan Paul, 1982.

Johnsen, William A. "Joyce's *Dubliners* and the Futility of Modernism." In *James Joyce and Modern Literature,* edited by W. J. McCormack and Alistair Stead, pp. 5–21. London: Routledge and Kegan Paul, 1982.

Jolas, Eugene. "The Revolution of Language and James Joyce." In *Our Exagmination . . . ,* by Samuel Beckett et al., pp. 77–92. London: Faber and Faber, 1972.

Kearney, Colbert. "The Joycead." In *Coping with Joyce,* edited by Morris Beja and Shari Benstock, pp. 55–72.

Kenner, Hugh. "Homer's Sticks and Stones." In *James Joyce Quarterly* 6(Summer 1969):285–298.

———. *Joyce's Voices.* Berkeley: University of California Press, 1978.

———. *The Pound Era.* Berkeley: University of California Press, 1971.

———. "Mauberley." In *Ezra Pound: A Collection of Critical Essays*, edited by Walter Sutton. Englewood Cliffs, N.J.: Prentice-Hall, 1963.

Kernan, Alvin. *The Death of Literature*. New Haven: Yale University Press, 1990.

Kershner, R. B. *Joyce, Bakhtin, and Popular Culture: Chronicles of Disorder*. Chapel Hill: University of North Carolina Press, 1989.

Kofman, Sarah. *The Enigma of Woman: Woman in Freud's Writing*. Translated by Catherine Porter. Ithaca: Cornell University Press, 1985.

Kojève, Alexandre. *Introduction to the Reading of Hegel*. Edited by Allan Bloom. Translated by James H. Nichols, Jr. Ithaca: Cornell University Press, 1980.

Kristeva, Julia. *Desire in Language*. Edited by Leon S. Roudiez. Translated by Thomas Gora, Alice Jardine, and Leon S. Roudiez. New York: Columbia University Press, 1980.

Lacan, Jacques. *Écrits*. Translated by Alan Sheridan. New York: Norton, 1977.

———. The *Four Fundamental Concepts of Psychoanalysis*. Edited by Jacques-Alain Miller. Translated by Alan Sheridan. New York: W. W. Norton, 1978.

———. The *Language of the Self: The Function of Language in Psychoanalysis*. Translated by Anthony Wilden. Baltimore: Johns Hopkins University Press, 1968.

Lawrence, Karen. *The Odyssey of Style in 'Ulysses,'* Princeton: Princeton University Press, 1981.

Leavis, F. R. *The Great Tradition*. New York: New York University Press, 1973.

Lehane, Brendan. *The Companion Guide to Ireland*. Englewood Cliffs, N.J.: Prentice-Hall, 1985.

Lernout, Geert. *The French Joyce*. Ann Arbor: University of Michigan Press, 1990.

Lewis, Wyndham. *Time and Western Man*. Boston: Beacon Hill Press, 1957.

Lidderdale, Jane and Mary Nicholson. *Dear Miss Weaver: Harriet Shaw Weaver, 1876–1961*. New York: The Viking Press, 1970.

Literary Essays of Ezra Pound. Edited by T. S. Eliot. New York: New Directions, 1968.

Loos, Archie K. *Joyce's Visible Art: The Work of Joyce and the Visual Arts, 1904–1922*. Ann Arbor: UMI Research Press, 1984.

Lowe-Evans, Mary. *Crimes against Fecundity: Joyce and Population Control*. Syracuse: Syracuse University Press, 1989.

Lukács, Georg. *The Meaning of Contemporary Realism*. Translated by John Mander and Necke Mander. London: Merlin Press, 1979.

Lyotard, Jean-François. *The Differend: Phrases in Dispute*. Translated by Georges Van Den Abbeele. Minneapolis: University of Minnesota Press, 1988.

MacCabe, Colin. *James Joyce and the Revolution of the Word.* New York: Harper & Row, 1979.

MacCabe, Colin, ed. *James Joyce: New Perspectives.* Bloomington: Indiana University Press, 1982.

MacCurtain, Margaret. "The Historical Image." In *Irish Women: Image and Achievement,* edited by Eiléan Ní Chuilleanáin. Dublin: Arlen House, 1985.

Maddox, Brenda. *Nora.* Boston: Houghton Mifflin Company, 1988.

Mahaffey, Vicki. *Reauthorizing Joyce.* Cambridge: Cambridge University Press, 1988.

———. "Wagner, Joyce and Revolution." In *James Joyce Quarterly* 25 (Winter 1988):237–247.

Malos, Ellen, ed. *The Politics of Housework.* New York: Schocken Books, 1980.

Manganiello, Dominic. *Joyce's Politics.* London: Routledge & Kegan Paul, 1980.

Martin, Timothy. *Joyce and Wagner.* Cambridge: Cambridge University Press, 1991.

McCarthy, Patrick A. *The Riddles of 'Finnegans Wake'.* Cranbury, New Jersey: Associated University Presses, 1980.

McCormack, W. J. "James Joyce, Cliché, and the Irish Language." In *James Joyce: The Augmented Ninth,* edited by Bernard Benstock, pp. 323–336. Syracuse: Syracuse University Press, 1988.

McCormack, W. J., and Alistair Stead, eds. *James Joyce and Modern Literature.* London: Routledge and Kegan Paul, 1982.

McGee, Patrick. *Paperspace: Style as Ideology in Joyce's 'Ulysses.'* Lincoln: University of Nebraska Press, 1988.

McHugh, Roland. *Annotations to 'Finnegans Wake.'* Baltimore: Johns Hopkins University Press, 1980.

———. *The Sigla of 'Finnegans Wake.'* London: Edward Arnold, 1976.

McMichael, James. *Ulysses and Justice.* Princeton: Princeton University Press, 1991.

Mellor, G. J. *The Northern Music Hall.* Newcastle-upon-Tyne: Hindson Reid Jordison, 1970.

Millett, Kate. *Sexual Politics.* New York: Avon, 1971.

Mitchell, Breon. "*A Portrait* and the *Bildungsroman* Tradition." In *Approaches to Joyce's 'Portrait,'* edited by Thomas F. Staley and Bernard Benstock, pp. 61–76. Pittsburgh: University of Pittsburgh Press, 1976.

Mitchison, Rosalind, and Peter Roebuck, eds. *Economy and Society in Scotland and Ireland, 1500–1939.* Edinburgh: John Donald Publishers Ltd., 1988.

Moretti, Franco. *Signs Taken for Wonders.* Translated by Susan Fischer, David Forgacs, and David Miller. London: Verso, 1988.

———. *The Way of the World: The Bildungsroman in European Culture.* London: Verso, 1987.

Munich, Adrienne Auslander. "'Dear Dead Women,' or Why Gabriel Conroy Reviews Robert Browning." In *New Alliances in Joyce Studies*. pp. 126–134.

Naremore, James. "Consciousness and Society in *A Portrait of the Artist*." In *Approaches to Joyce's 'Portrait,'* edited by Thomas F. Staky and Bernard Benstock, pp. 113–134. Pittsburgh: University of Pittsburgh Press, 1976.

Ní Chuilleanáin, ed. *Irish Women: Image and Achievement*. Dublin: Arlen House, 1985.

Ní Riain, Nóirín. "The Female Song in the Irish Tradition." In *Irish Women: Image and Achievement*, edited by Eiléan Ní Chuilleanáin, pp. 73–84. Dublin: Arlen House, 1985.

Norris, Margot. *The Decentered Universe of 'Finnegans Wake.'* Baltimore: Johns Hopkins University Press, 1976.

———. "Joyce's Heliotrope." In *Coping with Joyce*, edited by Morris Beja and Shari Benstock, pp. 3–24. Columbus: Ohio State University Press, 1989.

———. "The Last Chapter of *Finnegans Wake*: Stephen Finds His Mother." In *James Joyce Quarterly* 25(Fall 1987):11–30.

———. "Portraits of the Artist as a Young Lover." In *New Alliances in Joyce Studies*, edited by Bonnie Kime Scott, pp. 144–152. Newark: University of Delaware Press, 1988.

O'Brien, George. *The Economic History of Ireland: From the Union to the Famine*. Clifton: Augustus M. Kelley Publishers, 1972.

O'Connor, Ulick. *Celtic Dawn: A Portrait of the Irish Literary Renaissance*. London: Transworld Publishers, 1985.

Owens, Cóilín. "Clay (I): Irish Folklore." In *James Joyce Quarterly* 27 (Winter 1990):337–352.

Parrinder, Patrick. *James Joyce*. Cambridge: Cambridge University Press, 1984.

———. "The Strange Necessity: James Joyce's Rejection in England (1914–1930)." In *James Joyce: New Perspectives*, edited by Colin MacCabe. Bloomington: Indiana University Press, 1982.

Pecora, Vincent P. *Self and Form in Modern Narrative*. Baltimore: Johns Hopkins University Press, 1989.

———. "'The Dead' and the Generosity of the Word." In *PMLA* 101(1987): 206–215.

Pelzer-Knoll, Gudrun. *Kindheit und Erfahrung: Untersuchungen zur Paedagogik Walter Benjamins*. Koenigstein: Hain Verlag, 1986.

Perkins, Jill. *Joyce and Hauptmann*. San Marino: The Henry E. Huntington Library and Art Gallery, 1978.

Perloff, Marjorie. *The Poetics of Indeterminacy: Rimbaud to Cage*. Evanston: Northwestern University Press, 1983.

Platt, L. H. "The Buckeen and the Dogsbody: Aspects of History and Culture in 'Telemachus.'" In *James Joyce Quarterly* 27(Fall 1989):77–86.

Poirier, Richard. "Pater, Joyce, Eliot." In *James Joyce Quarterly* 26(Fall 1988):21–36.

Potts, Willard. "Stephen Dedalus and 'Irrland's Split Little Pea.'" *James Joyce Quarterly* 27(Spring 1990):559–575.

Pound, Ezra. *Personae: Collected Shorter Poems.* New York: New Directions, 1971.

Pound/Joyce: The Letters of Ezra Pound to James Joyce, With Pound's Essays on Joyce. Edited by Forrest Read. New York: New Directions, 1967.

Power, Arthur. *Conversations with James Joyce.* Edited by Clive Hart. Chicago: University of Chicago Press, 1974.

Reichert, Klaus, Fritz Senn, and Dieter E. Zimmer. *Materialien zu James Joyces 'Dubliner.'* Frankfurt am Main: Suhrkamp Verlag, 1977.

Riddel, Joseph N. *The Inverted Bell: Modernism and the Counterpoetics of William Carlos Williams.* Baton Rouge: Louisiana State University Press, 1974.

Rose, Danis, and John O'Hanlon. *Understanding 'Finnegans Wake.'* New York: Garland Publishing, 1982.

Rowe, John Carlos. "Modern Art and the Invention of Postmodern Capital." In *American Quarterly* 39(1987):154–173.

Scarry, John. "The 'Negro Chieftain' and Disharmony in Joyce's 'The Dead.'" In *Revue des Langues Vivantes* (Summer 1973):182–183.

Scholes, Robert. "Joyce and Modernist Ideology." In *Coping with Joyce,* edited by Morris Beja and Shari Benstock, pp. 91–107. Columbus: Ohio State University Press, 1989.

Scott, Bonnie Kime. *Joyce and Feminism.* Bloomington: Indiana University Press, 1984.

———. ed. and Introduction. *New Alliances in Joyce Studies.* Newark: University of Delaware Press, 1988.

Segall, Jeffrey. "Between Marxism and Modernism, or How to Be a Revolutionist and Still Love 'Ulysses'." In *James Joyce Quarterly* 25(Summer 1988):421–444.

Seidel, Michael. *Epic Geography: James Joyce's 'Ulysses.'* Princeton: Princeton University Press, 1976.

Setterquist, Jan. *Ibsen and the Beginnings of Anglo-Irish Drama.* Vol. 1. New York: Oriole Editions, 1951.

Spivak, Gayatri Chakravorty. "French Feminism in an International Frame." In *Yale French Studies* 62(1981):154–184.

Staley, Thomas F., and Bernard Benstock, eds. *Approaches to Joyce's 'Portrait.'* Pittsburgh: University of Pittsburgh Press, 1976.

Stoppard, Tom. *Travesties.* New York: Random House, 1975.

Templeton, Joan. "The *Doll House* Backlash: Criticism, Feminism, and Ibsen." In *PMLA* 104(1989):28–39.

Tenorth, Heinz-Elmar. "Walter Benjamins Umfeld. Erziehungsverhaeltnisse und Paedagogische Bewegung." In *Walter Benjamin und die Kinderliteratur,* edited by Klaus Doderer, pp. 31–67. Munich: Juventa Verlag, 1988.

Thornton, Weldon. *Allusions in 'Ulysses.'* New York: Simon and Schuster, 1973.

Tindall, William York. *A Reader's Guide to 'Finnegans Wake.'* New York: Farrar, Straus and Giroux, 1969.

———. *A Reader's Guide to James Joyce.* New York: Farrar, Straus and Giroux, 1959.

Torchiana, Donald T. *Backgrounds for Joyce's 'Dubliners.'* Boston: Allen & Unwin, 1986.

Trilling, Lionel. *Beyond Culture.* New York: Harcourt Brace Jovanovich, 1965.

———. *Sincerity and Authenticity.* Cambridge: Harvard University Press, 1972.

Tysdahl, B. J. *Joyce and Ibsen: A Study in Literary Influence.* New York: Humanities Press, 1968.

Wall, Richard. *An Anglo-Irish Dialect Glossary for Joyce's Works.* Gerrards Cross: Buckinghamshire: Colin Smythe, 1986.

Walzl, Florence L. "*Dubliners*: Women in Irish Society." In *Women in Joyce,* edited by Suzette Henke and Elaine Unkeless, pp. 31–56. Urbana: University of Illinois Press, 1982.

Weir, Lorraine. "The Choreography of Gesture: Marcel Jousse and *Finnegans Wake.*" In *James Joyce Quarterly* 14(1977) 313–325.

West, Rebecca. *The Strange Necessity: Essays and Reviews.* London: Virago Press, 1987.

Wilde, Oscar. *The Complete Works of Oscar Wilde.* New York: Harper & Row, 1989.

Williams, Raymond. *Problems in Materialism and Culture.* London: Verso Editions, 1982.

Williams, Trevor L. "Dominant Ideologies: *The Production of Stephen Dedalus.*" In *James Joyce: The Augmented Ninth,* edited by Bernard Benstock, pp. 312–322. Syracuse: Syracuse University Press, 1988.

Wilson, Edmund. *Axel's Castle.* New York: Charles Scribner's Sons, 1969.

Yeats, William Butler. *Selected Poems and Two Plays of William Butler Yeats.* Edited by M. L. Rosenthal. New York: Collier Books, 1968.

Index

Milton Keynes UK
Ingram Content Group UK Ltd.
UKHW020315010924
447596UK00012B/306